DADDY'S LITTLE SECRET

A Daughter's Quest to Solve Her Father's Brutal Murder

DENISE WALLACE

WILDBLUE
PRESS

WildBluePress.com

DADDY'S LITTLE GIRL published by:

WILDBLUE PRESS
P.O. Box 102440
Denver, Colorado 80250

978-1-942266-51-8   Trade Paperback ISBN
978-1-942266-52-5   eBook ISBN

Cover Design and Interior Formatting by Elijah Toten
Totencreative.com

To Hollie Lynn Steinke, who, like my dad, left me too soon

INTRODUCTION

Somewhere in my closet there is a sketch of my father, and I do not know where it came from. My oldest daughter Marissa's high school sweetheart was an artist. Perhaps he sketched the drawing of my dad from an old photograph; I never asked who drew it. Instead, I just pushed it toward the back of the closet to gather dust.

A decade went by before I came across the sketch again one day while rummaging through the closet. As soon as I realized that it was a drawing of my father, I quickly turned away. Who was this man? I loved him so much, yet it occurred to me that I had no idea who he really was. Why couldn't I look at his face?

I realized that I could not keep pushing my father out of my mind. What else was I not dealing with in my life if I could not even look at a picture? I decided then and there that I was going to dig up my father's past and learn who he really was. Then I would write a book about him, and about how he died ... his murder. I would order the court transcripts from the trial, but only after I had exhausted all of my memories of my father first. He had a larger-than-life personality, and I wanted people to know the father I knew. Only then would I seek to uncover the father I did not know.

In other words, I was going to face my fears. I was also going to assert myself as a now-single woman living in LA and go out and get a job in the film industry. I would wind up working for a picture car company, where I would find the vehicles needed for films and television shows. The job

1

would be far from glamorous and the warehouse would be dirty. But I was my father's daughter, and a little dirt was not going to hurt me.

And finally, I would live as my true self. Gone would be the clothes charged at Orange County boutiques and the membership at the Balboa Bay Club in Newport Beach. I would now wear Chuck Taylor sneakers and jeans and spend my days basking in the creative energy of Los Angeles. It would draw me in like sports fans cheering for their favorite player at a home game. I would write on my laptop at The Bourgeois Pig, the Hollywood hangout for writers on Franklin Avenue. Afterward, I would browse the books at the Daily Planet next door, which featured writers like Jack Kerouac and artists like Andy Warhol. Many would die as paupers, I knew, but their books would live on to tell their tales. And who could ask for more than that?

This true crime book is unlike most others, and I say that as a huge fan of true crime. I am well aware that there are exceptional writers out there who are capable of making you feel dirty, as if you have done the killer's deeds yourself. Writer's such as the legendary Ann Rule, who penned the dark story *Lust Killer* about a necrophiliac and murderer named Jerry Brudos. In her book, Rule describes Brudos as feeling "exhilarated" as he played with the dead body of his young female victim as if she were a "rag doll." Then there is the author and TV host Aphrodite Jones, who makes you feel as if you are inside the skin of the victim. In her true crime book *FBI Killer*, Jones writes about Susan Daniels Smith curling her hair to look pretty for the man who already knows he is going to kill her.

But what I am going to do is take you places that you do not go in other true crime books: places like the backseat of the detectives' car, the courtroom conference room with the prosecutor, and the journey of the victim's life—because

I was *there*. Much of the stories and dialogue in *Daddy's Little Secret* come from memories I have from growing up with my father, who often took me along with him when he went to visit his multitude of friends. This eclectic group included both males and females who were either gay or straight, alcoholic or recovering, affluent or poor. My dad fit into all walks of life, yet there was a separate path that he took when others were not looking. A dark path that was evil and unbeknownst to me. This book is going to go down that path.

As the author and daughter of the victim, I have tried to retrace my father's steps in a cathartic attempt to heal from the pain of losing the man I loved so much but did not really know. A man who had layers of secrets involving his sexuality and late-night deeds. Deeds that did not all take place behind the closed door of his bedroom.

It was Detective Boland and Detective Venetucci who first brought some of those deeds to light for me. With great sensitivity, they relayed the news to me that my father had led an alternative lifestyle. Though they attempted to shield me from some of the more sordid details, I was eventually bludgeoned with them as I read through the transcripts from the trial of my father's killer.

There were also numerous police reports and interviews that were conducted by the detectives. I was present for some of them that took place on my ride-along with Detectives Boland and Venetucci. Others I researched later. And then there were the private conversations that I engaged in with the prosecutor, Marc Shiner. Near the end of the trial I confessed a secret of my father's to him that I had never told anyone, a secret that I had pushed back into the far recesses of my mind.

I also met many of the employees of the Ritz Carlton Palm Beach that had worked along with my father. I saw their smiles when my father engaged them in conversation and heard their tales recanted by my dad many times. Any errors of fact are unintentional, some names have been changed to protect privacy, and some conversations have been reconstructed to ensure your ease of reading.

Several newspaper articles from the *Sun Sentinel* are also included in the book, although I turned down a request for an interview by a reporter that approached me at my father's funeral. At the time I could not bring myself to talk about how I felt about his killer. Since then my feelings have changed, and I have chosen to explain them here in this book.

It is my hope that you will be entertained by the story of my father. He was a complex and fascinating man who had his share of both good and bad traits. Perhaps more than his share, which always makes for a great character in both literature and film. There will never be another like him.

CHAPTER 1
The Banging

The banging was coming from Wes Wallace's apartment next door. Rose Mancini had heard it before on a couple of other nights. She and her husband were in bed, but unlike Frank, this night she lay awake. They were both in their sixties, and lately she had discovered she needed less sleep. A glance at the clock on her nightstand told her it was well past three in the morning.

Rose looked toward the bedroom's east wall and listened for more banging. Now she heard it again—and there was arguing, too. It sounded like Wes yelling at another man. She heard the words, "Get out! Just get out of here!"

Enough was enough. Mrs. Mancini nudged her husband awake. "Frank, do you hear that?"

"Do I hear what?" he asked, startled and annoyed. But a moment later there was another banging sound and more arguing.

Then there was another banging sound, this one much louder than the others.

"Do you think we should call the police?" she asked Frank.

"No, let's not pry. It's his own business," Frank Mancini said, then rolled over to go back to sleep. And sure enough, a few minutes later the banging stopped.

Rose and Frank lived in a senior complex where the neighbors walked their cats on a daily basis and plucked weeds from their potted plants whenever they wanted to listen in on a neighbor's news. Maybe if they lived closer to the tracks in West Palm, they would be more worried, but not here. The closest anyone around here came to danger was watching it on the late-night news.

Wes Wallace had only moved into the Lake Osborne Apartments a month before. The Mancinis had been there for years. Six weeks short of nine years. Originally they were from New York, but like so many other retirees, they chose palm trees over snow-covered firs. Lake Worth itself was close to the famous Palm Beach they liked to tour on vacations before they relocated, but without the expensive price tag.

Wes was a friendly enough neighbor, always taking the time to chat for a moment when they passed on the stairs. They had guessed he was in his fifties and perhaps used to be in the military because he wore his hair in what some might call a buzz cut. It was graying now, but one could still make out some reminiscent brown. It had seemed to Frank and Rose that Wes had more than his share of male friends. The Mancinis had both seen men come and go out of his second floor apartment. Wes appeared to be single, and they knew he lived alone. He had mentioned more than once he had a daughter and grandchildren out in California, but there was never mention of a Mrs. Wallace.

That next morning at seven on Sunday, June 6, 1999, Frank Mancini awoke to the smell of warm poppy seed bagels from the Original Brooklyn Water Bagel Company in Lake Worth. Since he and Rose had moved to Florida they had acquired the local habit of drinking iced coffee along with their daily bagel breakfast. The ice cubes at the Brooklyn Water Bagel Company were made out of decaf so they would not dilute when they melted. Both Frank and Rose liked their coffee that way.

Just as Frank reached the kitchen table, Rose set a cup of

coffee down next to the morning paper for him. The couple both preferred the *New York Times* to the *Miami Herald* and were grateful the *Times* was available less than five minutes away at the local drug store.

Rose joined her husband and picked up the front page of the paper that he had only just discarded. On it she saw there had been yet another boom in condo prices. Times were good for Frank and Rose. Over the last five years their unit had appreciated by 20 percent. The Mancinis were far from wealthy, but they had been able to retire at comfortable ages and enjoy senior living in Palm Beach County.

A wall of sticky heat hit Mr. Mancini as he opened his apartment door at a quarter past two in the afternoon. So did the beating Florida sun. Frank quickly grabbed a pair of oversized, dark green plastic sunglasses from a side table while almost simultaneously pulling the door shut. He had only walked a couple of feet before noticing the door to Mr. Wallace's apartment, number 209, was open. Remembering the banging sounds from the night before, Frank now felt obliged to check on his neighbor.

"Wes?" he called. No answer.

His second try was louder. "Mr. Wallace, it's Frank Mancini from apartment 210. Are you there? Can you hear me?"

Frank was alarmed by the silence. Finally, he pushed on the door until it was fully open. The living room was empty but for an inexpensive-looking, worn green sofa. In front of it sat a wooden coffee table that, in contrast, looked oddly antique. On the wall above it loomed a rather large painting of the ocean. His eyes were drawn to another oversized ocean painting on the wall of the dining area.

Suddenly, Frank noticed the protruding belly of a body on the floor beneath it. The feet were extended toward the kitchen. His eyes widened when he saw the condition of the corpse. Blood had seeped out and formed an expanded pool around the head and shoulders. There was so much of it, he could see it was still wet. Mr. Mancini stepped closer and recognized the heavyset body of his neighbor, Wes Wallace. He was lying on his back.

Why were his pants partially down? What had happened the night before? The guy was obviously dead. Mr. Mancini backed away and headed to his apartment.

"Honey, call the cops," Frank told his wife. "Wes is dead."

Rose's hands flew up to her face in horror. She reached out to grab her husband's arm. "What did you say?" She could not believe she had heard right.

"I said, Wes is dead," Frank repeated. Now they would have to call the police.

CHAPTER 2
The Bloody Sheet

Minutes later a police car raced up Lake Osborne Drive. The Mancinis were waiting outside on the ground floor of the chalk-colored senior complex that looked like a motel. Young red-headed Officer Devon Walsh and his older, savvy partner, Officer Bryan Reynolds, jumped out of the car and headed over to them.

"You the one who called?" Reynolds asked Frank Mancini.

"Yes, sir, I am. He's up there," the elderly man pointed to his neighbor's apartment upstairs. The officers hurried past the couple, who followed them up the stairs. They had trouble keeping up with the officers. Rose had arthritic knees that ached with every step. "It's pretty bad. I don't want my wife to see," Frank called out behind him, already running short of breath. "We'll be next door if you need us!" he yelled. "In apartment 210!"

The couple gazed up at the officers as they drew their guns and stepped inside the open doorway of Mr. Wallace's apartment. The Mancinis scurried inside their own after that, suddenly wondering if the killer could still be over there. The thought had not occurred to them until that moment.

From the open front door Officer Walsh could see the large body of Mr. Wallace resting in blood. Walsh was new on the force, and it was his first corpse. The effect was sobering. Reynolds had seen a fatal gunshot victim once. The guy had been shot twice in the chest, but there had not been nearly this much blood. The officer tried not to miss a beat in front of his greener partner. He preferred to appear cool and well-seasoned on each call.

Officer Reynolds nodded toward the kitchen for Walsh to investigate. A glance that way told him the killer had raided the cabinets for weapons, cleaning products, or both. There were also smears of what looked like blood on the counter. He stepped past the body and noticed that part of the carpet in the living room and hallway was wet. He could also hear water running. Gun first, he glanced into the small bathroom. The tub faucet was on low, and the tub was overflowing with water. Both of the bath mats on the floor were soaked. There were items in the bathtub, he noticed, but training had taught him to check the bedroom first to make sure they were alone.

It was obvious there had been a struggle there the previous night. There was blood on the bed. Though it had been stripped of most of its linens, the bed, oddly, still retained the fitted sheet on the mattress. It appeared the killer had left it there. Part of a cut electrical cord dangled from an outlet, and a light bulb and lamp shade lay on the floor with blood on them. Also on the floor were a glass tabletop and several scattered coins. One of the closet doors had been pushed in with apparent force, and the frame of the bedroom door had been shattered.

Minutes went by without a sound. Then more police began to arrive at the usually quiet senior complex. The Mancinis peered together through the blinds at the uniformed men invading their neighbor's home. The chaos had just begun.

CHAPTER 3
Night Beat

Lake Worth is the geographic and artistic center of Palm Beach County. Its name is derived from the body of water along its eastern border called the Lake Worth Lagoon. The city's motto, "Where the Tropics Begin," promises that it lies on the outskirts of paradise. Downtown Lake Worth boasts a historic theater, a museum, live music clubs, coffee houses, art galleries, and antique shops. Comprised mainly of service providers, such as salespeople and construction workers, Lake Worth is neither predominately blue collar nor white collar.

The city is also the birthplace of at least one mass murderer: Charles Whitmer, otherwise known as the Texas Tower Sniper. On August 1, 1966, at the University of Texas, Whitmer shot and killed seventeen people including his wife, mother, students, teachers, and police. It was the first mass murder to be nationally televised, and the broadcast touted the incident as "the murder spree that changed America."

Thirty-three years later in Lake Worth, there would be nine murder victims that year. The homicide detectives sent to investigate the murder of William Wesley Wallace were thirty-one-year-old Steven Venetucci and thirty-nine-year-old Daniel Boland.

Detective Venetucci was not just a dedicated detective, he was also the drummer for the department's rock band called "Night Beat," a local ensemble that aimed to encourage the notion that police officers are made of the same flesh and blood as the citizens they are sworn to protect. Over the years, Venetucci had developed his own interrogation style that apparently put people at ease and often led them to divulging more information than they normally would.

He also became aware of how many murders might be deemed utterly senseless. Among these was the death of an attractive twenty-seven-year-old mother of three who was strangled in the backseat of her Ford Fairmont, and a seven-and-a-half-month-old who was beaten in the head with a clothes iron by her twelve-year-old brother.

Steven Venetucci's work included a stack of death investigations that ran the gamut from accidents to suicides to questionable drownings. His job's long hours often took him away from his own family, and more than once he considered moving to another division. But in the end, Venetucci consoled himself with the knowledge and satisfaction that he had invariably done his duty and brought many killers to justice.

Detective Daniel Boland felt similarly about his work. Over a decade had passed since her death, but he still remembered a fifty-two-year-old golf pro shop employee named Cynthia Moffett. Mrs. Moffett had been killed at the Forest Oaks Golf Club in what appeared to be a robbery. She was shot twice in the torso and stumbled out of the store, falling dead a few steps from the shop's door. No arrests were ever made in the case. Boland stood at the podium in a room full of reporters, "I promise you that we're not going to forget her," he announced. "We're not going to go away." And while he had not solved the murder yet, it was still on his active list. It was still fresh in his mind. But not as fresh as the Wallace murder would become.

On Sunday, June 6, 1999, news vans and print reporters began arriving at 3080 Lake Osborne Drive in the afternoon. They had heard over the police scanner that a man had been stabbed in Lake Worth. *The Coastal Observer*, a local

newspaper "devoted to the interests of the peninsula of
Florida and particularly to Palm Beach County," was the
first to arrive. Wendy Newman, a perky photographer for the
small newspaper, snapped pictures of the yellow crime scene
tape and the police who had swarmed the second floor. A
brutal stabbing had been enough to warrant the interest of
the media, but a stabbing inside a senior complex had sent
them racing to the scene.

Reporters began approaching neighbors who had
gathered near the stairs of the building. The news people
wanted to know more about the man who had been killed
in the adult community. Most had not known Wes Wallace,
the husky fifty-six-year-old, who lived upstairs from them.
He had only moved in a month before and had mostly kept
to himself. One neighbor, Walden Thomas, knew Wes
had worked at the Ritz Carlton Palm Beach. He had seen
him in his security uniform and had spoken to him briefly,
welcoming him to the building when he first arrived.

The neighbors were shocked a murderer had lurked
among them in their serene, elderly community. Would the
killer come back? Would he rob them and stab their spouses
while they watched?

The thought prompted Harold Perelman, a condo official,
to arrange a meeting to discuss the safety of the remaining
residents. Neighbors were advised to pick up the spare key
that hid beneath the door mat or planter and hand it over
to a trusted neighbor or friend. They were also advised to
set timers on their lights and have their newspapers picked
up when they went away.It took until the next morning for
Venetucci to be able to view the crime scene. While Boland
had already been assigned to the case, department red tape
had caused Venetucci's assignment to be delayed an extra
day. Yellow crime scene tape made it clear to them which
apartment contained the murder victim. They made their

way upstairs and flashed their badges at the tall police officer who was standing guard outside. He gave them a quick nod as they entered the premises.

Stepping inside the living room on Monday, June 7, 1999, Detective Venetucci could see the body only a few feet away, but he moved to examine the modestly furnished living room first. He noticed the antique coffee table sharply contradicted the cheap sofa against the wall, and he reminded himself that people's furnishings often reflected different periods in their lives. He reassured himself that this was most likely the case at this crime scene.

Venetucci picked up a yellow photo album on the table and opened it. He stared at photo after photo of the victim and a pretty, young blonde. She looked to be in her early thirties. Some pictures also featured the woman holding a baby boy. Who was she? Venetucci kept turning pages until he came to a birthday card in the back of the album. He lifted up the plastic with a gloved hand, pulled out the card, and read the words: *Happy Birthday, Daddy. Love, Denise.* It was the victim's daughter. She was going to have to be told that her father had been murdered. He tucked the card back into the album and set it back down on the coffee table.

A further look around revealed there was definitely something missing from the TV stand in the room. The TV was there, but the bottom shelf was empty. Closer scrutiny revealed a coaxial cable had been left plugged into the wall. But where was the VCR?

On another wall, a wooden shelf caught his attention. From the outlines in the dust on the shelf's surface, Venetucci determined that something used to fill the empty space. Probably a stereo. The speakers were still there. He stepped over next to his partner, Boland, to view the body in the dining room. There did not seem to be any drag marks on the carpet, he noticed.

"What a pig," he hissed to himself about the killer when he saw all the blood that had seeped onto the gold carpet. The two men stood looking down at the large, uneven, red pool that had finally dried. There were numerous scratches on the victim's face and clotted, dried blood on his neck. Then something caught the detective's eye as he squatted down to scan the body more closely. There was what looked like bite marks on the victim's right wrist. This had definitely been a two-sided struggle.

Venetucci stepped inside the bathroom to have a further look. He was careful not to disturb anything. The Clorox bottle and milk carton floating in the tub showed the killer may have tried to destroy some of the evidence. Did that mean he had killed before? The detective's skillfully trained eyes went immediately to the light switch on the pale yellow wall. It was a place most killers overlooked when they cleaned up. He was not let down. There was a smudge of blood on the switch. Venetucci leaned over the tub to see what else awaited him. A gold lamp base, bed sheets, and a pillow lay eerily still in the cold bleach-smelling water.

A look in the bedroom revealed the killer had left one bloody sheet behind on the bed. Half of an electrical cord remained hanging from an outlet, and a light bulb and metal lampshade on the floor each had blood on them. From the looks of it, the killer had cut the cord with a knife. That would have left the room dark and could have caused him to overlook the fitted sheet. Another TV stand was missing its VCR, he noticed. There was also a white tissue on the floor at the end of the bed. The detective gazed over at the pushed-in closet door and noticed there was blood on a white, long-sleeved shirt that was hanging inside the closet. Then he saw the jamb on the door to the bedroom had been completely broken off. The door frame was also shattered. There must have been one hell of a fight in here, he thought to himself.

Sometime later, Venetucci started to head back down the hall. He stopped. The door to the hall closet was cracked open. The detective pushed it the rest of the way with his foot. He quickly scanned the contents of the shelves.

Then he saw them.

The boxes that the two VCRs and stereo had come in. Those could always be counted on for valuable clues: the serial numbers.

Over in the kitchen, Boland was gathering details. He could see the cabinet doors under the sink had been left open. He left them as he found them so as not to disturb any prints.

At the time of the crime, the processing of ten-print fingerprint submissions could take weeks or even months. But that summer the Integrated Automated Fingerprint Identification System would be launched. This would greatly hasten the process.

Venetucci and Boland exited the victim's apartment and started back down the stairs. Two elderly women headed upward toward them. One in white capri pants caught sight of the two detectives. She looked only mildly alarmed. "They're sending the police, now, along with the paramedics?" she remarked to her female neighbor. Ambulances were a common sight at the senior complex. Surely this was just another case of a heart attack or respiratory complication? Not this time.

That day the *Sun Sentinel* printed a story confirming that a Lake Worth man had been slain in his Lake Osborne Drive home in the early hours of Sunday morning. Detective Boland was quoted as having said, "We believe he met somebody and they went to his house and they had a fight." The article claimed a gun had not been used in the murder and that exactly what weapon had been used would not be known until autopsy results were in. The victim was William Wesley Wallace, and his 1986 Acura Legend was also missing from the scene.

Thousands of elderly readers would see the article that day and feel vulnerable inside their own homes. Many would place calls to the Lake Worth Police Department requesting extra patrolling of their neighborhoods, but even that would not be enough to calm their fears.

CHAPTER 4
Poster Boy

It was Saturday, June 5, 1999, the last day of Wes Wallace's life. He had woken up late on the hot, sunny morning and fixed himself some bacon, eggs, and toast. At six feet and 252 pounds, Wes loved to eat. He was an excellent cook and was fond of using the favorite recipes of celebrities that he found in magazines, such as Farrah Fawcett's coconut cream pie and Liz Taylor's chicken with avocado and mushrooms.

Wes even possessed a surviving copy of Liberace's little-known cookbook called <u>Liberace Cooks! Recipes from His Seven Dining Rooms</u>. The copy was hidden behind his Betty Crocker edition. Wes had emulated Liberace's tactic back in the seventies by telling some high-school football players at the European Health Spa in Fort Lauderdale that he would not give them personal training unless they brought their entire team over for a pool party. Just as with Liberace, the unscrupulous scheme had worked. The boys had showed up with Speedos on underneath their shorts. Soon they were splashing in the pool and downing chili dogs that Wes's wife, Lynda, had served on their best china. That had been Wes's idea: humor with an obvious sexual undertone.

After breakfast, Wes took a five-minute drive over to Lake Worth Presbyterian Church. He cruised by slowly, peering intently over his steering wheel at the well-manicured grounds. Though he had been brought up in the Bible Belt of North Carolina, Wes had not attended worship services there. He had gone to the church on this day for another reason: Derek Carney.

Carney was a twenty-two-year-old white male who had been sleeping on the church grounds. Wes wanted to once again offer him a place to stay for the night and was hoping the young man would take him up on the offer this time. The young heroin addict had discovered he could shoot up in the bathroom of the church despite his filthy, disheveled appearance and not get caught. Most other churches kept their facilities locked at night, but the co-pastor, Reverend Bill Withers, had a notoriously kind heart. The first time he had come across Carney sleeping on the church lawn, he had woken him, invited him in for counsel, and taken him to breakfast.

As Wes passed in his car, the reverend gave him a wave from the open door of the church. Wes waved back at him and grinned, then threw his head back and took a long drag on his Marlboro cigarette. Outside the church, an aging wooden sign quoted a verse from the Bible: COME TO ME, ALL OF YOU WHO ARE WEARY AND CARRY HEAVY BURDENS, AND I WILL GIVE YOU REST.

Wes's interest in gaining Carney's attentions would go unrequited that morning, so he then decided to drive over to the Gardens Mall in Boynton Beach to kill time. Perhaps he would browse the latest sunglasses collection at Michael Kors that he had read about and dog-eared in his *GQ* magazine. Such endeavors amused him.

The entrance to the Gardens Mall was bursting with a profusion of the crimson bougainvillea variety called "Don Fernando," and Wes loved to window shop at the luxurious 1.4-million-square-foot shopping center that featured a Nordstrom, a Saks Fifth Avenue, and a Bloomingdale's. Though his taste was sophisticated, he could no longer afford luxuries since his divorce in 1974 had rendered him broke. It was a state in which he still found himself even twenty-five years later.

As Wes strolled through the mall, he was suddenly stopped by a larger-than-life poster at Abercrombie & Fitch. It featured a handsome young man with tightly muscled abs barely concealed by an open flannel shirt. Wes decided to step into the store.

Inside, floor-to-ceiling shelves framed the sides of another life-sized poster, this time of a sexy young male and female about to kiss. The slogan read: YOUNG LOVE IS A FLAME; VERY PRETTY, OFTEN VERY HOT. Wes stepped closer to the huge photograph and stared at the shirtless couple.

"Can I help you?" offered a slender male salesperson who would later remember him.

"What? No, I'm just looking," Wes answered, startled at the high voice that seemed to have come out of nowhere. "No, thank you," he added emphatically with a forced, broad smile. But he could not resist placing a hand on the soft fabric of a blue, pre-wrinkled plaid shirt and pulling it free from the stack. Holding it up in front of him, he stared at his blocky image in a mirror and saw the shirt was much too narrow to cover his shoulders, much less his protruding belly. He then half-folded it carelessly and tossed it back onto the pile. He wandered out of the store, glancing back one more time at the alluring life-sized poster that had originally beckoned him inside.

Up ahead in the mall was Cafe Chardonnay, one of Palm Beach County's most superb restaurants. Wes walked over and squinted at the mounted, gold-framed menu for quite a while, the hostess later recalled. It featured foie gras and port wine lacquered grilled filet mignon that soared out of his price range.

After that he had most likely continued through the mall. Over the next few hours Wes's exact whereabouts would remain unknown.

CHAPTER 5
"We Think He Was Gay"

Back at the crime scene on Monday afternoon, the stoic forensic investigator from the state autopsy lab, Cleighton Thomas, was the next to arrive. Donned in gloves and booties, he joined the nine crime scene investigators, detectives, and supervisors and began taking photographs and documenting drops of blood and the layout of the apartment. It was a long and tedious process. Technicians also began labeling the sections of blood trail that led from the bedroom to the dining room. Oddly, there was no blood in the hall. They photographed in detail the gold lamp base, Clorox bottle, milk carton, bed sheets, and pillow that lay submerged in the bathtub. A closer look revealed a paper towel was stuck in the drain. It had caused the water to overflow into the hallway and part of the living room area. Over a thousand photographs would be taken.

Thomas began to videotape the crime scene from the outside to the inside of the apartment. He switched from video to still photographs as the camera panned along the pale yellow walls of the bathroom. There he documented the bloody red smudge on the light switch. The forensic investigator focused in particular on the blood-stain pattern of the fitted sheet that remained on the mattress in the bedroom. Close attention was also paid to the closet door that had been pushed in, the broken door jamb, and the half-cord that dangled from an electrical outlet on the west wall.

In the bedroom, two crime scene investigators followed

behind Thomas and carefully stripped the white fitted sheet from the bed. They placed the sheet into a large, clear plastic bag and sealed it closed. The flat sheet and pillow that lay submerged in the tub would have to be transported to the lab in a separate, sealed plastic container. Though the water and bleach left little chance of any DNA evidence, everything had to undergo testing regardless.

In order to get the blood off of the light bulb that lay on the floor of the bedroom, crime scene investigator Ralph Rinaldi had to use a sterile swab in conjunction with water. He placed the swab onto the bulb, broke the tip of it off so it would become part of the sample, and put the tip and the bulb into a plastic container and sealed it. Each piece of evidence had to be packaged separately so there would be no chance of cross-contamination, and each sealed bag had to be signed and dated.

The dimmer switch over the dining room table in Mr. Wallace's apartment was turned all the way up, above the lifeless Wes, who lay on the floor. The crime scene investigators, detectives, and supervisors all bent over his body along with Thomas. Together they observed the several long, thin scratches on his face, likely caused by a knife, though no weapon had been found at the scene. There was also dried blood on his neck. It was impossible to tell how deep the wound was because of all the dried blood. They were careful to step around the rest that had pooled into a large, misshapen puddle on the gold carpet. All of them wore booties and gloves.

"Hey," Boland said, nudging his partner. "The guy's not wearing a watch." The tan lines on the victim's right wrist made the detective think of the TAG Heuer 1000 watch that his wife, Karen, had bought him for Father's Day the previous year. His son, Mike, and his daughters, Kiley and Lindsay, were still in grade school, so his wife had taken them shopping and picked out the watch. He loved the one she had chosen and wore it every day.

Boland knew Florida law stipulated that if a theft occurred during the commission of a murder, it would fall under the category of special circumstances, which would then put the death penalty on the table. The guy better hope he got away with it, Boland thought to himself, or else he could be looking at lethal injection.

"We think he was gay," Venetucci stated when one technician remarked about the victim's pants being partially down. The vast male porn collection in Wes's bedroom had been seen by everyone present. The chance of the killer being a female still had to be considered, but already none of them believed a woman had committed the crime.

Brown paper bags were placed over Wes's hands to contain any evidence, and clear tape was wrapped around the victim's forearms to seal the tops of the bags. A set of bite marks could clearly be made out on the victim's right wrist. They were deeper on one side than the other. Crime scene investigators lifted the body into a body bag and zipped it closed. They laid the body bag on a wheeled gurney, carried it down the two flights of stairs, and placed it into a coroner's van.

The body would be sent to the Palm Beach County Medical Examiner's Office. Though the inner autopsy rooms were cold and clinical, glossy, walnut plaques on the outer walls memorialized fallen heroes of the police departments in Palm Beach County. No deaths were ever forgotten.

Back at the senior complex, elderly neighbors had gathered below the stairs of the building to gawk at the morbid process as the coroner's van pulled away. Gasps and looks of horror prevailed throughout the group. One woman in her navy-blue gardening apron turned and clutched her husband. She lowered her head and buried it into his chest.

Detectives Venetucci and Boland decided to question the Mancinis next. Venetucci knocked on apartment 210. Rose Mancini answered the door immediately. The couple had been waiting for a visit from the police. Although Frank Mancini had found the body, Rose Mancini had heard the argument, so Venetucci decided to begin the questioning with her. He asked if she had seen Mr. Wallace the day before his death. Rose said she had not but she had clearly heard his voice that night through the wall yelling at another man to get out. Banging sounds had accompanied the yelling as well, she told him. This was a senior complex where the residents were nosy. They knew if their neighbor had not paid property taxes or if there was hoarding of ceiling-high stacks of newspapers that were becoming a fire hazard. It had definitely been a brazen move on the killer's part to risk being seen or heard by a resident—unless he had not planned to kill the victim. If death had been accidental or the result of self-defense, that would take premeditation off the table. Killers got off easier when they did not mean to kill. The ones who did, on the other hand, could get the death penalty.

CHAPTER 6
"Were You Aware of His Sexual Orientation?"

The Ritz Carlton Palm Beach is a sprawling, sand-colored hotel that covers seven acres of Atlantic beachfront property. Its name brilliantly capitalizes on the island of Palm Beach's reputation as the playground of the rich and famous, but it is actually located in the nearby town of Manalapan.

Hundreds of palm trees and other plantings frame the hotel's 3,000-square-foot oceanfront terrace. There are two pools and an evening fire pit outside. The hotel's supper club boasts of local fare such as line-caught fish, and the spa shamelessly refers to its open-air sanctuary as "The Self Centered Garden."

The help, however, did not eat at the supper club nor enjoy the benefits of the spa. Instead, they scurried inside the inner maze of the hotel through hidden hallways and separate elevators. This underground world was the one the detectives wanted to investigate to learn about the life of former employee Wesley Wallace.

Later in the afternoon on Monday, the detectives decided to interview fifty-one-year-old Marion Carlyle first. Ms. Carlyle was the hotel supervisor who wore a double-breasted blazer with gold buttons and a no-nonsense expression. She spoke a bit haughtily when she received Detectives Boland and Venetucci in an open area of the second floor, which had 180-degree views of the Atlantic Ocean, Palm Beach, and the Intracoastal Waterway. This particular section of the 3,000-mile <u>inland waterway</u>, called the Palm Beach Inlet, is an artificial cut through a barrier island that connects the northern part of the Lake Worth Lagoon with the Atlantic Ocean.

After admiring the breathtaking views, Boland began the questioning by asking Ms. Carlyle about Wes's duties at the hotel.

"He was an unarmed security guard. Much of Wes's job was about monitoring the actions of others," she stated. "If he witnessed any strange activities, such as trespassing, he had to be able to handle the situation with confidence. He also had to be able to assert himself whenever the situation required it." It did not occur to the hotel supervisor that this aspect of a security guard's job was very similar to that of a detective's.

"It was crucial for him to monitor the property on a set schedule," she continued. "He had to make it a part of his regular routine to keep watch over all of his designated grounds."

"And what were those?" Ventucci asked.

"It varied," she stated. "Sometimes he monitored the closed circuit TV surveillance inside the main guard booth. Sometimes he was in charge of guarding the employee entrances, delivery entrances, or service entrances. Sometimes he guarded the hotel grounds and parking areas, and sometimes he patrolled the guest corridors and areas inside the hotel."

They learned Wes had been a prompt and reliable employee who had been respectful of people's privacy. After working there for only a year, he had even been entrusted with the guarding of celebrities' rooms. On one occasion he had been in charge of guarding the Rolling Stones' Keith Richards's room. The famous musician had gone above and beyond the Do Not Disturb sign and posted his own crudely handwritten sign on the door that read Go Away. He had then holed up for five days before finally emerging to check out in a nearly deathly looking state. Wes had been careful to fend off the prying eyes of his young coworkers. Some were die-hard Stones fans who were prone to idle gossip.

Unknown to Wes's employer, he had been able to maintain his sobriety the last ten years of his life by attending AA meetings as often as two times a day. An autopsy would later reveal his liver to be in perfect condition upon his death.

The supervisor had not been sure of her employee's sexual orientation but did recall he had brought a male guest to the Christmas party. "He was a lot younger than Wes," Ms. Carlyle elaborated. "He seemed a little uncomfortable to be there. I think they stayed for about an hour and then left."

"Did you notice anything else unusual about Wes?" Venetucci asked.

"No, not that I recall," Ms. Carlyle told him. "But I really didn't work that closely with him."

The detectives thanked the supervisor for her time and took the imperial stairs down to the first floor of the massive hotel. Polished, sand-colored marble shone from the floor as they stopped to question the poised, ever-smiling staff.

Only one of Wesley's co-workers appeared to have known of his sexual preference—a fair-skinned, middle-aged chef named Leonard Fairbairn. The "out and proud" gay chef was slipping a chocolate soufflé into the double-decker convection oven when the detectives sought him out.

"We'd like to ask you a few questions about one of your co-workers," Boland began, taking in the massive kitchen that looked like a stainless steel explosion to him.

"Which one's that?" Fairbairn replied in a soft voice.

"Wes Wallace," the detective clarified.

"Oh, yes. Wasn't he murdered?" the chef asked with a pained expression. "I heard about that. It's just awful. What is it that you all want to know?"

"Well, for starters, how long had you known him?" Detective Venetucci asked.

"I'd known Wes ever since he started working here about a year ago. He'd come in checking to see what I was cooking quite a lot," Fairbairn said. "Sometimes I'd give him a little taste of something I whipped up. He liked that and was always asking me to give him the recipes."

"Were you aware of his sexual preference?" Boland asked the man.

"Oh, heavens, yes. I knew Wes was nelly the first time I saw him," Leonard admitted. "He was checking out Gaby, one of the busboys here. Oh, and he'd asked me if I'd been to Roosters."

"What's Roosters?" Boland asked.

H. G. Roosters was a popular gay dive bar in West Palm Beach replete with neon lights and aquariums, one of which held a giant, glowing octopus. The place featured go-go boys, a drag bingo night, a Miller Lite draft night, and a cookout night.

"I go there, but unfortunately most of the gay bars up here are train wrecks in slow motion. They all have 'retro music.' It's just dated, honey," the chef explained. "Not like in Miami. The other sad part is that you've either got twenty-one-year-old power bottoms or grandpas who hide giant kiddie porn collections in their basement." Leonard rolled his eyes. "Take your pick. Oh, and if you approach someone without an invitation, you're destined to get a 'you can't sit with us' glare. It's dreadful."

The detectives tried to imagine such a scene. It took some effort.

Venetucci cleared his throat. "Was Wes seeing anyone at the hotel?"

Leonard shook his head. "No. Wes wasn't that type of queen. He was into one-night stands."

"And where might he have gone to pick up someone?" the detective wanted to know.

"You mean other than the local bars? There aren't any sex clubs in West Palm. You have to go farther south for that."

The chef was referring to places like Slammer in Fort Lauderdale. Slammer was a private membership club that could only be found from the road if one knew to look for the discreet yellow sign with the numbers 321 that was posted outside of a chain-link fence. Patrons had to bring their own booze; they did not serve alcohol. Inside there was a large, guarded locker room changing area and a huge play space filled with slings, cubicles, benches, positioning chairs, an elevated walkway, and other nooks and crannies. The place was stocked with free condoms and most of the men wore flip-flops so as not to step in anything unseemly.

"But if you want to go out in West Palm, it depends which night of the week it is. There's 'Eye Scream Sundays' at Privé out on Okeechobee Boulevard. I like to go there if I strike out on Friday and Saturday night at Roosters," Leonard admitted.

Privé Lounge boasted a carnival atmosphere on Sundays that featured candy-adorned shot boys, scantily clad, glittered muscled go-go gods, and circus-inspired acts. Patrons were encouraged to wear their food-inspired colors: red cherry jubilee stood for "I'm Taken"; split banana yellow stood for "Hmm Maybe"; mint green chip stood for "I'm Single"; and orange sherbet stood for "Looking for a Third." There was a live DJ in the house on Sundays, one-dollar Jolly Rancher Jell-O shots, and two-dollar Panty Droppers.

"Anyone who strikes out there is black, gay, and a drag queen," Leonard explained. "That's two strikes too many."

"How was Wes as an employee? Anything unusual about him?" Boland wanted to know.

Leonard thought about it a moment. "Hmmm. The most unusual thing I ever saw Wes do was come ask me to clean a fish. We're supposed to go above and beyond here at the hotel as far as service is concerned, and apparently one of the guests had been out fishing and caught a 200-pound dolphin—the fish, not the friend. Anyhoo, the guest said that the fish was in his car, and he asked Wes if he would get him some extra ice. Well, Wes comes running to me with this cooler and says, 'Leonard, will you clean this fish?' Now, this was no small task, mind you, given the size of that fish. But I said I would do it, because Wes knew just how to ask, and apparently, while I was cutting up the dolphin, he cleaned the guest's cooler. He was something, that Wes. I'm sure he got quite a tip after that."

"Sounds like you must've liked him. Did everyone at the hotel like Wes?" Venetucci asked.

"Well, no," Leonard remembered, frowning. "There was one security guard who hated him, I believe, but Wes hated him, too. Wes called him Super Snoop—not just behind his back, either—to his face."

The detectives decided to interview this employee next, so they exited the hotel and walked around the grassy side of the building to the main guard booth. A plump security guard in a golf cart passed them. The detectives watched as it traveled down a sloping path of sand right onto the beach behind the hotel and turned the corner. It turned out to be the guard they wanted to speak with.

Melvyn Clacher was a bloated security guard with flushed cheeks and an angry scowl. He liked to complain to anyone who would listen that he had not been justly paid for his overtime, and Wes had apparently grown tired of hearing it.

"He'd say stuff to me like, 'Mel, if you think you didn't get paid right, that's you and the hotel's business. Why don't you stop whining about it and go on back to your booth,'" Mel told the detectives. "But it wasn't just about me! It could happen to him, too! He just wouldn't listen."

"How long did you work with Wes?" Boland asked.

"About a year. I'd been here twelve and a half years when he started," the fifty-three-year-old security guard said, puffing out his chest.

"Were you aware of his sexual orientation?" Venetucci asked.

Clacher's eyes bulged. "He was gay?" There was clear surprise in his voice. "Well, I'll be. I had no idea. That's a surprise to me."

"Did the two of you get along?" Boland asked, though he had already heard that they did not.

"Hell, no, we didn't get along! Everybody here knows he called me Super Snoop," Mel complained. "He even had the new guards calling me that. He'd introduce them to me and say, 'So-and-so, this is Super Snoop!'" The man's face was turning redder.

Boland tried to keep from smiling. "Do you know why he called you that?"

The security guard sighed. "Yeah. There was one night about, I don't know, three or four months after Wes started working here. Anyway, I was patrolling the employee parking lot—it was my job!" he cried, holding out his hands.

Boland nodded in agreement with the overly defensive man. It seemed to calm him a bit, and he continued.

"Anyway, I thought I saw someone inside this white car," Mel explained. The detectives' ears perked at the mention of the color "white."

"It was dark out, and the lights in the parking lot aren't that good, so I cupped my hands like this," the guard demonstrated with his hands, "and I leaned forward like this to look in the back window. Then I could see that it was just another security uniform hanging inside the car. Well, out of nowhere, Wes starts yelling at me from this golf cart. He says, 'What the hell are you doing, you Peepin' Tom! Get the hell away from my car!'"

The detectives looked at each other in unison. It was odd behavior on Wes's part to become so irate that a fellow security guard was checking out his car. Perhaps it had been in Wes's best interests that he was doing so. Would it not have been more appropriate to ask first? they thought, wondering if there was more to the story.

"Then he rides over, jumps off the cart, and gets in my face. He says to me, 'I better never catch you anywhere near my car again, Mel, you hear me? This is private property!' he says, banging his finger down on the car."

"What did you say?" asked Venetucci.

"I tried to tell him that I was just doing my job, but he kept interrupting me. I couldn't get a word in, he was so furious about it! He kept calling me a 'nosy sumbitch' saying that I was in everybody's business. I'm a security guard!" the man said in astonishment.

"And what happened after that?" Boland asked.

"Well, ever since then he called me Super Snoop. He'd say, 'Look who's here! It's Super Snoop' or 'Peep in any of the guest's windows today, Super Snoop?' I never look in any of the guests' windows!" Mel looked defeated. The detectives would have felt sorry for him if the incident had not been so funny. Yet there was an eerie element to it, too. What had Wes been afraid the other guard might find inside his car?

The next employee the detectives sought out was a forty-five-year-old African American maid named Roberta Mosley. Roberta was a descendent of a long line of hotel maids from Palm Beach's muddled history. Her grandmother had worked at Henry Flagler's famous hotel, The Breakers.

She had lived in a rooming house that was destroyed during the legendary burning of the Styx, a black community on the blooming new island of Palm Beach. Roberta had seen and heard of the rich behaving badly through a collection of stories, some of which were hers.

"Wes used to love to hear me tell him about every new guest that checked into the hotel," she told the detectives sadly. "They all had something interesting about 'em if they made it here," she recalled, humor edging her voice. "I learned long ago from listening to my Grandma Harris that rich people can do some really funny things sometimes, but you can't get mad about it. You just got to move on." Roberta straightened her apron and smiled as a hotel administrator walked by.

"Like what?" Boland asked, taking the bait.

"Like coming to the door with no clothes on. I told Wes the last time I saw him that if that old white dude Mr. Bishop came to the door nekkid one more time, I was gon' throw the sheets on him and tell him to make the bed hisself," Roberta exclaimed. Boland and Venetucci smiled at the image that was fraught with racist undertones.

"Well, Wes thought that was the funniest thing he'd heard. He told that story to everybody," she remembered with a smile. "And he was always teasing me after that, telling people, 'Don't mess with Roberta. She'll hang you up by your britches if you get on her bad side. Don't do it!'" Roberta went on.

"How long did you work with Wes?" Venetucci asked.

"Oh, I got here long before Wes did. I've been here nineteen years," the maid declared with earned pride. "And Wes picked up on the guests' rascally ways right away," she continued. "Rich people will steal towels from the hotel just like a poor person will. They don't like to pay for things if they don't have to. Wes knew," she confided. "He used to

33

tell me, 'Roberta, you make sure you check those whiskey bottles in the minibar. You never know what those rich folk might be fillin' 'em back up with.'"

The detectives thought about this with a frown. Boland made a mental note to remember the tip.

"What kind of man was he?" he asked.

"Oh, Wes was a character. He was just about as nice as he could be to me, but he didn't like Melvyn," Roberta remembered, shaking her head. "He used to say to me, 'Roberta, you tell me if you see Super Snoop comin'.' That's what he called him—Super Snoop," she giggled. "'I can't stand that nosy sumbitch,' he'd say. 'He gets in everybody's business.'"

"Were you aware of Wes's sexual preferences?" Venetucci asked.

The maid's eyebrows raised. "You mean he was gay?" she asked. "No, huh uh. I didn't know that."

"Did you ever see any unusual behavior from Wes?" Boland asked. Roberta thought about this for a moment.

"Well, one thing I thought was kinda strange was something he did right after he came back from visiting his daughter and grandchildren out in California—they were all he talked about, God bless his soul. Anyway, he brought Clay, the valet, some bottles of this Fiji water."

The detectives listened closely.

"He said, 'Clay, I know you travel all over to go surfing and you like this Fiji water. Well, I found some while I was out in California.' But they sell that water in the stores right here," the maid explained quizzically. "Wes didn't know that. He carried those bottles back on a plane all the way from California," she said. "Now, why would he do something like that?" Roberta asked the detectives.

They had a pretty good idea why. The detectives decided to interview Clay Acheson, the valet, next. They found him out front by the enormous, horseshoe-shaped driveway of The Ritz Carlton. The spry, blond valet in his early twenties had just returned from parking a white Cadillac in the heat. He hung the keys on a hook at the podium, tossing his blond locks to the side as he stood up to face the detectives.

"What can I do for you guys?" Clay asked in a friendly voice when he saw Boland's brass badge.

"Mr. Acheson, I'm Detective Boland and this is Detective Venetucci. We're investigating the murder of Wes Wallace," Boland informed him.

"Oh, right! I heard about that! What a bummer. He was such a cool dude," the valet remembered.

"What do you mean by 'cool'?" Venetucci wanted to know.

"Well, he was always like, 'What's going on, Chapstick?'" he explained casually in an animated voice. "I don't know what it meant, but he called me that all the time," the young man added, shaking his head with a smile.

"How long had you worked with Wes?" Boland asked.

"Umm, about three or four months, I think. I haven't worked here that long," Clay admitted.

"Did you ever socialize with him outside of work?" Venetucci wanted to know.

"Nope. Never did that, although he did talk about coming over to my place to check out some of my boards sometime. I make surfboards on the side. It's kind of a hobby," the valet explained, his eyes panning the parking lot for guests. "He was talking about having me make one for his grandson one day when he got older. I told him, 'Sure.'"

"Did he ever ask you to come over to his place?" asked Boland.

Now the young man turned to eye the detective, suspiciously. "Hey, where's this going?" he inquired skeptically. "You think the guy was a homo or something?"

"Is that a 'yes'?" Boland pressed.

"I don't know, maybe," Clay remembered, clearly searching his memory. "Maybe he did." The realization Wes might have been a homosexual was slowly dawning on him. "Hey, how was he killed, anyway?"

"He was stabbed in his bed," Venetucci answered. "He bled out a little while later in the dining room."

"Whoa! Are you serious?" the valet asked, picturing the grisly scene. "That's bogus!" he exclaimed, shaking his head. "Aren't there like eight pints of blood in the human body or something? I think I read that somewhere."

"Anything you can tell us about him would be helpful," Boland prodded.

Clay looked up again. "You mean like homo stuff? Is that what you're asking? I don't know, man. I'm not a homo. I mean, to each his own, you know, but …"

"Did you ever see any unusual behavior with Wes that you can think of?" Venetucci asked.

Clay thought about this for a moment. "Yeah, all of it, now," he confessed. "That explains a lot. You got my head spinning, dude. Now it makes sense, why he was always coming out here talking to me and bringing me food and stuff," Clay recalled. "And water."

"But he was never aggressive with you or anything like that?" asked Boland.

"No, not at all," the young man said adamantly. "I told you he was a cool dude. I liked the guy. I'm sorry he's dead."

The detectives expressed their dismay as well. They headed back to their car, pondering what they had learned about Wes from all of the hotel employees at the Ritz Carlton. "Okay, the guy was in the closet except when he was around other gays. That much we know," Boland began, as they briskly walked. "Most people liked him and thought he was friendly, but one guy got on his bad side and, let's face it, Wes bullied him pretty hard. He humiliated the guy in front of his co-workers."

"And what was that about Wes going ballistic over the guy looking inside his car?" Venetucci asked.

"Yeah, that was definitely a hot spot for the guy. He seemed pretty paranoid about it for some reason," Boland agreed. The detectives got back into their car and left the grounds of the hotel for the day. Over the next few weeks, they would eventually interview every employee at the Ritz Carlton, Palm Beach.

CHAPTER 7
Lee's Trail

As police continued to scour Mr. Wallace's bleak apartment for evidence, Media Affairs Captain Rick Bradley had begun to talk to the reporters parked outside the department. The sun reflected off his badge as he held his head high before the crowd. It was Tuesday, June 8, 1999.

The purpose of his message was to release information that could draw in potential witnesses. Like the newspapers, Bradley only disclosed the basics: William Wesley Wallace had been slain in his Lake Osborne Drive home early Sunday morning. He was believed to have gotten into a fight with someone, and his white 1986 Acura Legend was now missing. "The neighbors next door to Mr. Wallace heard an argument," he explained, and one of them had found the body.

Such grisly evidence as the bloody submerged sheets and pillow, the gold lamp base, and the Clorox bottle would be withheld. They would serve as qualifiers for anyone who came forward about the murder. Only someone with inside information would know about these items. The story would eventually froth with all the elements that both the media and the public craved: murder, sex, and a Palm Beach trial, but for now, the homosexual aspect would be withheld.

The fact that the crime had occurred inside a senior community made it all the more frightening. Channel 4 reporter Angela Rae approached one of the residents of the Lake Osborne Apartments while the woman was out walking her cat. "It's just horrible," the woman exclaimed. "To think that it could happen to any of us. It just makes you want to stay inside and pull down your blinds."

Detective Boland observed the prying news reporter on TV and pondered his next move. He was going to have to get word out to Mr. Wallace's daughter in California. The thought of calling her and breaking the news over the phone seemed cruel. It was doubtful she knew about her father's sexual activities, and learning of it after all these years was sure to alter her reality. The double blow of hearing about his murder on top of it was likely to be traumatic. No, the news should be delivered in person. Boland decided he would let the Orange County Police Department know and they could send an officer out to the daughter's home. It was the decent thing to do.

***

Late Tuesday afternoon, Boland was at his cubicle at the homicide unit when the desk sergeant told him Wes Wallace's missing white 1986 Acura Legend had been located behind Don Ramon's. The Mexican restaurant's back parking lot was a notorious car-dumping site for criminals. "Jesus!" Boland cracked, "Does every God damned car thief in the county eat at that place?" Now he picked up his phone. "Lance," he barked, "we just found that '86 Acura from the homicide last night. I'm going to need a flatbed to transport the car to the police impound for cyanoacrylate fuming."

Boland knew simply dusting for prints in the vehicle would not work because the sweat in a print will dry after a very short time. The body's amino acids, however, can remain for months, and cyanoacrylate, otherwise known as super glue, naturally clusters and solidifies these acids, which ultimately leaves a sticky image of the fingerprint. Of course the disadvantage of the super glue technique is that it damages the interior of the vehicle. The Acura, which now belonged to the victim's daughter, would be declared a total loss by the insurance company once they were done checking it for prints.

On Wednesday, June 9, 1999, an article in the *Sun Sentinel* read:

"Police got a major break on Tuesday when they found the car belonging to a man who was killed on Sunday. Neighbors heard an argument at the Lake Osborne Drive apartment of William Wesley Wallace in the early morning hours on Sunday. About 12 hours later, a neighbor discovered his body and called police. Lake Worth police said they think Wallace met somebody and they went to his house, where they had a fight. Police did not say how he was killed. On Tuesday at 2 a.m., the Palm Beach County Sheriff's Office found his 1986 Acura Legend in a commercial parking lot along Military Trail in an unincorporated area near West Palm Beach. Police still want to know where Wallace was on Saturday night."

After an extensive three-hour examination of the car the next day at the Lake Worth auto processing station, the dusting procedure failed to yield any fingerprints. Inside the covered center console of the car, however, was a black wallet that contained Wes's old North Carolina driver's license and a social club card that offered discounts at various businesses. Lying on top of it was ten dollars in the form of a five and five ones. Oddly, there also was a brown wallet on the driver's side floor area tucked underneath the floor mat. This one had twenty-eight dollars in it along with Wes's current Florida driver's license, six credit cards, an ATM card, and a Ritz Carlton ID. This brought to mind a pertinent question for the detectives: Why did the victim have two wallets?

***

The victim had been a security guard the last twelve years of his life. Alcohol had gotten him fired from his branch manager job at North American Van Lines in 1987. This had prompted the decision to leave his home state of North Carolina and start a new life near his daughter, who lived in Delray Beach, Florida, at the time.

Wes spent the next several years working security for employers such as The Polo Club of Boca Raton. The Polo Club is an exclusive golf and tennis club known to host professional golf and tennis matches. Wes and his daughter had come to watch athletes like Venus and Serena Williams play. He had also worked security for Lake Worth Community College.

It was while working at the college that Wes would come to discover John Prince Memorial Park, just a five-minute drive from the campus. The park was also only a mile and a quarter from Wes's apartment on Lake Osborne Drive, where he would later be found brutally murdered. Venetucci and Boland decided to pay a visit to what was then regarded as a notorious gay cruising site.

The 726-acre county park was nestled on an isolated piece of land that was primarily surrounded by water. Hidden deep inside the murky marshlands was a nature trail that led through the mostly scrub habitat. The trail was a reliable location to find limpkins, also known as crying birds. These lanky, annoyingly loud creatures could be seen strutting through the sawgrass sticking their long beaks into snails they found in the marsh—swallowing them whole. Stalkers by nature, the crying birds appeared to mimic the gay hustling that was going on along the beaten dirt path that encircled their private lair. This shrouded haven was ideal for anonymous sex.

There were three entrances to John Prince Park, which made for easy access, as well as an easy escape from the police. One was on Sixth Avenue, one was on South Congress Avenue, and one was on Lake Worth Road.

One trail known as "Lee's Trail" was the most accessible and notorious of the gay cruising paths. It ran deep into the park and joined the main trail that ran along the water's edge. There, middle-aged studs could bend twenty-year-old pretty boys called twinks over the marshy bank and not be seen from the road. In less than five minutes what they did would be over and quickly forgotten. Barely a word would be exchanged.

There were various and distinct types of men that were drawn to the natural hookup site. Age and build were often factors, but the details were more interesting than the act itself. First, there were bears and cubs who were ruggedly masculine; then, there were Marys and muscle Marys who were softer versions. Next, there were twinks who were one step away from being transvestites; and last, there were tired old queens who had been down the drag path and looked weathered and worn.

Detectives Venetucci and Boland stepped through the grass that was longer than the grass at most parks, due to the fact that the place was a marsh. Venetucci thought of his son, Dominic, who was only one year old. He was just learning to walk, and high vegetation like this would surely give him trouble. The thought made him smile. Finally they spied the orange 1967 Dodge van up ahead that was known to be driven by John Latham. It was parked in a clearing away from the clusters of coconut palms and paradise trees. A figure was sitting in the driver's seat.

Latham was a fit man in his early thirties with a thin beard and a confident air about him. He looked perplexed as the detectives quickly approached the window.

"Afternoon, Mr. Latham, is it?" Venetucci began.

Now the man looked alarmed. "Yes?" he answered, his voice a bit higher than usual.

"We're looking for anyone who knew this man," the

detective stated, holding up a color photo of Wes. Latham studied the strapping man in shades before him. He looked tough. At six feet tall and burly, it was clear the man had lifted plenty of weights over the years. Though his belly stuck out underneath his shirt, his shoulders and lats were exceptionally broad. They almost extended off the sides of the photo.

Latham relaxed a little. "Yeah, I know that guy. He used to come here all the time. A cop who was here yesterday said he's dead."

"He is," Boland confirmed, stepping closer to the window, his arms folded. "What was your relationship with him?"

Latham chuckled. "Oh, I didn't have a relationship with him. He would just drive up and talk to me sometimes when I was here."

"When was the first time?" Venetucci asked.

Latham looked off into the distance as his mind traveled back over the last few months. "Probably in December," he recalled. Florida was just as warm in December as it was in April or May. The snowbirds flocked down south and swam in the ocean, while the locals pointed at them amusedly from the beach. Most would not be caught dead going in the water unless it was at least eighty degrees.

The man explained he tended to visit John Prince Park in the late afternoons. He would choose a secluded spot like this one that was peaceful and quiet to get away from his sister and his three teenaged kids, who lived with him. Latham had a pilot's license. He enjoyed sitting in his van watching the planes land, he said. He liked to listen to them on his scanner.

Venetucci and Boland both looked over at the dash. They noticed his scanner was not on.

Latham went on to explain Wes drove slowly through

the park quite often. "In the beginning, he didn't pay any attention to me, and I didn't pay any attention to him," he said. But Latham had a noticeable vehicle. It was an orange 1967 Dodge van.

One night when Latham was on his way home, he looked into his rearview mirror to find that Wes was behind him. He had seen Wes's white Acura several times in the park, so it made him somewhat nervous, he said.

Venetucci and Boland glanced over at each other, skeptically. Who was he trying to kid? This was not this guy's first time around the block at John Prince, they thought. The park was known to be a spot for gay cruising, so why would Wes following him make him nervous?

Latham said he pulled over to the right, and Wes drove past him, then brazenly pulled directly in front of his van. Latham was not happy about that. He pounded his hands on the wheel until Wes stepped on the gas and drove off.

Boland asked him if he thought Wes had seen him. "Oh, he saw me," Latham said. A couple of days later he'd been sitting in his spot in the park when Wes drove up. Latham told them that Wes pulled up next to him and apologized for following him. There were a lot of times after that when Wes would just drive up and start a conversation. It was clear to the man that Wes wanted sex. "He was extremely persistent," Latham explained, but he just chose to change the subject with Wes.

Latham told the detectives that Wes cruised the park a lot. He saw him go by his van maybe twenty or thirty times.

"Was he ever violent toward you?" asked Boland.

"No. He never threatened me or anything," Latham answered. "The whole thing was just creepy."

"Did you ever go back to Wes's apartment with him?" Detective Venetucci boldly asked.

"Absolutely not," Latham replied.

CHAPTER 8
Bite Marks

On Wednesday, June 9, 1999, Venetucci was eating strawberry pancakes at The Clock restaurant. His wife, Michele, usually made him breakfast, but she was down with the flu, so he was relishing the opportunity to have what she would call "the equivalent of eating chocolate cake for breakfast." Afterward, he left and picked up Boland at his Lake Worth home. Boland had passed on the invitation to breakfast, saying he had already had his super-green shake with antioxidant- and nutrient-packed vegetables. Venetucci was sorry he had asked.

They pulled up outside the massive stucco and glass Palm Beach County Sheriff's Office Crime Laboratory. Coconut palms swayed in the restless breeze overhead as Venetucci parked the black, government-issued Crown Victoria. Boland grabbed his notebook and pen, and they headed inside.

The detectives were led into a chilly, fifty-foot-long autopsy room. Wes's bluish-gray body was already out on a gurney waiting for them under harsh lights that cast eerie shadows in the corners. A stainless steel table full of shiny dissection tools like scalpels and forceps sat to his right. The body bag had already been unzipped.

Carrie Alred, the elfin thirty-four-year-old autopsy technician dressed in a white lab coat introduced herself. She wanted to know what had happened.

"Some kind of lover's spat, we think," asserted Venetucci.

"A lot of blood was found on the victim's bed."

Alred had a strange look on her face. She knew women rarely resorted to murder and violence was an even rarer occurrence for dispute resolution. Women were much more fond of using poison to kill someone. It was easy to disperse during their expected role of caretaking. And women, in general, did not like to make messes. Probably, Alred thought, because they knew they would likely be called upon to clean it up afterward.

"We think it was a guy," Boland added.

"Oh," Alred uttered.

Wes lay stiffly on his back in front of them. Doctor Jon Thogmartin, the balding medical examiner with small, round glasses soon joined the three of them. He cut open the bag and quickly noted the ample amount of blood around the victim's neck. A lab photographer began taking flash photographs. The clicking sound of the camera echoed throughout the cold vault of a room.

There were several abrasions and scratches on the right side of the victim's face that crossed in some places. None were deep, and all lay in straight lines as if they had been made with the edge of a tool. His blue, chapped lips had been split with a cutting instrument as well. Contusions or purple bruises marked both of his upper arms.

Thogmartin stepped over to the victim's right hand, which had two small scratches on it. The detectives dutifully followed. They each noticed bite wounds on the victim's right wrist. There was also some kind of wound on the back of the victim's left hand.

"These are mandibular marks," the medical examiner remarked clinically of the bite marks.

"What do you make of that, doctor?" Boland asked curiously.

"That means that the lower partial of the killer's teeth bit into the victim's wrist. Something had to have been pressing down on the killer's head at the time." His brow furrowed and he frowned at the thought.

"Something or someone," surmised Venetucci.

The doctor nodded in agreement.

Thogmartin and Alred removed Wes's blood-soaked white Ralph Lauren shirt, blue shorts, and boxers. They placed them each carefully into evidence bags. Swab samples were taken of the inside of the victim's mouth and anal opening to be tested later for DNA. Next, the victim's face and body were washed down with a narrow, black hose. The detectives watched as watery blood ran down the grooves on the sides of the examination table into a shiny, stainless steel collection sink.

Thogmartin carefully documented each injury by mapping out each one onto an outline of the face or body on his clipboard. Each wound had to be measured in length and depth and width.

The autopsy dragged on until the detectives finally relocated to an upper observation deck. Staring down at the morbid process made Boland think of all the victims who had ended up at the crime lab because of some violent bastard. *God, I hope I never have to see either one of my daughters here,* he thought grimly. Unfortunately, his years in the field made him painfully aware of that possibility, therefore, he vowed to perform a thorough background check on both of his daughters' male suitors in the future.

Venetucci's mind was on the murder weapon, which had not been found at the scene. He looked over the evidence list from Wes's apartment, which chronicled page after page of other items that had been seized: the gold lamp base, the bloodied bed sheets and pillow, the Clorox bottle, the milk carton, fingernail scrapings, tissues from the wastepaper basket, and more. The forensics team would have to establish whose blood was on what and label everything for the possibility of a future trial.

Eventually Thogmartin came up to visit, mindlessly wiping his gloved hands on his lab coat. "The mortal wound is on the right side of the victim's neck, right underneath his jaw," he reported as the detectives leaned back and listened. "It's a crescent-shaped wound that's three-quarters of an inch long. Although it was only an inch deep, it partially penetrated Mr. Wallace's external jugular vein, as well as a branch of his internal jugular vein. I believe the weapon was a thin blade with a dull edge," he said frowning. "The tip of the knife was dragged across the victim's skin." After the brief update, he diligently went back downstairs to finish his work.

By eleven that morning, Thogmartin and his colleague had finished the main exam. They were now upstairs in Thogmartin's third floor office. The two doctors laid out all of the printed photographs of Mr. Wallace's body. Each one had small marks on it that mapped out all of the injuries. There were twelve wounds in total on the victim's face and neck that appeared to have been made by the same knife. Each one measured between one-half-inch and one-inch long. The neck wounds all seemed to be inch-deep jabs that had been delivered with approximately the same amount of force.

Thogmartin found himself wondering what kind of killer attacked his victim in this way. It was hardly a display of rage. The doctor remembered seeing a twenty-three-year-old Hispanic female victim once that had suffered multiple stab wounds. She had incisions that were five inches deep. One had severed her windpipe and rendered her immediately unable to breathe. Her boyfriend had apparently discovered she had slept with his brother. It had been a crime of passion according to a jury of his peers. What kind of crime had this one been?

Venetucci found himself wondering the same thing. Something was nagging at him. It was the way the medical examiner had described the murder weapon. It was dull. Venetucci knew criminals. They were mostly cowards who made sure their blades were sharp before going up against an unarmed victim. And the most common knives used in stabbings were kitchen knives. Those were known to be sharp, too. Also, what kind of killer wielded small jabs at his victim? It was almost as if the person had been backed into a corner.

When the detectives got back to the station, they learned the Palm Beach Sheriff's Office pawn shop division had come up with a serial number hit on one of the VCRs they had entered. Pawn shops were required by law to enter the serial numbers of items that had been sold to them into the National Crime Information Center database as well as the state's version. Recorded in the pawn shop's log was the name of the seller: Tyler Montegut. Boland did a search in the Integrated Automated Fingerprint Identification System and came up with Montegut's fingerprints a few hours later. The guy had a history of selling drugs and receiving stolen items for payment. It was likely he was not the killer. This was not going to be an open and shut case.

CHAPTER 9
"Put a Shirt on Boy!"

Detectives Boland and Venetucci flew to Richmond International Airport the next day to interview Montegut. The African American young man had just moved back to his mother's house in Richmond, Virginia, and had come into possession of Wes's Sony VCR only days before his move home. The detectives believed young Montegut had been face-to-face with Wes's murderer.

In a phone conversation Montegut had asserted to Boland that the VCR had been given to him in a black duffle bag, and that Wes's name and address were still on the tag that was in his possession. Boland and Venetucci's superior, Lieutenant Paul Patti, felt it possible that having the bag was a valuable step forward in the case and approved the transportation and expense request for Boland and Venetucci to make the trip out to Virginia.

After landing at the airport, Boland and Venetucci picked up a burgundy Chevrolet Caprice at Hertz Rent-a-Car and drove toward Richmond. On their way, Venetucci noticed a stark law enforcement ad on a local city bus and pointed it out to his colleague: AN ILLEGAL GUN GETS YOU FIVE YEARS. A tough new state-wide program had been implemented called "Virginia Exile." It assured that any criminal who was caught carrying a gun during the commission of a crime was to be "exiled" to federal prison for five years. Venetucci and Boland would later learn the same message had been placed on fifteen billboards citywide and that there were TV commercials, traffic reports, and over one million supermarket bags bearing the same message.

The detectives were headed to a section of Richmond called Church Hill, which was reputed to be one of the most dangerous neighborhoods in the country. They pulled up in front of a dilapidated two-story, red-brick house with salmon-colored, wrought-iron railing. Before getting out of their rented vehicle, both men noted the assortment of neighborhood street types who had observed their arrival and automatically checked the readiness of their side arms. Being well-schooled law enforcement officers, as they got out of their vehicle they automatically recorded the accusing faces they saw around them.

It was Detective Boland who pulled open the ripped screen door and knocked on the worn wood behind it.

Venetucci noticed an African American woman in her fifties had come to a window and was now peeking behind one of the lace curtains at them and frowning. A few moments later she reluctantly came to the door and opened it a few inches. "Hep y'all wid somethin'?" she asked.

Boland flashed his badge for her, and her frown deepened. "Ma'am, we're here to see Tyler Montegut," he explained.

"We just have a few questions for him," Venetucci added.

Unconvinced, the woman looked him up and down skeptically. "Ya'll wait where you at. I juss be a minute," she replied, shutting the door.

The woman whom they took to be Mrs. Hanita Montegut, Tyler's mother, then turned to call up a staircase. "Tyler! Get youself down here, boy! Po-lice is here. Dey wants to talk wich you!"

Several seconds later a lanky young man in his mid-twenties leaned out the door of an upstairs bedroom. He was shirtless. "Yeah?" he demanded suspiciously.

"Two white po-lice here to talk wich you!" the

woman said again.

"What they want?" Tyler demanded.

"You bess put a shirt on, boy, and don't come down them steps lookin' like no heathern!" she ordered. "Yo' momma raise you better'n that!"

A minute later Tyler reappeared at the top of the stairs in a brown T-shirt. He shuffled down the steps, shoulders hunched.

"Now what these po-lice want *this* time, huh?" Mrs. Montegut inquired of her son, folding her arms over her plain cotton dress. "What kinda mess have you gotten youssself into now?"

"Mama," Tyler replied, "my biness ain't yo biness. Din I tole you that I was gon' get you money for them bills? And ain' that what you wanted?" Tyler asserted.

"I want a son that done have no laws comin' around lookin' for him every time we go to sit down and eat," she rasped.

"But you wants food on the table for Ruthie and Charmaine, don't you?" he argued, referring to his sisters.

The detectives knocked on the door once again, louder this time. Mrs. Montegut opened the door for them.

"I guess you two can come on in," she told them.

"Thank you, ma'am," Boland mumbled, as the woman shut the door behind them. "I'm Detective Boland from the Lake Worth Police Department and this is Detective Venetucci," Boland stated.

"Yeah?" Montegut asked carelessly. "What you guys want?"

"We're here about that duffle bag you said you have," Boland explained. "We want to talk to you about that."

"Oh, yeah? So you that cop that called," the young man remembered. He relaxed a little, then looked over at his mother, nervously. "Okay, let's go outside," he told the detectives.

"Yeah, you better go outside," his mother warned. "I don' wanna hear none about no nonsense you been up to lately."

Tyler led the detectives back out onto the porch. He pulled up a wooden chair for himself and motioned for them to sit on the three-seated swing. It moved slightly when they sat down. "You guys came all the way out here for that bag, huh?" Montegut asked, shaking his head.

"Tell us when you got it," Boland began.

"Look, man, I don't know what day, okay?" the young man recalled.

"What time of day was it? Morning? Afternoon? Night?" Venetucci asked.

"Oh, it was mornin'. Early mornin'. I remember that," Montegut recalled.

"What were you doing when you got the call?" Boland asked. "Did the guy call or just come over?"

"Oh, Travis don't have no phone. He just come on over," Montegut remembered. "I was sleepin'. Probly ... I dunno know, seven o'clock in the mornin' or somethin' like that."

His mother peeked out from the behind the curtain, frowned again, then let it drop in disgust.

"Did you notice if he had any cuts on his face or arms?" Boland asked.

Montegut shook his head. "Nah, I don't 'member. He looked just like he always did—dirty."

"What else?" Venetucci coaxed. "Can you tell us what he looked like?"

"Travis?" the young man asked, then laughed. "Scrawny. That white boy was scrawny. Hair kinda like yours," he said, pointing at Boland's dirty blond crew cut. "He wasn't that tall neither. Maybe five-six or somethin' like that."

"Do you know his last name?" Boland asked.

"Nah," Montegut said.

"Did he have any facial hair?" Venetucci pressed.

"He wasn't clean shaven, if thas what you mean," the young man answered. "I wouldn't say he had like a beard or moustache or nothin', though," he said, laughing again. "Dude didn't even look old enough to grow one."

"Any tattoos? Piercings?"

"Nah."

"So what did he want?" Boland asked.

Montegut chuckled again. "Rocks. Travis always wanted rocks," he said. Crack cocaine.

"How many times had you sold to him before?" Boland asked him.

Montegut thought about it a moment. "I don't know, forty, fifty times. Somethin' like that," he estimated.

"And what all did he have with him?" Venetucci wanted to know.

"He had a shoppin' cart with a couple of VCRs in it, a stereo, and some other shit." Montegut said he took a look at the stuff and immediately noticed the stereo had no speakers and he wasn't interested in purchasing it. Travis tried to get him to change his mind. Tyler still was not interested. He would give Travis thirty dollars worth of rocks for one of the VCRs. No more. Again, Travis tried to convince him to buy the stereo. Montegut did not know that the young man allegedly had just killed a man and was trying to sell his possessions.

"Travis gave me one of the VCRs in that black bag, and I gave him some rocks, like he wanted. Then he took off, and I went back in the house," Montegut explained.

"Any idea where he went after that?" Boland asked.

The young man shook his head. "Nah."

"When did the VCR get pawned?" Venetucci wanted to know.

"Me and my girl took it to Cash America the next day,"

Montegut answered. Cash America was a pawnshop on Dixie Highway in Lake Worth, Florida, that ironically featured "confidential pawn loans."

"What's your girlfriend's name?" Boland asked.

"Tina. Tina Heidel," Montegut answered. "She white, like you," he said, smiling. "I gots me a white girl."

Boland informed the young man that if they caught the killer they would be subpoenaing him as a witness at the trial. They would also need a DNA sample from him and molds of his teeth. "Where's the bag?" the detective asked.

Montegut got up and went inside to get it, while the detectives sat on the porch swing, eyeballing the neighborhood. Montegut returned a few minutes later with a black canvas bag about two feet long in his hand. The bag's creased American Airlines tag had the deceased's name and old Delray Beach address on it. It had been worth the trip. The bag definitely belonged to Wes. They also had the first name and physical description of the alleged killer. They were getting somewhere.

CHAPTER 10
Sugar Mountain

Since the detectives had flown out to Virginia and rented a car, they decided to make the extra three-hour trip over to Greensboro, North Carolina, to interview several of Wes's friends from when he had lived there twelve years prior. Before leaving Florida, they had compiled a list of names, phone numbers, and addresses from Wes's address book. There was no shortage of names for them to choose from, but they had narrowed it down to a half-dozen for the sake of saving time and expenses.

The first names on the list were Mike and April Rogers, who lived in a middle class section of Greensboro called Lindley Park. It was less than two miles away from the Lindley Park Pool. The place was a popular summertime hangout for April's teenaged nephews. It gave them something to do on hot summer nights other than hang out on the hoods of their cars in the parking lot of the Roy Rogers restaurant.

April and Mike Rogers's house was a small, slate blue bungalow with a foundation, front porch supports, and chimney that were all made of milk quartz. The glazed, opaque rock had been chosen by April's grandfather when the house had belonged to him. It was native to the Carolina Slate Belt, which ran through Guilford County and produced most of the state's gold, as well. Out back, there was a paved patio inside a large fenced-in yard with room for their dogs. April was a dog catcher, and Mike was a painter. She happened to be squatting down outside filling her husky's water bowl on her lunch break when the detectives pulled into the driveway.

"Ma'am, I'm Detective Boland from the Lake Worth Police Department in Palm Beach County and this is Detective Venetucci," Boland announced. April stood up as tall as her five-foot-two frame would allow. She was forty-six, yet still wore her dark hair in a youthful ponytail.

"Palm Beach?" she repeated in surprise.

"Yes," Boland confirmed. "You and your husband's names came up during an investigation, and we'd like to ask you a few questions, if we may."

"*Our* names?" she asked. "I don't know why our names would come up. Okay. Well, Mike's not home, but I've got half an hour or so."

The three of them went in through the side door of the house and sat down in the small living room. April let the detectives sit on the chocolate-colored, leather sofa and she took the recliner, though she kept it in the upright position. Years ago, a large felt picture of a black panther adorned the wall above the couch. Now it bore a portrait of April and her husband. They were old drinking buddies of Wes's who had managed to ease up off the alcohol over the years without the help of The Program—Alcoholics Anonymous.

Boland informed April of Wes's murder, and her mind traveled back over the years as she grieved.

"How did he die?" she asked.

The detectives explained Wes had been stabbed. They witnessed a look of horror descend over the woman's face.

"Stabbed? Oh my Lord," she cried.

Venetucci then asked her what kind of man Wes had been.

"Wes used to call up and ask me what I was cookin' that night," April recalled sadly. "Then he'd show up with a case of Pabst Blue Ribbon. He was a lot of fun. Mike and I really liked him," she added. "He'd lean over the pot of chili I was cookin' and tell me how good it smelled, then he'd ask me if I'd caught any dogs that day. He always wanted to know if I'd caught any dogs."

Sometimes they would all creep down the wooden stairs past April and Mike's waterbed to the basement where they would play pool. "Wes did more talkin' than playin'," April remembered. "It was really Mike and I who loved to play."

"How long had you and your husband known him?" Venetucci asked.

"Oh, I'd say about twenty years. We met Wes at a BBQ that my friend had one summer. Mike and I had been playin' horseshoes out back, and he wanted his daughter to learn how to play. That little girl was the world to him," April remembered as her eyes teared up. "Oh, Lord—she must be fallin' to pieces right now."

"Was he working when you knew him?" Boland asked.

"Yeah. I believe he was a bartender," April managed to say.

"When had you seen him last?" Venetucci wanted to know.

"Umm, Mike and I took a trip out to Florida back in '95, I think? We had lunch with Wes and his daughter at some restaurant on the beach that he wanted us to go to. They served crab. Wes told us we had to try the crab."

"Was anyone else with him at the time?" Boland asked. "Did he have a girlfriend or anyone special in his life?"

"No, Wes didn't have a girlfriend. Come to think of it, he never had one that we ever knew of." April pondered for a moment. "Oh, but I mean, we knew he'd been married and all that. We'd just never seen him with anyone." April and Mike were not sure of their friend's sexual preference, but they had their suspicions. They really did not know much about their friend's personal life.

"Did you and your husband stay with Wes when you were in Florida?" Venetucci asked.

"Oh, no. His place was much too small," she said. "We stayed at a little motel down the road."

"Was that the only trip that you and your husband made out to Florida to see him?" Boland wanted to know.

"Yeah, that was the only one. We did go to Sugar Mountain with Wes and his daughter one time, though, to go skiin'," she recalled. "That time we all shared a room with two double beds. Wes pulled in a cot for his daughter."

"Did anything unusual happen on the trip?" Venetucci pressed.

April looked puzzled. "No, not that I recall. There was this boy down in the gift shop, though. He was a cute kid a couple of years older than Denise, I think. Maybe fourteen or somethin'. Anyway, Wes invited him to come light sparklers with Denise that Wes had brought," she explained. "So Wes and that kid lit sparklers in the snow. I think Wes had even more fun than Denise that night lightin' those sparklers. He was like a big kid with that little boy. You should've seen it." Boland scribbled down some notes as his partner shifted positions on the couch.

"Was Wes violent at all that you recall?" Venetucci asked.

April thought about that for a moment. "You know, we never saw him get violent, but then we always hung out with him at our house. Mike and I are on a budget. We don't really go out to bars," April confessed. "I do remember Wes tellin' us years ago that he'd gotten into some bar fights. It was hard to picture him getting mad at anyone or makin' anyone else mad. He was always so friendly when he drank. Him and Mike never had a problem. I do remember drivin' him to the supermarket one time to pick up some more beer," April said. "Wes said he'd had his driver's license suspended, so Mike and I let him sleep on the couch whenever he came over during that time. That way he wouldn't get stopped for drunk drivin' again. That's all I know," she concluded.

Wes's driver's license had been suspended for ninety days after his first DWI, Boland discovered. After his second one, it had been suspended for a year. He and Venetucci thanked April for her time and walked back out to their car. They had four more names on their list.

CHAPTER 11
The Fashion Designer

The next name on the list was Bill Drew. Boland and Venetucci took a drive over to Aycock Park, a prestigious area that had been developed back in the late nineteenth and early twentieth centuries. The section was one of three local historic districts in Greensboro, the other two being Fisher Park, which was near Wes's old apartment, and College Hill, which was near University North Carolina at Greensboro.

Bill's house had been constructed back in 1912, before the first skyscrapers had begun appearing on the north side of downtown. It featured a white, Neoclassical Revival facade with a full-height portico of paired Ionic columns, a wraparound porch supported by Tuscan columns, and unusual corner bay windows with curved plate glass.

Since Bill was a fashion designer, he had chosen to place mannequins in the corner windows that could display his chic, elegant clothing. The resulting look was that of the Victorian era storefront section of South Elm Street that the Old Greensborough Preservation Society had rallied to save.

The detectives stepped up to the front porch, and Boland rang the brass, Victorian twist doorbell. Bill appeared after several long moments and ushered them into the stylish parlor that was lit by a brass, gothic candle chandelier. The stocky gentleman sported a comb-over that was graying and complained about a bunion that was giving him trouble. He offered them each a seat in one of the peach, Victorian balloon-backed chairs and then sat down himself.

The fashion designer had been flipping through a copy of *Fine Line Hosiery,* the detectives noticed. It lay open, facedown on top of the gold-trimmed Toscano Madame Antoinette end table beside the gold, antique French phone that he had owned for two decades. He was getting ready for Greensboro Fashion Week, a local designer runway show that was the biggest fashion event of the year in North Carolina.

Bill had met Wes way back in the eighties when gays had not yet become visible in the bigger metro areas, much less in the South. Sheriff Gerald Hege of Lexington, North Carolina, had changed all that in the nineties when he went on to become nationally famous as the law enforcement officer who always dressed in riot gear, drove a squad car that had been souped up by NASCAR mechanics, and painted all the jail cells pink. He also liked to dress his prisoners in colorful children's pajamas.

It was around the time when the Tarheel Leather Club had organized bar nights, AIDS fundraisers, and toy drives all over Guilford County. Their home bar was the Palms, but they had also been known to frequent Warehouse 29, the most popular gay bar in Greensboro back in the eighties, where Bill had met Wes. Though the drinking age in North Carolina was eighteen, one had to either be twenty-one or older to enter or be signed in by a member who was twenty-one or older. All newcomers had to fill out a membership form to get in, and despite the inconvenience, the club drew redneck guys all the way from rural Virginia on a Friday or Saturday night.

The open warehouse with the black canopy over the door featured a large outdoor patio and sand volleyball court for afternoon events. At night, the club lit up with something for everyone: drag shows, go-go boys, fan dancers, pageants, and contests. Bill had met Wes on drag-queen night at the bar back in 1982. They had gotten along like old friends from the start and hosted dinner for each other on countless occasions.

"Oh, no," Bill cried when he heard the news of Wes's murder. "Not Wes. Oh!" he moaned.

The detectives patiently allowed the man a few moments to grieve.

"Wes was a dear friend of mine. He was such an enchanting fellow—an exuberant old soul!" Bill reached for a tissue from the brass filigree tissue box and dabbed at the tears he could not stop from coming. "Oh, I just can't believe it."

"How long had you known him?" Boland asked.

"Almost twenty years," Bill managed to say.

"When was the last time you saw him?" asked the detective.

Bill said he had not seen Wes in several years.

"Had you known about his sexual orientation?" Venetucci asked.

"Yes," Bill said. "But what does that have to do with anything? Why can't people just live their own lives?" he sobbed.

When Bill learned Wes had been stabbed in his bed and managed to crawl to the dining room, he nearly screeched in horror. "He *bled out*? Poor, poor Wes," he said, still overcome with emotion. "How awful! How hideous!"

This question and answer session was more than Bill could bear. He would need a day to collect himself, he said. Boland said he and Venetucci would show themselves out and call on him again tomorrow. They knew from experience that they would not be able to glean any new information from a hysterical character witness. Better to give him a chance to calm down.

CHAPTER 12
Grease Monkeys and Hard Hats

The next name on the detectives' list was Cathy Rordin, so they set out for the lower-middle-class section of southwest Greensboro called the Hewitt Area. Often referred to as Hewitt Area-Pomona, it was also Wes's place of birth. Fifty-one percent of the people in the Hewitt Area are African American, while only 31 percent are Caucasian. Cathy and Wes had both found themselves attending Baptist churches that were founded before the American Revolution. Even then, African Americans, both slave and free, had been treated as equals to white members at the churches.

Cathy lived in a Craftsman-style bungalow that featured battered stone porch supports, wide overhanging eaves with scrolled exposed rafters, and a low-pitched roofline. She had thought the structure looked like something out of *Grimm's Fairy Tales* when she'd moved in.

Cathy had been a waitress at the Red Baron Lounge where Wes had worked as a bartender back in the early eighties. It had been a smoky hotel bar that catered to blue-collar workers. The waitresses had worn black Danskin leotards and miniskirts with bright red sashes. At six feet one inches, Cathy had long bangs and biscuit-colored hair that fell just short of her shoulders. She had to bend down to get through the door. Like Wes, she was an alcoholic.

"No, I haven't seen Wes in a few years," she told Boland when he asked. Wes had given her a call back in 1998, and she had told him her mother had died. Boland informed her

Wes had died, as well, but that he had been murdered.

"What? Wes was murdered!" she cried. "Why would anybody want to murder Wes?"

The detective said that was what they were trying to find out. They relayed the manner of Wes's death to the woman as she lit up a cigarette.

"What kind of man was he?" Boland asked.

"Wes just liked to drink and smoke," she remembered. "Oh, and eat. Wes loved to eat. He and the other waitresses and I would come back to my place sometimes and drink beer and shoot the shit," she reminisced, taking a drag on her Marlboro Light. "Wes was a riot. He was always sayin' 'Cathy, you're so tall, why don't you quit waitressing and play basketball.'" It was the way he said it, she remembered. His face would light up with laughter, and he would pat her on the back of one of her long, stockinged legs. He had not been able to reach her ass from the chair. The one time he had slapped her ass by mistake he had apologized over and over again, he had been so embarrassed about it.

"How long had you known Wes?" Venetucci asked.

"I think I started working at the Red Baron in 1981, so, how long's it been now? Almost twenty years?" Cathy deduced. "Wes started working a couple of months after I did. He replaced the older bartender I didn't like—Mark or Mack or something. Wes was a lot more fun to work with."

"How so?" Boland pressed.

"Well, he was always glad to see me. He'd smile and ask me how was I doing, and he really wanted to know, you know?" Cathy remembered sadly. "That's just how he was."

"Was he a good employee?" Venetucci asked.

"Oh yeah. He kept the regulars comin' in. He'd remember their names, what they drank and whatnot. Everybody loved Wes," Cathy said as she took another drag on her cigarette.

"And was there a love in Wes's life?" Boland asked.

The question made Cathy laugh. "Wes? No. Huh uh. He liked to buy drinks for the cute guys at the bar, though," she said.

"So he was gay? Did he tell you that?" Venetucci wanted to know.

"Look, Wes didn't say he was gay, but he didn't say he wasn't, either. All I know is what I saw," Cathy confessed.

"What was that?" Venetucci asked.

The former waitress thought back over the years of working with Wes. "He would flirt with the guys. Especially the young ones. I remember because he liked the ones I liked," she recalled. "Sometimes I'd get kinda mad, you know, because he'd be talking to 'em and I couldn't get a word in!" Cathy laughed again. "That was Wes. He was real loud, and he always had the attention of the room."

"Had you ever known of him to be violent with anyone?" Boland asked.

"Violent?" Cathy thought about this for a moment. "Well, I seen him get mad at some customers, but I never saw him hit anyone or anything," she told him. "We had some Carolina boys in blue down there, you know. Some grease monkeys and hard hats that would get crocked and wanna fight. Wes would just tell 'em 'Go on, get outta here, you sumbitch, before I knock you in the middle of next week!' or something like that," Cathy explained. "You didn't want to mess with Wes. He had a look in his eyes that could scare the bejesus outta you."

The detectives looked at each other, then Boland took a look at his watch.

"You guys want some lemonade or somethin'?" Cathy offered sweetly, standing up. "It's mighty hot out there today." They declined the offer and thanked the woman for her time. They had more of Wes's friends to see.

CHAPTER 13
Stroke Play

The next name on the list was Jan Sealy. Boland and Venetucci took a drive over to Starmount Forest, an upper-middle-class section that was home to the Starmount Forest Country Club, which had held the first women's US Open for stroke play in golf. Since 1974, Jan had lived in a red-brick Colonial home with fluted Corinthian columns that she had acquired in an amiable divorce. Beneath the windows was a tiered, manicured hedge in the shape of topiary. It was a family friendly neighborhood, where the kids played outside and people left the keys in the ignitions of their cars.

Jan was a former beauty with long, white curls and fingers that were good at pointing out other people's faults. She had met Wes in AA. Their daughters were the same age, and the two girls had played together a lot over at Jan's. She had not talked to Wes in years and was shocked to hear about his death. "Wes was murdered?" she asked. "What happened to him?"

Boland told the woman about the grisly murder, and she cringed from the picture that formed in her head. "How long had you known him?" he asked.

"Wesley and I met through Dr. Clemmons," Jan explained to Boland. "He was a psychologist in The Program who'd seen both Wesley and me," she went on. "My drink of choice was wine. White wine. I'd fallen off the wagon a second time back in 1981, and Wes had been there for me then. He'd had a few more months in AA than I'd had, and he used to tell me, 'Jan, you know you can't drink—it makes you crazy. Now how are you going to raise Mary if you're crazy?' he'd say. Then he'd come over to the house and pick me up, and we'd go to an AA meeting."

The woman said Wes had a sense about people and a way with them. "He'd had a lot of years in sales, and you could tell. He knew what made people tick, and he'd use it on you in a non-threatening way," she smiled sadly as she lit up a cigarette. "Thank God it worked on me."

"What was the nature of your relationship with Wes?" Boland asked.

"Oh, Wes and I were just friends. I was seeing a guy named Don at the time, and he didn't mind Wes coming over at all. He was actually glad to have some help keeping me sober," Jan confessed with a laugh. She had not known of Wes's sexual preferences, nor had she cared, she said. They were both in The Program working the steps. The two had young daughters to raise. And they were both divorced, so the job was even tougher.

"Did Wes help anyone else in AA?" Venetucci asked.

"Uh, huh. More than one. I believe Wes was sponsoring a young man when I met him," Jan stated. "And he was real friendly. He liked to welcome in the newcomers and make them feel at home. It helped him to help others, I think. It really did. 'Your story is the key to unlocking someone's else's prison' was the quote he liked to use. I can still hear him say it," she said with a sad smile as she took a drag on Virginia Slims.

"Did you know of him to be violent?" Boland asked.

"Wes? No, not that I know of. I never saw anything like that," Jan claimed. "Why would you ask that? Wasn't Wes the one who was murdered?"

"We're just trying to get the whole picture, ma'am," Boland explained.

"Do *you* think he was violent?" Jan continued.

"We don't know."

"But you must think he was or you wouldn't have asked."

"It's just a routine question, Ms. Sealy," Boland responded. Jan did not seem to believe him. "Look, despite what you've seen on TV, murder is not a very common crime, but it's more common among people who put themselves in high-risk situations."

"Like violent ones?"

"Yes."

Jan thought about this for a moment and took another drag on her cigarette through her long fingers.

"What else did you and Wes do besides go to AA meetings together?" Venetucci asked in an attempt to change the subject.

"Well, Wes and his daughter went to church with Mary and me sometimes up at Starmount Presbyterian," Jan recalled. The church was a mile away from Starmount Country Club out on Sam Snead Drive where Lynda's father had bought them a membership after she and Wes were married. Wes found it amusing that some of the golfers from the aristocratic club had formed a group at the church called the Slicers and Duffers. He joked that it had been a sneaky way for the country club members to say 'No Jews allowed.'"

"We also took the girls ice skating at the Carolina Circle Mall quite a bit," Jan added. "It was indoors, so they had it year-round."

"Was Wes a good father?" Boland wondered.

"Oh, yeah. He doted on his little girl, I mean, she was all he had." Jan took another drag on her Virginia Slims. "One time we took the girls to this kids' disco in the mall," Jan remembered, smiling. "It was called Current Events or something. Anyway, there was this real tall young black man there. He was the best dancer in the place, and he had on a pair of those bell-bottoms that we all had back in the seventies. You know the ones?" she recalled, laughing at the memory.

The detectives nodded. They did.

"Well, Wes went up to the guy and asked him, 'Will you dance with my daughter?' and the guy told him 'no.' But Wes wasn't taking 'no' for an answer. He kept on bugging that guy until he finally agreed to dance one song with Wes's daughter just to shut him up," Jan said. "I don't think his daughter even wanted to dance with him. But you didn't say 'no' to Wes. It didn't work. I never forgot that," she said.

As they left Jan Sealy's home the detectives would not forget it either. A man who would not be denied his wishes and desires might be capable of who knows what to get his way.

CHAPTER 14
Hustling the Hustlers

The last name on the list Boland had compiled from Wes's personal address book had been printed in darker ink than the rest of the names. The page had also been worn, which signaled to the detective that this person may have played a more significant role in Wes's life.

Boland pulled the rented burgundy Caprice into the circular driveway of the sprawling, white, Queen Anne home. A hexagonal gazebo jutted out from the left, while a second-floor turret sat further back on the right. Both detectives got out of the car and ventured up the gray, tumbled-stone walkway, taking in the dramatic feel of the property.

Dr. Howard Adcock greeted them at the door and guided them into the grand foyer. From there, he led them through the French doors of the great room, out the back, and onto the Camelot river blend pavers where they had a seat at the wrought-iron table on the patio.

Although it was June, the temperature that afternoon was still a cool seventy-six degrees. There was a mild breeze, the professor noticed, as he stared out at the low-hanging Spanish moss that swung slightly from the laurel oak in his garden like gray feather boas.

Dr. Adcock was a sophisticated, elderly gentleman who had a very slow and eloquent way of speaking. He had served as head of the Department of Drama and Speech at the University of North Carolina at Chapel Hill before retiring at sixty-five with the esteemed title of Excellence Professor.

Many productions headed by Adcock had been performed overseas. His students had entertained GIs and always had a number of civilians from other countries in the audiences, as well. When Howard and his troupe were in Munich, they went to the Munich Opera. When they were in Paris, they went to the Comedie Française and the Paris Opera. After both performances, they had chosen to meet at the Lido, one of the city's famous show clubs. The professor's career at the university had lasted an impressive thirty-four years.

Detective Boland began the conversation: "Doctor, we're here from the Lake Worth Police Department investigating a case involving a Mr. William Wesley Wallace. Your name was listed in his personal address book, and that's why we wanted to meet with you today. Do you know Mr. Wallace?"

"Yes, I know Wesley," Adcock articulated with a heavy southern drawl.

"I'm sorry to have to inform you that there's been a homicide. Mr. Wallace has been murdered," the detective continued.

There was a long silence while the professor processed what he thought he had just heard. "Say that again, please?" he asked politely. "Are you telling me that Wesley's been murdered?"

"Yes, I'm sorry to say he was. That's why we're here, sir. Can you please tell me what the nature of your relationship with Mr. Wallace was?" Again there was a long silence.

"Why, Wesley was my best friend."

"How long had you known him?" Venetucci asked.

"Oh, I've known Wesley for a long, long time. Twenty-five years," the elder professor recalled.

"Where did you meet him?" Boland asked.

Adcock took a few moments to search his memory then responded in measured diction. "Well, I first met Wesley in the Back Room of the Cat's Cradle. It's a live music venue that's located less than a mile away from the University of North Carolina at Chapel Hill."

The Back Room of the Cat's Cradle is a dark, industrial space that has exposed wooden rafters and a large, well-lit stage. Its cash-only bar serves beer from a big plastic cooler, and the performer of the night sometimes grabs a stool and stands in the middle of the crowd. It's a place to withdraw or, as some might say, to "cool out" in-between bands if you want to speak to someone privately.

"My acquaintance with Wesley was actually cultivated quite slowly. We first met when he was married. He and his wife, Lynda, had just had a daughter and were living in Greensboro. Wesley was fortunate enough to have married into a relatively prominent family. As I recall, Lynda's father owned North State Chevrolet downtown."

"What was the nature of your relationship with Wes?" Venetucci asked.

"Eventually we became like brothers," the professor explained. "Wesley had a male sibling with whom he was never close, and I had a brother with whom I was never close, and we sort of filled in for each other. Our relationship was something that *blossomed* over several years."

"Did you ever socialize with Wesley and his wife?" Boland asked.

"Oh, yes. We went on a trip to London in the early seventies and had a marvelous time together."

"When was the last time you saw Mr. Wallace?" Venetucci asked.

"Oh, I had just been out to Florida to visit Wesley the first week of June," Adcock answered.

"Did you know that that was the week before Mr. Wallace was murdered?" Venetucci asked.

"How disturbing! Oh, I had no idea," Adcock replied. "I stayed at his condominium."

73

"Were you aware of Wes's sexual preference?" Boland asked.

"Well, I do recall that he occasionally enjoyed being with men but he also enjoyed being

with women at the same time, or *so I was led to believe.*"

Now Adcock paused. He appeared to be deeply saddened to hear of his friend's death. It took him a minute or so to compose himself before he went on in a much more candid manner. Adcock then revealed that, given Wesley's sexual propensities and lifestyle, he was not at all surprised that he had been murdered. He knew Wesley engaged in casual sex with men much younger than himself, many within their teens or early twenties. He had warned Wes that these interludes were high-risk behavior.

After making half a page of fevered notes, Venetucci then asked the professor if he would elaborate.

"Well, for instance, Wesley told me he always kept two wallets. If somebody—some 'trick,' one of these anonymous street urchins—wanted money from him, Wes could show them a wallet that had very little money in it. He didn't believe in paying for sex especially when there was so much free sex around."

Boland listened intently, and Venetucci continued to take notes.

"I frequently scolded him," Adcock went on. "He had wonderful taste in furniture and his apartment had lovely décor, and I was concerned that someone, one of these parasitic itinerant street scum, might try to take some of his belongings."

The professor went on. "You see, I've worked with young people at the university, and I am well aware of some of their rampant substance abuse issues. And more than once I also warned Wesley that someone might want to rob him when he picked one of them up in his car."

For Boland and Venetucci, Adcock's information about Wes's two wallets shed a whole new light on the crime.

Once the detectives were back in the privacy of their rented vehicle, Boland decided to recap what they had learned from their trip to Richmond, Virginia, and Greensboro, North Carolina. "Okay, so, we've got a duffle bag with an ID tag with Wes's name and address on it from a dealer that got it off the killer. We got a pretty decent description of him: He's thin, blond, and around twenty years old. We've got friends of Wes's who knew of him as a drinker, and friends who knew of him as sober. We've got a clothing designer who can't stop crying long enough to tell us much about him, and a theater professor who says that Wes told him he used to carry two different wallets and refused to pay for sex."

The detectives looked at each other and digested the collection of evidence they now had. It was like none they had ever encountered before. The trip had been a fruitful one; that was for sure.

"He was hustling the hustlers," Venetucci concluded.

"Yep," Boland agreed. He started up the car, and they continued their search for information about the enigma named William Wesley Wallace.

CHAPTER 15
"Did You Know About His Alternative Lifestyle?"

On Thursday, June 10, 1999, I pulled my green SUV into the stone-lined garage after returning home from the drug store in Dana Point, California. With my long, blond hair and fine, Scottish features I was the dutiful wife of my husband, Rick Reilly, who had achieved success in the investment banking world. I ascended the bottom steps of our three-story home. As I turned the corner from the landing and looked up, I found my husband peering down at me from the edge of the first step. Rick had a handsome face and a prominent chin. Many thought he looked like the actor Charlie Sheen. "Did you find all the things you wanted at the drug store?" he asked; he sounded odd. I knew instantly that something was wrong. My husband was not the least bit attentive and had no interest whatsoever in shopping. What was going on?

I flew up the rest of the steps and turned into the adjoining kitchen and den, where my infant son spent most of his time. His highchair sat at a breakfast bar that jutted outward above the newly laid, gray marble in the kitchen. Had my son fallen and hit his head on the floor?

Little Blaine was playing on the carpet with his favorite castle game. In his hand was one of the red, plastic balls. He dropped it into one of the turrets of the castle, and it briefly reappeared. The ball then slid across the top, disappeared inside the castle, and dropped out of an opening with a thud.

No, my son was fine. "What's wrong?" I demanded, knowing already that it was bad. I could feel it.

Rick was leaning forward on the sofa with his forearms

on his knees and his hands intensely clasped. He had news.

"Honey, come sit down," he coaxed. I slipped onto the nearby loveseat. "While you were at the store, a policewoman knocked on the door. She asked for you, but I told her you weren't home." Rick handed me a scrap of paper. "She gave me this to give you."

I read the two-sentenced, typed message in black ink on the white paper. "There's been a homicide. Call Detective Boland at the Lake Worth Police Department." The note included a phone number.

I knew now. It was my father.

I stared at the paper and read over the words again. Oh, God. Daddy. What did you do? I thought.

My hand flew up to my lips near my long blond locks. I had just talked to my father the week before on the phone. My husband had wanted him to get us a discount at the Marriott in Palm Springs, California, through the Ritz Carlton, where he worked. The call had irritated my dad. He had seemed to be distracted, and I was sorry that I had imposed on him by asking him for a favor. Those irritated words of his had been the last ones I would ever hear.

I jumped up and stretched across the breakfast bar to grab the cordless phone. I had no idea that this simple motion was about to alter every memory I had of my father. Reading the typed number off the paper, I dialed the phone and waited. A female voice answered in a business-like tone after the second ring. "Lake Worth Police Department," she stated.

"Detective Boland, please," I asked the faceless voice.

"One moment." The woman transferred the call to the detective, who picked up the phone immediately.

"Detective Boland," he answered.

"This is Denise Reilly," I began, "I'm—"

"Mr. Wallace's daughter," he interrupted, "I've been waiting for your call."

I sat in silence. The detective was on the other side of the country, yet he already seemed to know me. It was surreal. "I'm sorry but your father's been the victim of a homicide. Did you know about his alternative lifestyle?"

My mind was still trying to process the first sentence. It was like I had given a computer one command, then given it another one before it had time to process the first one. My hard drive was full, and it would stay that way for a long time.

"N-no. I didn't," I managed after several moments. "How did he die?"

"He was stabbed in the throat," Detective Boland told me. "I'm afraid he bled out."

I tried to process this next piece of information. "How long did he suffer?" I whispered hoarsely.

"We don't really know. It could've taken between four and ten minutes for him to die. Everyone is different," the detective gently explained. He added that some of the items in Wes's apartment had been stolen along with his car.

"What items?" I wanted to know.

"Two of his VCRs and his stereo," Boland said.

Was this why my father had been murdered? I wondered. For some cheap electronic equipment?

"We still don't know the motive for the murder," the detective confessed, as if he'd somehow read my mind. They needed me to fly out to claim my father's body and personal effects, he said.

I uttered the word "okay" and ended the call. Then I sat there, alone, in complete silence. How could my dad have possibly been gay when he had gotten so angry at me at the age of fifteen when he thought I had a girlfriend? I could still hear his voice in my head yelling the words at me: "Denise, are you gay?" I immediately felt betrayed in the midst of my grief. It was just too much to handle all at once. I would remain stunned for days to come.

CHAPTER 16
The Porn Collection

By the afternoon of Friday, June 11, 1999, Boland had a hunch about the case that he planned to run by the lieutenant once they finished inside Wes's apartment and got back to the station. Over the years, he had learned to constantly reassess the facts in light of new evidence. Those who jumped to conclusions got tunnel vision, he liked to say, which only got in the way of justice. Boland strongly believed that if a person had chosen law enforcement as a career they had chosen the warrior's path, and a true warrior did not just know how to fight, he knew how to do the right thing.

The facts were not adding up for him. To start with, they had discovered Wes had carried two different wallets—one with money and credit cards in it and one with very little money in it. What did that say about Wes's character? he wondered. But what was really troubling him was a particular pornographic video that had been found inside the deceased's bedroom closet called *The Taking of Jake*.

The front cover of the video featured a tanned, slender, muscular young man who was nude. Only a couple of teasing inches of his shaved, pubic area were visible between the white-skinned outlines left from a Speedo bathing suit. On the back of the tape was a scene from the video in which a young blond-haired man was tied up with rope and left unable to defend himself. The plot summary described two Jakes who headlined "a cast of sex-hungry studs" in the full-action video where "intrigue, danger and explosive sex" rattled the calm of Jake's world. Was one Jake meant to dominate the other Jake? Boland wondered. What if the other Jake had not been a willing participant and had decided to fight back?

Boland's hunch was that the killer had set out to defend himself from a violent Mr.

Wallace and had ended up killing Wes in the process. "I'm telling you, something's not right," Boland would later tell Lieutenant Paul Patti. "We've got no forced entry and one hell of a struggle. What if the tables got turned once the guy got to the apartment?"

"Just work the scene," the lieutenant would tell him. Patti knew it would ultimately be left up to a jury to decide whether the crime had been an act of self-defense or not. In the meantime, there was still a killer on the loose.

Boland and Venetucci combed through the rest of the pornographic videos in

Wes's closet with titles like *Dominant Male Luke Fucks Cross Slave* and *Jason Gets His Tight Ass Trained!*

"There's a definite slave and master theme going on here," Boland commented, showing the two tapes to his partner.

"Yep," Venetucci agreed, picking up another one called *Fuck Slave Ian Gets It Good.*

There were also black leather pieces of S&M gear in the bottom left drawer of the bureau. Boland had never understood why some people were into sadomasochism. He knew the sadist was supposed to exert control and inflict pain over the masochist, who was supposed to enjoy it in return. To each his own, he mused. It was not his cup of tea.

The particular piece that Boland noticed first was called a Big Bear Harness. It had a black front centerpiece with two D-rings and a wide, black centerpiece that was designed to give the male a nice looking chest without the harness looking like a miracle bra. Lying nearby was a black leather hood with a detachable blindfold and gag that laced up the back.

The item was deeply disturbing to Boland as it conjured up the image of a gagged person screaming. "Check this out," he told Venetucci, who had been staring at a whipping device called a Barbed Wire Leather Flogger. It had a weaved handle that was covered with black leather barbed wire and strings.

"That looks like a whole 'nother level of S&M," Venetucci remarked seriously about the blindfold and gag. He looked back down into the drawer and noticed a white, folded paper in the bottom corner. Picking it up, he noted that it looked like some sort of instruction manual for the flogger by the company Authentic Ruff Doggie Styles. The detective turned to a page entitled "During a Scene." It read:

"If you make a mistake and hit harder than you intended, acknowledge the slip for what it was and re-establish rapport with your bottom by touching or talking to him. An error need not 'blow' the whole scene—no worthwhile bottom will panic because you're not perfect, but he may need reassurance that you know what you're doing and are in control. If a bottom feels a top is incompetent or is exceeding his limits and won't stop, he could easily panic or become terrorized. Such emotional wounds may make it difficult for the bottom to enjoy subsequent S&M action, and they can even generate psychic stress that impairs other areas of his life. If he wants to quit the scene and the top doesn't, it's the top's responsibility to persuade—not bully—him into continuing. Anything else is brutality, not consensual S&M."

"Looks like the guy liked to have a party," Venetucci remarked. The detectives agreed that they would not mention the items to me—Wes's daughter—once I arrived from California.

CHAPTER 17
"Who's the Man in the Hawaiian Print Shorts?"

"Can I show you where the pillow is? It would help make you more comfortable," the blond flight attendant from Miami asked me during the flight to Fort Lauderdale. She had to ask twice. I sat back up properly from leaning against the window of the plane, only half-hearing the words. It was Friday, June 11, 1999.

"What? No. No thank you," I managed as I turned back toward the white, familiar clouds of my porthole. As the plane veered away from the Pacific Ocean on its path to the Atlantic, my thoughts once again turned to my father's next-door neighbors who had heard the argument coming from his apartment but had not called the police. If only I had been there, I thought with some anger. Why had they not called? What harm would a false alarm had been? I continued to stare out the window. I had flown dozens of times throughout my childhood from Fort Lauderdale to North Carolina to visit my father. I had also collected dozens of golden wings from Eastern Airlines—pins I had received while traveling as a minor.

My father had always ignored the protests of airline staff and met me at the bottom of the giant metal stairs that they rolled out to the plane. "Daddy!" I would cry, as he would pick me up in his arms. Each time the airline personnel would stop their scolding of him and smile with their hands clasped in front of them when they witnessed this act of mutual devotion.

"What do you want to get at the grocery store?" he would ask as we walked away from the plane, hand in hand. "My refrigerator's empty. I've been waiting for you to shop to get all your favorite foods."

"Yuck!" I would always answer. I suffered from motion sickness regularly, as well as asthma and allergies. "I'm sick, Daddy! Can't we go later?" I would ask, as we walked to the terminal.

"You're sick?" he would tease me each time. "You're always car sick or plane sick! What am I going to do with you?"

Those memories felt as real as yesterday.

Once in Florida, I stepped through the doors of the Fort Lauderdale airport with my bag. I was alone. My husband stayed behind to tie up some things at the investment banking firm. He would catch a flight before the funeral, he had promised, and his sister would watch our infant son and my twelve-year-old daughter, Marissa, from a previous marriage, while we were in Florida.

The wave of wet Florida heat always seemed to come with the sound of the tropics. To me it was like home. I had always loved the way the sunlight reflected off the green of palm fronds in the midst of a gray-clouded rain shower. The rays looked almost silver when the clouds were hiding the sun. Florida was known for having downpours on only one side of the street at times. The rain would last only a few short minutes before the sun would come out and shine again. It was as if the deluge had never happened. I wished life's deluges were that short and simple.

The Hertz shuttle bus squeaked to a stop in front of me outside the busy airport. I climbed aboard mindlessly with my bag for the jerky, five-minute ride, with mostly empty seats around me. The girl at the Hertz counter rented me a black Grand Am and told me to enjoy my stay. I was not looking forward to the trip.

The ride on Federal Highway brought back countless memories, though South Florida was an ever-changing mecca. Elaborate nightclubs would boast a new name and be the hottest place to go for a few months, only to be bought out and revamped several months later. There were many new ones that I did not recognize as I passed by.

The drive took me through Pompano Beach, Lighthouse Point, and Boca Raton. They were all cities I had lived in as a child. My journey finally ended just over the border of Boca in Delray Beach. My mother had a condo there across from the Intracoastal. She was in the middle of a two-week visit to China and would not be able to attend her ex-husband's funeral. I could still hear my mother's words in my head: "I'm so sorry that happened to your daddy, sweetheart," she had said over the crackly telephone line from 7,000 miles away.

"Did you know he was gay?" I had asked her.

"Yes," my mother had told me. She had known. A call to my old friend Alyssa Wilde had yielded the same response. "You knew the whole time?" I had asked her.

"No, not until after we grew up. My mom told me that Wesley used to wear her dresses," she had said. I had been dumbfounded. How could I have been so close to my father and not have known he was gay when others around him had known?

I distractedly turned the key in the lock of my mother's modest condo and pushed open the door. After setting my bag down in the living room, I immediately went to the kitchen phone and called Detective Boland. He and his partner would be right over, he said.

When I answered the firm knock at the door twenty-five minutes later, I found two plainclothes, handsome men holding photo albums in their arms. They were full of pictures of me and my father. There were probably plenty of my daughter and son, too.

In the doorway the detectives eyed me in my ivory silk blouse as I led the way inside. They entered the dining room and sat down at the simple, beech wood table together, extending their condolences about my father. Boland then got out his notepad and pen, and Venetucci began the questioning this time. "What kind of man was your father?" he asked me.

This was not a simple question. My father had been sober for ten years. I liked to think that he had been a different person when he had not been drinking, but just how different I could no longer guess.

"My father was the most complex man I've ever known," I told him. "He could make friends with anyone and light up a room, or he could sit by himself for hours and you had no idea what he was thinking."

"Did he ever hit you?" Venetucci asked.

"No," I answered quickly.

Boland suddenly set down his pen and opened up one of the photo albums. He set it in front of me on the table. "Who's the man in the Hawaiian print shorts?" he asked. "Who is the man smiling with your father on the boat?"

"I don't know," I found myself saying over and over again. None of the men they showed me looked familiar. I had moved to California three years before and had not made any trips back to Florida. My father always came to California to visit me during that time.

"We were very close," I admitted. "I came first with him, and he always made me feel that way," I said, remembering the way my dad would put his hand over mine and tap his fingers in a distracted manner. "He'd take me to see a play or a film, and we'd always discuss it in the car on the way home," I explained. I declined to tell the detectives that my father and I had often snuck into more than one movie at the air-conditioned theater in order to stay out of the summer heat. My dad's dilapidated apartment did not have air conditioning.

"He also took me horseback riding, emerald mining, and panning for gold," I remembered. "Oh, and camping," I added. "One time my dad took me whitewater rafting in the Grand Canyon. We went down the Nantahala River in North Carolina, too." I failed to mention that in order to save money on the Grand Canyon trip, my dad had decided not to rent a car once we had flown to Colorado. Instead, we had hitchhiked on the side of the road, catching rides from random strangers.

"My dad had no filter," I suddenly admitted. "He would talk to me the same way he would talk to an adult, even when I was only nine or ten years old."

This statement seemed to get both of the detectives' attention. Boland looked up from his notes, and Venetucci stared even more closely at me.

"His friends were shocked that he'd taken me to see *The Exorcist* when it came out," I recalled. I had been only six years old when the film made its debut in 1973. The young child actress, Linda Blair, had shocked the American audience by spewing pea green vomit directly between the eyes of a priest.

"Why do you think my father was gay?" I suddenly thought to ask.

The detectives looked at each other. "Mrs. Reilly—" Detective Venetucci began.

"Denise," I interrupted.

"Denise, the reason we think your father was gay is because we found a large number of homosexual videos at his apartment—heterosexual ones, too, but mostly homosexual ones." He watched me digest this information.

"How many?" I asked.

"More than fifty," Detective Boland offered. "Actually, closer to a hundred."

Silence overtook the room. I listened to the words, and my mind traveled back over the years. The detectives watched closely as it was happening.

"Denise, does it seem real to you that your father was murdered?" Venetucci asked curiously.

"No. It actually feels more like a movie."

"People react to news like this in different ways," he explained. "Everyone's different. So you had no idea your father was gay?" the detective coaxed.

"No. I wondered sometimes about some things, but I didn't know. And I didn't ask. If my father wanted to talk about his personal life, he would have. It wasn't my business," I explained.

"But you saw things," asked Detective Boland, "over the years."

"Yes," I confirmed.

"Like what?" asked Venetucci. His curiosity was sincere.

"Well, one of his best friends was gay. His name was Bill. I remember going over to his house when I was little. It was in downtown Greensboro in North Carolina. It was really big, and it had these—these dress shop windows on the corners, with mannequins in the windows. I didn't really understand whether it was his business or his house. It seemed to be both. I just remember Bill sitting in this big chair and thinking that he was gay, that it was funny that my dad had a gay friend when my dad wasn't gay." Again the detectives looked at each other. Detective Boland jotted down notes.

"Was there anything else?" Boland prodded.

I thought about this. "Well, there was one time, when I was older," I began.

"How much older?" Detective Boland interrupted.

"I don't know … eighteen?" I answered. "I surprised him one day," I explained. "It was morning, and I stopped by to see him without calling, like I usually did. The screen door was unlocked, and I opened it and called out to him. He answered from the bedroom. It was open, and I went in to see him.

"There was a man sitting on the bed next to him. I didn't recognize him. He was a lot younger than my dad, and he wore a beret. My dad introduced him to me. He said the guy was a decorator. It was like there was ice in the room. We were all really uncomfortable. And there was something else."

"What?" asked Venetucci.

"There was a picture of a young guy in a frame on top of the TV. I didn't recognize him, but I remember thinking: What man keeps a picture of another man in a frame who's not a relative? Anyway, I never asked him about it. I figured if he wanted to tell me about it, he would."

The detectives listened, expressionless. They'd been trained not to give away what they were thinking. That could cause a person to clam up.

"When's the last time you saw your father?" asked Boland.

"Three weeks ago. I had asked him to come out to see his new grandson. He was born on my dad's birthday. My dad flew out and took me and my son to Pasadena. We stayed at the Ritz Carlton there." The memories of that last trip came flooding back. I suddenly felt like crying.

Boland explained that they needed to understand who my father was at every level and in every part of his life, and since he was not married and I was his only child, I was probably the only one who really knew.

"My dad was an alcoholic," I began. "AA was a big part

of his life. He hadn't had a drink in ten years, and I was proud of him for that. A lot of times he went to two meetings a day to stay sober," I explained.

Venetucci nodded. "We understand your father worked at the Ritz Carlton in Palm Beach."

"Yes, he did," I confirmed.

"We also know that he'd only been living at the Lake Osborne Apartments for a month.

Where did he live before that?"

I thought about this for a minute. "I don't remember the address, but I know where it is. It's just a few blocks from here."

"Can you show us?" asked Detective Boland. "It would help us to see where your father spent his time."

I was surprised at the request, but I obediently grabbed my bag and followed the two detectives out to their Crown Vic. It was the first time I had ever ridden in a police car. I felt vaguely guilty even though I had done nothing wrong. I was also starting to feel a sense of purpose. If they needed my help to find my father's murderer, I was going to do whatever they needed.

Once past the initial shock of finding myself inside a police car, I was not really that surprised to be there, though I refused to admit to myself why that was. The black Crown Vic traveled north on Federal Highway and made a left just past Atlantic Avenue. I directed the detectives toward the yellow guesthouse where my father used to live. The house was oddly situated on the other side of an alley behind a Wachovia Bank where my father used to walk over and do his banking. He had always used Wachovia. The institution had been founded in Winston-Salem, North Carolina—one of the triad cities, which included High Point and Greensboro, the city of my birth.

My father could also walk a couple of blocks south into

the downtown Delray section called Pineapple Grove to The Green Owl Restaurant and Shea's Bakery. They were two places he often frequented. He liked to people-watch there. Another couple of blocks west brought him to the railroad tracks of Dixie Highway, a road that spans from Miami, Florida, all the way to Detroit, Michigan. I knew it also to be the dividing line between the proverbial right and wrong side of the tracks.

The guesthouse my father had lived in was divided into two tiny apartments. He had occupied the downstairs unit, which consisted merely of a kitchen, a bedroom, and a bathroom. The entire structure matched a large yellow house on the property. It had been owner-occupied by an elderly woman with cancer, who had been bedridden and cared for by a live-in nurse. Upon her death the property had been sold, and my father had been asked to move out. He had then relocated to nearby Lake Worth.

The property was rather quaint and homey, yet there were no trees or surrounding fence, therefore, the businesses on each of the four sides had a clear view of the property. There was no privacy at all. It was almost as if it had been picked up and placed in the middle of a commercial zone.

In front of my dad's unit, however, was a half-wall that was enclosed on each side to form a cement porch. Once the sun went down, it made an excellent refuge for young men in The Program. I had stumbled across more than one vagrant on the porch. My father had sponsored many of them over the years. He often claimed with annoyance that once they were fed "they kept coming around like cats."

The detectives pulled slowly into the alley alongside the wall of the yellow guesthouse. They peered up at the two-story structure. "So this is it?" Boland asked.

"Yes," I confirmed.

"Let's see what the neighbor has to say." The detectives

exited both doors and climbed up the side stairs to the upstairs tenant's apartment. Boland knocked on the door and was greeted by a tanned, wrinkled, middle-aged gentleman. The man told them that he thought his former neighbor, Wes, had been into some kind of charity work because he was always feeding the homeless. He did not know him very well and said he was glad the undesirables had stopped coming around since Wes had moved. The neighbor had hated having to keep his windows closed and locked at night in the Florida heat.

"What about the main house?" Boland asked me.

"The landlady died," I told him. "That's why my dad had to move."

"Where to now?" Venetucci wanted to know. "Where'd your father spend his time?" The two men stared at me in the backseat.

I decided to direct them across the tracks and over a few blocks to a halfway house for recovering addicts called The Bridge. Since it was so close to the guesthouse where my father had lived, he had sometimes taken me on a detour there. "I want to see who's in there," I could remember him saying when we were on our way somewhere. He would peer into the open doorway of the small, dirty white structure that the detectives and I were staring at now. We could see a lone folding chair in the shadows.

Venetucci opened the car door and stepped out to search for some sign of life. He found none. His partner grabbed a poster, a hammer, and a nail from the trunk. I watched through the rear window as he tacked up a black and white poster of my father's face. Below were the words: DO YOU KNOW WHO KILLED THIS MAN? A $10,000 reward was being promised to the provider of any information leading to the conviction of the killer.

"How many of those are you going to put up?" I asked

tentatively. Seeing my father's face in this way was startling.

"Just that one," Boland told me. "Word will get out around town," he added, backing out of the alley.

CHAPTER 18
Vampire

After leaving The Bridge, I led the detectives to a yellow halfway house called Fresh Start next, where my father had claimed to have sponsored some of the residents. "I'm going to take this new kid I'm sponsoring to a five o'clock meeting," he would say, as he drove by with me in the car. Then he would peer up at the yellow house to see if anyone was around.

Since my father's sobriety, he had seemed to be behaving as the responsible one who rounded up new AA members and kept them on track. I had not really paid attention to my father's activities with these young men. Though he had candidly shared more about his life than he should have with me as a child, there had still seemed to be some missing piece of his puzzle, some imaginary line where the conversation stopped. For instance, why had he stopped celebrating Christmas Day with me after he and my mother had split up? What did he do on that day? I wondered. He would spend Christmas Eve with me and then send me to my Grandmother Williams's house the next day. "Christmas is a personal day between me and the Lord," he'd tell me. "You go to your grandmama's and see your uncles and your cousins."

And why did he get so irate when my mother's boyfriend had stopped by to see him one day by surprise. "He's nosy, and he's snoopin' in my business," he told me. "You tell him I said *not* to come around here! I don't go snoopin' around your mama's house, tell him."

My father could get so angry at times, seemingly without reason. One time when I was eighteen, he had stopped speaking to me for six months because I had given him my old station wagon and it had a leak in the back. "The roof leaks!" he had bellowed at me. "Why would I want a car with a leak? It's no good like that!" he yelled.

"Well, I didn't know, Daddy," I had told him. "What's the big deal? It's not in the front."

My father had never explained what it was about the leak that had angered him so. Instead, he had merely stopped speaking to me for months. I had been so hurt that I had wracked my brain to try to figure out a way to get him to have dinner with me on his birthday. Finally, I had come up with the idea of leaving a card at his front door with a fifty-dollar gift card in it for The Firehouse Restaurant in Boca Raton. Then I waited for a call from my father on his birthday. I never received one. Finally, at eight I drove over to The Firehouse and peeked into the window of the restaurant. My father was seated at a table having dinner with a young man. I had trudged back to my car in puzzlement. Then the next day he had called me and thanked me for the card. Now I was in the back of a detective car trying to help two detectives find his killer.

Venetucci and Boland recognized the halfway house as having been nicknamed "the heroin house" because of the circling dealers that awaited the relapses of its residents. The house was known for loud fights and mounds of trash heaped on the curb. The owner had been accused of "warehousing" people by way of patient brokering and the acceptance of kickbacks. There had been allegations of fraudulent overbilling and excessive urine testing. Addicts were allowed to live rent-free while insurance companies were billed exorbitant amounts for them to attend intensive outpatient meetings for alcohol and drug abuse.

Boland pulled up to the house next to the white van that was parked out front. He could hear arguing coming from inside. He and Venetucci stepped out of the car and walked to the front of the house. The door was being cracked open by a bony hand. They heard a disheveled male staff member say, "I want my check when I come back. You owe me from last week, too." He pulled open the door and spotted the detectives. "You got company," he said to the unseen figure before leaving the house. The staff member stared back at the detectives with bulging eyes as he walked down the walkway.

Inside, a haggard woman in her forties with wire-rimmed glasses was poring over medical insurance forms behind a desk. An ashtray full of cigarette butts was overflowing to her left. She looked up at the detectives over her glasses as they entered the office.

"Yes?" she rasped in a gravelly voice.

"I'm Detective Boland from the Lake Worth Police Department," Boland announced, flashing his badge.

"What's this about?" she asked defensively. "One of the residents do somethin'? We can't watch them 24-7 around here."

"We'd like to know if you've ever seen this man," Venetucci asked, placing the photo of Wes down on the desk in front of her.

The woman peered down at the picture. "No, I ain't seen him. Why? He a criminal or something?"

"He's a homicide victim," Venetucci informed her.

"A homicide victim?" the woman repeated. "You think somebody here killed him?"

"We don't know," Boland answered. "We'd like to talk to the residents."

This sent the woman rising to her feet. Boland could

sense her uneasiness. "You got a search warrant with you?" "Don't worry. We're not searching anyone. We're only interested in the murder," he assured her, looking around at the disarray of her desk. His eyes settled on a drawer that was cracked open. He could see four bottles of pills and a pack of Marlboro Lights cigarettes inside. The woman quickly leaned against it with her thigh and shut it.

"Okay, then. The ones who aren't at IOP, you know, intensive outpatient program, should be in their rooms," she told them, sitting back down in the creaky swivel chair. "Watch out for Ian in five. He can be pretty moody this early."

The detectives headed down the hall to a door on the right and knocked on it. There was a crooked, gold, peel-and-stick number one stuck to the front.

"Who is it?" an annoyed male voice called out from inside.

"This is Detective Boland. We need to ask you a few questions," the detective announced. "Open the door, please." Several moments passed before a haggard man in his mid-thirties came to the door. Boland held up the picture of Wes. "Have you seen this gentleman?" he asked.

The man shook his head without looking at the photo. "No."

"Take another look," Boland ordered.

The man obeyed, though annoyed. "I told you, I ain't seen him," he uttered, closing the door.

"Okay, thank you," Venetucci said to him through the door. The detectives moved on to door number two and knocked. Several moments passed before Boland knocked again. The detectives continued down the hall and knocked on door number three. A sickly-looking young female came to the door and pushed back her sandy-colored hair with her fingers. She was rail-thin with dark circles beneath her hollow eyes.

"Have you seen this man?" Boland asked, holding up Wes's picture.

The young woman touched the photo with bony fingers and a haunted look in her eyes. "No," she uttered, shaking her head and closing the door. Venetucci and Boland exchanged glances before heading down to door number four. They could hear retching coming from inside as if someone was vomiting. Boland knocked and allowed a minute to pass before knocking once again. A young, blond-haired man in his twenties came to the door, wiping his mouth with the back of his hand. Boland showed him the picture of Wes. "Have you seen this man?" he asked.

The young man took a look at the photo. "Yeah, why?" he inquired.

"Where did you see him?" Venetucci asked.

"Across the street in his car," the man answered.

The detectives looked at each other. "What kind of car?" Boland pressed.

"I don't know. It was white," the man said.

"Did he say anything to you?" Venetucci asked.

"Yeah. He asked me if I wanted to go to an NA meeting a couple of times," referring to Narcotics Anonymous.

"And what did you say?" Boland asked him.

"I said 'no,'" the man answered. "It was weird. He said, 'You know you're supposed to be going to meetings,' but he wasn't part of the staff here or anything."

"How long ago was this?" Venetucci asked.

"Probably a month ago. I'd just gotten here and, I don't know, it was almost like he knew it," the man replied. He told the detectives that he had seen Wes drive slowly around the corner another time after that. He had been looking up at the house.

There was no answer at door number five, so the detectives returned to their car. "Where to now?" Boland asked me. I led them to a clubhouse called Crossroads that was a couple of miles away. Crossroads was a simple, green and white Alcoholics Anonymous meeting house with metal push bars on the doors. I recognized it immediately as the place where my father had attended AA meetings sometimes as often as twice a day.

Boland parked the Crown Vic and got out along with Venetucci while I stayed in the car. He had never seen the place before. They entered through the front metal and glass doors just as an AA meeting called Not High Noon was winding down. A tan, creased man in his late thirties standing at the podium had just finished up speaking. He was clutching a bronze AA token that commemorated his second year of sobriety.

Boland and Venetucci spread out among the small crowd and started asking members if they had known Wes. Many were rising from their metal folding chairs and discarding Styrofoam coffee cups in the trash. There was an air of humble camaraderie about the place. Venetucci had cornered a young man and was quizzing him when Boland came upon the speaker at the podium when they came in. The detective introduced himself and showed him the picture of Wes. A look of recognition fell over his face.

"Do you know this man?" Boland asked.

"Yeah, I know him," he admitted disapprovingly. "He's a vampire."

"Excuse me?" Boland uttered.

"A vampire. Look, one of the unwritten rules of AA is when someone approaches you and offers to be your sponsor, run for the door. Do not walk. Run," he said.

"Why's that?" the detective wanted to know.

The man sighed. "The newcomer is supposed to seek out the sponsor to avoid coming across a sponsor who collects slaves," he explained.

"Slaves?" Boland repeated.

"Sex slaves," the man spelled it out for him as if he were quoting a term from *AA For Dummies.*

"In what way are they slaves?" the detective asked.

"They're preyed upon by some controlling bastard during the lowest point of their lives when they're the most vulnerable," the man elaborated.

"And you think that's what Wes was doing?" the detective asked.

"It sure looked like it to me," the man answered, waving to a female member who waved back.

"What made you think this?" Boland pressed.

The man's eyes met with the detective's. "Look, today's Friday, right?"

Boland nodded.

"I don't usually come on Fridays, but the last time I did, I saw Wes. At Midday Miracles, I saw Wes. Serenity Hour— Wes. Got it?"

"The guy came here a lot," Boland guessed.

"Uh huh. And he was always going up to the guys—the young ones—trying to be their sponsor," the man told him.

"Did you ever say anything to them? You're the leader of the group, right?" the detective asked.

"There *is* no leader," the man explained. "Everyone's on their own here."

Boland absorbed the new information and moved to question some of the other members. Several of them recognized Wes, though none admitted to going home with him, if they indeed had. The detective then sought out Venetucci, and the two headed back out to the car.

"Who was that you were talking to?" Boland asked his partner.

"This guy, Heath," Venetucci told him. "He said Wes had come up to him on his first night at AA and asked him if he wanted a sponsor. The guy told him he didn't know who he wanted or if he was even ready for that yet. Know what Wes told him?" Venetucci asked.

"What?" Boland asked interestedly.

"That he needed to look for a sign as to who it should be. Then guess who showed up as a customer at the guy's work the next week?"

"Wes."

"Uh huh. How 'bout you? You find out anything?" Venetucci asked.

"I learned a new word," Boland answered. "Vampire." He explained that it had a different meaning in AA than the traditional bloodsucker in a black cape.

The detectives then got back into the car with me.

"Did anyone recognize my dad?" I asked.

"A few people did, yes," Venetucci confirmed.

I sat back against the seat and stared out the window. The thought that the killer could have been one of the people that my dad had been helping was disturbing to me. AA was my father's sanctuary. It was his comfort zone, I thought. I was not aware that one of the members had just described my father as a predator.

The next stop in the investigation was a XXX video store, which had not been my idea. I asked why the detectives had chosen it. They explained that many of the adult videos found at my father's apartment had been purchased from this XXX store. Upon investigation, the detectives had learned that the Yellow Pages featured three separate listings for the business at one address: Palm Beach Adult Video & Theater, Palm Beach Book & Video, and Palm Beach Adult Theater.

The stark, gray building that was surrounded by a chain-link fence was located in a residential area. A blue Dumpster on the next street had carelessly rolled to the edge of the road. It was clear to me that it set the tone for the people of the neighborhood, who apparently did nothing to fight for the morality of the city through its zoning laws. This was evident by the sign next to the video store that boasted yet another title: Adult Theater & Video Booths. I felt sorry for the kids in the neighborhood and immediately thought of my son back at home. The place was sleazy. I wondered, how could my father stand to shop here? I shuddered at the thought.

Inside, the detectives had to pass by the heterosexual pornography section first in order to find the homosexual section behind it, where Wes had purchased his movies. Some still had the bright orange sticker on them from the store. The graphic videos featured tanned men in various positions. Black leather seemed to be a common theme. Boland and Venetucci had no desire to enter the back of the store where there were thirty peep show booths and private viewing rooms. Instead, they chose to question the heavy, bearded worker behind the counter.

"Do you recognize this man?" Boland asked, holding up a photo of Wes.

The worker placed his fat hands on the counter and leaned forward to take a look. His belly pressed against the side.

"Yeah, I've seen the guy," he said.

"He's been in the store?" Venetucci asked.

"Yeah. Haven't seen him lately, though," the worker admitted. This was understandable. It had been almost a week since Wes had been murdered, and Dr. Adcock had been out to visit him during the week prior to that. His old friend had flown out to see my father just as he had returned from spending a week out in California with me.

"Came in a lot, did he?" Venetucci guessed.

"A fair amount, yeah," the worker confirmed.

"What kind of videos was he into?" Boland asked.

"Mmm ... gay porn. Heavy domination," the worker replied. "He wanted me to let him know when any new flicks came in."

"What about S&M gear? He ever buy any of that?" Venetucci asked, looking around.

"We don't sell that stuff here," the worker said.

"No?" Venetucci asked in surprise. "You don't have like a room in the back with any of that stuff?" he added.

"We got lots of rooms in the back," the worker confirmed. "But none with any of that stuff. You gotta go to an S&M place for that."

"What about any of the peep shows?" Boland asked. "The guy ever check out any of those?"

"No, we only got chicks back there," the worker replied. "This ain't Miami."

By this point in the investigation, the detectives were starting to build a picture of Wesley Wallace. And it was not always pretty. Thankfully, this was the last place that I would go with them. I had enough for the day. The detectives dropped me off at my mother's condo and headed back to the station.

"I feel bad for her," Boland remarked, as I walked away from the car. "Having to find out all this sleazy stuff about her father after he's been murdered."

"I do, too, but don't forget, she grew up with the guy. They were close. She *knew* him," Venetucci stated.

"She didn't know about his sexuality, though," Boland said, pulling away from the curb.

"Yeah, but she had an idea," Venetucci insisted.

Boland looked at him.

"What?" Venetucci asked.

"You got that sound in your voice again."

"It just seems like there's something she's not telling us about her father," Venetucci explained. "Remember when I asked her if he ever hit her?"

"Yeah," Boland answered. "She said 'no.'"

"But she answered really fast. Like she didn't want to talk about it," Venetucci said. "I don't know. It just seems like she knows more about her father than she's telling us, that's all."

"Well, we're just gettin' started," his partner said. "Let's see what else we can find out." Boland knew Venetucci's hunches about people were often right, however they couldn't glean any more information from me than I was willing to give. I was not a suspect in the case, therefore, they would have to look elsewhere for clues.

CHAPTER 19
Pump It Up

The gas prices in Palm Beach County in 1999 were the priciest in all of Florida since the gas tax was used to pay for roads and mass transit. Many chose to go down to Broward County to fill up their tanks, but the detectives still decided to check out the surveillance videotapes at every gas station within five miles of the crime scene. Perhaps Wes had stopped to gas up his car on the night of the murder, they reasoned. Boland and Venetucci found that most of the owners of businesses were trying to lower their exposure to crime by using surveillance equipment to monitor all exit and entry points of their premises. Fortunately, most were willing to cooperate with the police and provided any assistance they could with an investigation.

Some even offered to review the video they had from the appropriate time frame during the early morning of June 6, 1999, to see if there was anything noteworthy suggesting further investigation might be fruitful. Most of the video surveillance equipment in the five-mile radius included a feature called Smart Search, which allowed for the selection of any area or areas of recorded video during a certain time period. If, for example, one was looking for someone dipping into a cash drawer, they could highlight just that area of the tape, hit a button, and the playback would then jump to any sections where movement occurred in that area.

The video surveillance from the BP gas station on Congress Avenue in Lake Worth was equipped with the

Smart Search feature. Upon analysis, it showed Wes had been there just before two in the morning on June 6, 1999—within just two hours of his death. He had driven into the lime green station's parking lot in his white Acura and parked next to pump number seven. The price on the flip sign with the green and yellow sun logo read $1.249 for unleaded fuel, but the relatively high price did not seem to bother Wes. He stepped up to the door of the small convenience store with the fluorescent pink flamingo Florida lottery sign in the window.

According to the grainy closed circuit television system's video that the detectives had gotten from the gas station, Wes walked past the brown coffee dispensers on his right and straight back to the fountain drink machine. Grabbing the largest-sized paper soda cup, he filled it with ice and Diet Coke, then capped it with a plastic lid. Next, he grabbed a straw, removed the paper covering, and thrust it through the slitted "X" in the center. As Wes turned back around, a disheveled young male seemed to catch his attention. He watched the wiry man in a red T-shirt and jeans for several seconds as he bent to scan the candy bars. After finally selecting a Baby Ruth, the young man stood up and sauntered over to the counter. Wes approached from behind him and watched as the tired male Hispanic clerk took the man's money through the opening of the protective booth.

When the young man's transaction was finished, Wes did something odd. He set his soda down onto the counter without purchasing it and followed the man out of the store. The area of the gas station near the pumps was extremely well-lit. The man could clearly be seen trekking across the pavement to the sidewalk. Whether Wes called out to the guy or not would never be known, but something caused the man to turn his head around and look at Wes. He then turned back around and continued to walk out onto the sidewalk in the dark. Wes hurried over to his car, jumped in, and shut the door. He flipped on his headlights and followed after the young man, who was just passing a streetlight and coming up to a chain-link fence that separated the gas station from a side street. This time Wes could be seen saying something to him from his open car window.

It was at that point that both Wes's white Acura and the man went off camera. There was no way to know if the guy had gotten into the car with him or not. Boland and Venetucci were both disappointed at their misfortune. If only the camera had been pointed a few more degrees to the left they might have seen what had happened next. Was this the killer? Had Wes solicited sex from the man, or had he lured him to his apartment by some other means? Was the man still in the area?

The tape left many unanswered questions. Their next course was to give the surveillance videotape to forensic experts, who had many techniques that could enhance recordings to bring out the details. They hoped it would provide a clearer picture of the man's face.

The questioning of the gas station clerk had not yielded much information. He had been tired at that hour and had not remembered Wes at all, which was not surprising since he had not actually purchased anything at the counter. The clerk vaguely recalled the young man in the red T-shirt but did not recognize him as someone who came in on a regular basis. The detectives left after only ten minutes.

A forensic artist drew a sketch of the man that was released to the public through Channel 4 News. The detectives also showed the sketch to the drivers of cars that were stopped at the intersection of Tenth and Congress Avenues since it was right next to the BP gas station. Some thought Wes looked familiar but then changed their minds. Others simply shook their heads. After an hour's worth of questioning under the

blazing hot sun, Boland suggested they walk across the
street to show the sketch to the worker at The Check Cashing
Store. Venetucci was happy to get out of the heat, as well.

The simple store with the blue roof sat just in front of
a double billboard that loomed over it and dwarfed its size.
Signs in the windows read ADVANCE DE PAGO and CASH FOR
GIFT CARDS. Venetucci followed Boland inside and up to the
counter. A weathered Cuban man in his fifties stood behind
the counter writing on a pad of a paper. He looked up when
the plainclothes detectives entered.

"We'd like to know if you've seen this man," Boland
asked, flashing his badge and setting the sketch down on the
counter in front of him. The man picked up the drawing and
studied it for a moment.

"Yeah, I've seen him—if it's the same guy," he answered.
The detectives looked at each other. It was the most confident
ID they had had of the red-shirted guy so far.

"Has he been in the store?" Venetucci asked.

"Every Friday," he responded. They could not believe
their luck.

"Comes in to cash his paycheck," the man explained.

"We'll need his name," Boland ordered. The man said he
would check his records. He then reached down underneath
the counter and pulled out a logbook. The detectives waited
patiently in the cool of the air conditioning. Sweat was now
showing through their shirts.

Finally, the man looked up from the book. "Kevin
Conner," he announced. They now had a name to go along
with the face.

Back at the station, the detectives entered Conner's
name into the computer and discovered he was a twenty-
four-year-old white male who lived at the Congress Motel
and Apartments in Lake Worth. He was also a dishwasher
at the Atlantis Country Club in the nearby city of Atlantis,

which featured an award-winning golf course on Champion UltraDwarf greens.

Conner had no criminal history, and his driver's license showed only three speeding tickets and a failure to yield citation. On Monday he found himself in the interrogation room of the Lake Worth Police Department sitting across from Venetucci. He was intently pulling bits of cuticle from his fingernails.

"What can I get for you, Kevin? Would you like a Pepsi or a 7UP?" Venetucci began.

"7UP is fine," Conner answered cordially. The detective stepped out of the room and returned a couple of minutes later with the suspect's beverage. Conner cracked it open and took a sip.

After a few basic biographical questions, Venetucci got to the early hours of June 6, 1999—the last few hours of Wes's life. He explained to the suspect that he had been seen on surveillance videotape at the BP gas station. "So we know you got there around two o'clock in the morning," he stated. "Where were you coming from?"

"Home," Conner answered. The detective nodded.

"Anybody see you there?" Venetucci asked.

"Nope. I live by myself," the suspect answered.

"The BP is about a mile and a half from there. That's quite a long walk in the dark. Where were you headed?" he pressed.

"To my girlfriend's who lives near there. She told me she'd come home right after work that night at two, but she didn't," Conner explained.

"So, what'd you do then?" Venetucci asked.

"Waited outside her house until like 2:45, then walked back home. I don't have a cell phone, so I couldn't call her."

"What's her name?"

"Maria Hernandez," Conner answered.

"I'll need her address," the detective added, while writing on a notepad. He explained that Conner could call it in to the station later if he did not know it. "Where does she work?"

"The Esco Bar," he answered. "She's a waitress there." The Esco Bar was a South American restaurant named for drug czar Pablo Escobar. It featured live music and Colombian dishes like *picada* and *pechuga asada*.

"Don't waitresses usually have to clean up and do set up work for the next day after a place closes?" the detective wondered. "She wouldn't be home yet, would she?"

"The place closes at six, but her shift ends at two," Conner clarified for him. "The girls who stay till six would do all that."

The detective nodded again thoughtfully. "So why didn't she pick you up? She would've been going right by your place, right?" Venetucci asked.

"Nah, she doesn't have a car, either," he explained. "She gets a ride with one of the waitresses there, and she said the girl ended up wanting to go out after work so Maria had to go with her."

Venetucci wanted to get to the part of the morning where Wes spoke to him from his car. "What did he say to you?" he asked.

"That guy? He asked me if I knew where to go to have a good time," the suspect told him. "I said, 'No.'"

"Then what did he do?" the detective pressed.

"He asked me if I wanted to go to his house to watch some fuck movies," Conner said. "I ain't into that," he chuckled.

"So you told him no," Venetucci guessed.

"Damned right I told him no. He was pretty persistent, though," he continued. "He kept saying 'Come on, you can make some money.'"

"So then what happened?" the detective asked.

"I just told him 'Get out of here, dude. I ain't into fags,'"

Conner stated simply. "Then he finally took off."

An interview with Conner's girlfriend, Maria, revealed that she and Carmen, another waitress at the Esco Bar, had gone to Pit Row bar after work. She had not seen Conner that night at all, although she claimed to have told him that she would meet him at her house after her shift ended. Carmen had wanted to go see a bartender that she had just begun dating, so Maria had gone along to the bar with her in order to eventually get a ride home.

Carmen confirmed she had, indeed, wanted to stop at Pit Row after work and that Maria had not told her of her plans to meet with Conner. Venetucci found this odd. Did Maria not care that her boyfriend had walked all the way from his apartment on Congress Avenue that night to see her? It was a long walk just to turn around and walk home again, he thought.

The story was hard to believe. Conner remained a suspect, and a DNA sample was obtained with swabs from the inside of his cheek. They were handed over to forensics for testing. They would also have molds taken of his teeth. Meanwhile, there were plenty of other people on the detectives' list.

CHAPTER 20
The Tip Line

The Lake Worth Police Department's tips line had already lit up with over one hundred telephone calls about the murder of Wes Wallace. Although some were too vague to pursue, the rest had to all be checked out. The crime had been brought to the attention of the public on all of the local television stations, cable stations, radio, and newspapers. Television press coverage of the murder would typically conclude with: "If you know something about this case, or any other serious crime in Palm Beach County, call Crime Stoppers at 1-800-458-TIPS. If your information leads to an arrest, recovery of stolen property, or seizure of narcotics, you may be eligible for up to a $1,000 reward."

The validity of any information about the murder that was received on the tips line was first checked by the program coordinator, then disseminated to an overwhelmed Detective Boland. Each caller was assigned a special code number and advised to call back at a specified interval of time to check on the progress of the case. For anonymous purposes, the caller was to only be identified by that code number.

The first tipster that Boland spoke to was an elderly woman who claimed she had seen a black homeless man taking a dump near Lake Osborne. Apparently, it was not the first time she had seen the vagrant. She believed he lived down by the water and often drank alcohol until he became very loud. The trail next to his "nest" was similar to the one in John Prince Memorial Park that lay just on the other side of the lake. The senior complex could be seen from the dirt path. Because of this, the woman feared that the man might have followed the victim home on Lake Osborne Drive—the route she also took home. Boland said he would check it out.

Boland and Venetucci drove over to the Lake Osborne Apartments, parked along the curb across the street, and got out of the car. After a couple of minutes of looking around, they spotted a well-trodden path and followed it through the marsh in search of a make-shift camp by the lake. Venetucci's mind was on his daughter, Juliana, as they walked. She was turning three years old that weekend, and his wife had been planning a birthday party for her. He reminded himself that he needed to stop by the store when he got off work to pick up balloons for the party. Then his mind focused on the scruffy, black homeless man in front of him who was spreading out a brown, rumpled jacket on the ground next to him. A pile of dirty clothes lay to his left.

"Afternoon, sir," Boland began, flashing his badge. "What's your name?"

"Fred Bowery," the man answered. "Something wrong?"

"We'd like to know if you've seen this man," Boland continued, showing Bowery the photo of Wes.

The homeless man squinted at the picture, holding up his hand to block the sun. "Nah, haven't seen him. Why? He do something?" the man asked.

"Someone killed him," Venetucci answered. "You wouldn't know anything about that, would you?"

"Nah, not me. I jus' stay down here, don't bother nobody," Bowery said.

"Well, now that's not entirely true," Boland said. "Apparently you bother at least one of the residents in the senior complex across the street. A lady said you tend to get mighty loud out here at night."

Bowery thought about this. "Is that so. Must be that old

lady that keeps slowin' by the road in her car to take a look at me. I was thinkin' 'bout makin' a stalkin' report. Guess I'm glad you guys showed up today."

This caused Venetucci's eyebrows to raise. "A stalking report?"

"Yep. Guess I need one o' them strainin' orders," Bowery added.

"It's 'restraining order.' And the woman needs to have abused you. Did she abuse you in some way?" Boland asked, skeptically.

"Well, not yet, but I'm afraid she might," the man answered.

"You're afraid, huh? Well, if she does, let us know," Boland continued, sarcastically. "What were you doing last Saturday night?"

"Last Saturday?" Bowery asked, scratching his bearded chin. "Let me check my calendar. It's up here," he said, tapping the side of his head.

"You do that," Venetucci told him.

"Hmmm. I believe I was right here," the man claimed.

"All night?" Venetucci asked.

"All night," Bowery confirmed.

"Anyone see you?" Boland asked.

"Nope. Not even the old lady. She left me alone that night, I believe," the man said.

Fred Bowery turned out to have been charged with two counts of loitering and one count of aggressive panhandling during the previous year. The last time he had been picked up, he had walked into a flower shop, fallen flat on his back, hit his head on the floor, and passed out. The flower shop owner had reported that Bowery's eyes had rolled back in his head and that it had scared her. Afterward, Bowery had spent a couple of days at a homeless shelter called the Clean Time Inn in Lake Worth, which insisted he remain sober. Not having been able to live up to his end of the bargain, he now lived down by the lake.

The next lead Boland followed up on was a twenty-nine-year-old man named Raymond Steel, whose criminal record dated back to 1992. He had been arrested seventeen times in Florida on charges including assault, possession of methamphetamine, robbery, and resisting arrest. The majority of his crimes had been committed in the West Palm Beach area.

Steel had also recently participated in the South Bay Correctional Facility riot that ended in the death of a corrections officer. During the riot, several officers were assaulted and taken hostage. Sergeant Ricardo Rivera was consequently killed when inmates attacked him with a food tray. The hostages were held for several hours by participants in the riot, while other prisoners took food service carts out of the dining hall and kitchen and stacked them on top of each other to climb onto the roof where Rivera had been beaten. It took hours for authorities to control the riot, which involved hundreds of inmates. An active felony escapee warrant had been issued against Steel that had remained outstanding until police had picked him up. Steel had been located at his girlfriend's house in Lantana Beach and taken to the second floor interrogation room of the West Palm Beach police station.

The escaped inmate leaned forward in his straight-legged chair and sneered aggressively at Boland. He looked as if adrenaline was coursing through his veins like he had just come out of the prison riot. The single, hanging overhead light cast ominous shadows onto the long, metal table before them. Boland leaned forward in his wheeled chair and met Steel's gaze.

"I heard you had a little fun back at South Bay," he began sarcastically, "That you and the boys stacked up some food carts like Legos and made it out onto the roof."

"Whatever," Steel grumbled.

"Looks like you made it farther than that. You're here talking to me now," the detective conceded.

The escapee relaxed a little. "Yeah, I did. So what do you want? Why am I here?" The inmate was smarter than a lot of criminals, Boland knew. It took one with brains to pull off an escape like that. He eyed the man with interest for a moment.

"I'm working on a homicide at a senior complex in Lake Worth. Someone said they saw you near the place last Saturday."

"I got nothin' to do with no murder," Steel growled.

"Well, I wouldn't say that's entirely true. You were involved in the murder of Sergeant Rivera back at the prison, weren't you?"

The inmate became visibly angry. "That wasn't me," he seethed.

"Oh, no? Well, who was it, then?" Boland pressed.

Steel leaned back and folded his arms behind his head. "I ain't no snitch."

"I'd say you're in a hell of a lot of trouble right now. That prison murder isn't my problem, but this one is." Boland pounded his finger on the table for effect. "Why don't you tell me where you were and what you were doing on Saturday around midnight after you escaped?"

Steel's eyes scanned the wall as he thought back to Saturday. "I was at Liesel's. Same place they picked me up."

"They checked her house that night." Boland leaned in toward his suspect. "You weren't there."

The inmate placed his forearms precisely on the table and stared into Boland's eyes. "Just 'cause they didn't find me don't mean I wasn't there," he snickered. Steel claimed he had hidden in a two-foot-by-two-foot air conditioning vent at the end of his girlfriend's hall. When the police apprehended him the next day, they had caught him sleeping. He had mistakenly figured they would not be back.

The police would get swabs from the inside of Steel's cheeks. Meanwhile, Boland would check up on one other escapee.

Wayne Clarke was a forty-four-year-old mental health patient who had escaped from the Florida State Mental Hospital in Chattahoochee. The institution had earned the nickname "The Mattress Factory," as some of its patients had been put to work making mattresses in the old powder magazine building back in 1876. The dilapidated structure was the subject of a historic preservation project designed to transform the building into a museum and conference center upon its completion.

Clarke's mother lived in Lake Worth and had been surprised to find her son on her doorstep, instead of at River Junction Work Camp on the campus of the Florida State Hospital, where he had lived for the past two years. The police had been less surprised. They had picked him up and brought him to the West Palm Beach Police Station to be questioned by Boland.

Unlike Steel, Clarke sat passively in his chair as if he were sitting at his mother's dinner table. His plump midsection pressed against the cold metal, his bald spot shiny under the bright light. He claimed to know nothing about Wes's murder and said that he had not left his mother's house since he had arrived on Saturday—a fact which she adamantly confirmed. Clarke was placed in a cell to await transfer back to Chattahoochee. Swabs from his cheeks would also be compared to those held in evidence.

Boland and Venetucci went over the suspects that had been interviewed over the last couple of days. The most likely one to be guilty of Wes's murder was Conner. He'd actually been seen on tape talking to Wes within two hours of his death. His alibi had been hard to believe, even though his girlfriend had confirmed it. Girlfriends of suspects had been known to lie. They would have to wait to see what the evidence revealed.

CHAPTER 21
The Gay Scare of '57

Allie Wallace was not happy to be pregnant with an eighth child. She was thirty-eight years old and past what she felt were the proper childbearing years. She gave birth to William Wesley Wallace on August 18, 1942, in Pomona, North Carolina. Wesley was named after the Scottish hero William Wallace, the legendary Braveheart—the thirteenth century Scottish warrior who had led the Scots in the First War of Scottish Independence against King Edward I of England. Both the Gibsons, Allie's family, and the Wallaces, the baby's father's family, were of Scottish and English descent.

Wesley was the youngest in a family of eight children. There were six girls and two boys. The other son had been named after his father, Edward Lee Wallace. He was seventh in the line of children. The sixth was Wesley's favorite sister, Margaret. She was the only one who did not twist washcloths forcefully into his ears while bathing him to discourage him when he wanted to tag along. Instead, she let him follow her to her girlfriend's houses or on errands around the neighborhood. Even on their daily trip to school, she did not mind his company. The fourth and fifth were a set of twin girls that had been named Hildred and Mildred, but went by the endearing terms, Hon and Pig. Third in line was red-headed Billie, who went by the nickname, Bill. Then there were Doris and Helen, the oldest.

The Wallaces grew up poor in the Bible Belt where

alcohol was frowned upon by the God-fearing folk of the Carolinas. Edward, the father, was a blue-collar worker whose wife stayed at home with the children. Even at the end of her life, she never learned how to drive a car. Their home was an old converted church made of wood that weathered over time into a pitted, dusty gray. A swinging chair on the front porch gave Allie a view of her young'uns when they played in the park across the street. Grass did not get much longer and greener than it did at that park. Far from flat, the land there sloped down in a small valley. It then rose high on the other side under thick maple and elm trees, licking the sides of a stony creek.

The old church house opened up to a front living room with a wood-burning stove. Maw, as Allie would be called in her later years, would often rock in her rocking chair in this room, sometimes laughing a bit to herself in the dim light as she recalled the memories of her life. She wore her long, gray hair tied back in a bun that she let down twice a day to brush. It easily passed her bottom. Folgers Coffee cans were scattered throughout the house for Maw's peach snuff residue. Snuff is a chewing tobacco product of the Carolinas that was common for people—even women—to chew and spit when the flavor ran out.

A long hallway off the center of the living room opened to bedrooms on each side for the eight children to share. There were a total of five bedrooms in the house. Edward would die in one of the chenille-covered beds from a heart attack at the age of fifty-six. It would be the same age at which his youngest son, Wesley, would die.

The kitchen and den lay at the back of the house. Eggs were cooked every morning right in the bacon or sausage-patty grease in a cast-iron skillet. The leftover grease would likely be poured into a glass jar that Maw would save under the kitchen sink for when they needed lard or butter; grease was cheaper. The metal kitchen table and chairs would remain there until long after Maw's death from osteoporosis at age eighty-nine. On the large back porch were wooden steps that led down into the yard, where an outhouse sat under a gnarled apple tree. Even with teeth missing in her later years, Maw loved the green apples and strawberries from her backyard.

Wesley hated strawberries. He also hated school and usually brought home Ds and Fs, though no one seemed to notice. There were already too many kids to keep track of by the time he came along and never enough presents at Christmas time.

Perhaps it was because of the lack of attention at home that Wesley was a mischievous child. In grade school he often found himself sitting behind a girl with pigtails in her hair. Instead of paying attention to the lesson, he preferred dipping the end of the girl's pigtails into the jar of ink on his desk. This often led to detention for Wesley and a visit to the principal's office for him and his mother. Another favorite prank of his involved placing frogs on railroad tracks with his friends. The boys would stand away from the tracks and watch in gory fascination as the train turned each frog into a bloody, flattened mess.

By the time Wesley was in high school, most of his sisters were already married. Pig and her husband, Dewey Moore, had a tobacco farm, and Bill had married a chicken farmer. They both lived in farm houses and grew crops of vegetables, like corn and okra, right on their properties.

Wesley was different. Wesley's best friend in high school was a Farrah-Fawcett lookalike named Becky Rawlins. They were so close that Becky felt comfortable changing in front of Wesley. She even let him try on her flowered, cotton dresses, giggling at his silly reflection in the mirror as she helped him with the tight zipper. Sometimes her mother or father would knock on the door, and Wesley would have to sneak out the window in Becky's dress. He would hover to the side until they were gone. The two would remain friends throughout adulthood, where Becky would continue to feel at ease with Wesley and allow him to see her in her bra.

Another friend of Becky's and Wesley's from high school was Lynda Williams. Lynda was a shy student with short, sandy curls. She wore the horn-rimmed glasses of her time, like many of the other girls, and played the clarinet in the school band. Her father owned a Chevrolet dealership with two other partners called North State Chevrolet in Greensboro. Everyone, including Wesley, had heard the best-known car jingle of the fifties, "See the USA in Your Chevrolet," sung by Dinah Shore. He had heard it on the radio as well as on two of Shore's Chevy-sponsored television shows. Wesley had also seen the ads all over the billboards, magazines, and newspapers. Therefore, when Lynda told Wesley that her brother, Tommy, was going to test drive the new '57 Chevrolet Bel Air Sport Coupé out in an open field, he insisted she take him to see it. The sleek, black car raced around in circles in the grass that day right before Wesley's wide, young eyes. Even the Chevrolet competitors had yet to see the new model.

Meanwhile, something else was happening in Greensboro that would later be called "The Gay Scare of '57."

On February 4, 1957, a Guilford County grand jury emerged from its closed session and issued handfuls of indictments unlike any before or since. They accused thirty-two men of being homosexual. After witnesses named the men during police interrogations, the suspects were tried one by one in a Greensboro courtroom for what they called "crimes against nature." It was the largest attempted roundup of homosexuals in Greensboro history, and it marked one of the most intense gay scares of the fifties. Unlike sweeps of the following decades that involved raids on public parks and gay bars, the trials focused on private acts that had been conducted behind closed doors. The purpose was to remove people from society who were feared to prey upon the youth and to protect the town from what a presiding judge called "a menace." Twenty-four of the convicted individuals received prison terms from between five and twenty years, and some were assigned to highway chain gangs.

The convictions triggered the beginnings of a panic among gays in Greensboro. Many sought to curb their behavior, at least outwardly, by marriage.

Wesley was one of them.

He and Lynda were both fifteen in 1957. Lynda was the first to get a car the following year on her sixteenth birthday. It was a red, '59 Chevy Impala. Soon the two were cruising the streets of Greensboro with Wesley behind the wheel. Sometimes they would park on a hill on High Rock Road near Reed's Gold Mine and make out. Lynda loved Wesley's adventurous spirit. "A lady died out on this road a long time ago," he would whisper in her ear, peering out the window in the dark. "If I put the car in neutral, she's supposed to come and push us up the hill," he would say, looking back over the seat behind them. Each time they made the trip, Wesley would slide the car into neutral and tell Lynda to stay quiet while they waited. Then he would grab her sides and shout "Boo!"

"You get me every time!" Lynda would squeal.

He was always taking her on some new adventure. One time they went to explore the Robinson Rock House Ruin over in Charlotte. "My daddy told me this house was owned by some of the Wallaces back in the 1850s," Wesley told her, as they trudged through the patches of grass and red Carolina dirt. "They lived in a big plantation house over there called the White House," he said, pointing proudly toward the southeast. "But their slaves lived here in the Robinson house."

It quickly became obvious to Lynda that Wesley was acutely aware of the social and economic gap between their two families. She, however, could not care less. Lynda loved all of Wesley's sisters and felt bad for him that they seemed to get all of his mother's attention along with his brother. "*I love you more than anyone,*" she would say to him time and time again in his arms, "and that's all you need." This always caused Wesley to smile. She felt special to be the only one in his life who showered him with attention. It brought out the mothering instinct in her and made her care for him all the more. What more could a guy want?

Unlike Wesley, Lynda was not poor. He was fascinated when she invited him over to her house one day and he saw that she had a pink and white, life-sized playhouse in the backyard all to herself. Most amazing of all, she did not have to share it with her two brothers. Wesley and Lynda shared a silly, keen sense of humor. It was rich girl/poor boy from different sides of the tracks, and the relationship worked for them just fine. Lynda's father, Thomas, sat her down for lunch at The Princess Café in Greensboro when she was seventeen and told her she should marry Wesley. He had high hopes for him.

The two were married the summer they both turned twenty in a big church wedding full of family and friends. Wes's fellow seaman friend, Wayne "Dutch" Eakins from the navy accompanied the newlyweds on their honeymoon. Lynda did not oppose the idea, and they did not speak much about it. Like all other girls her age, she was happy just to be getting married. After the wedding, she went on to study liberal arts at the University of North Carolina at Greensboro and worked part-time as a switchboard operator.

Wesley served in the navy as a cook, and the newlyweds

went to live on a nearby naval base. Lynda was happy to have the other wives to talk to and did not understand why Betty, one of the wives at the base, kept carrying on about her husband. It was "Jimmy this" and "Jimmy that." Did the woman not have any interests of her own? Lynda kept busy with her studies and saved the money from her part-time job. She was very frugal and was shocked to hear that another navy wife, Norma, was sneaking money out of her savings to buy clothes. The woman lived in constant fear of the day her husband would inevitably find out.

Lynda's conscience, on the other hand, was clear. She had no real worries, and her days went by uneventfully, though something strange did happen three months into Wesley's short stint in the navy. One night when he was home on leave, she heard him talk in his sleep. His words were clear enough that Lynda could make them out: "I killed a man." It was not an inconceivable thing for a man in the service to say. The only odd thing: Wesley had never been in combat, nor had he ever spoken about any sort of accident that had happened aboard the ship. Perhaps it was just a nightmare. Lynda decided not to ask him about it and told herself that if he wanted to talk about it, he would. Wesley never did.

Three months later Wesley was discharged for having flat fleet. Their daughter had been conceived on one of Wesley's layovers in Charleston, South Carolina. He was ecstatic to find out he was going to become a father and eagerly waited for the day to come.

I was born to William Wesley Wallace and Lynda Lou Williams on October 8, 1967, in Greensboro, North Carolina. My parents named me Lynda Denise Wallace after my mother. Like the Wallaces, the Williams were Scottish and English on both sides.

Unlike my parents, I was an only child and would always be one. My father went to work for my grandfather at North

124

State Chevrolet selling cars. He had an outgoing personality and a sincere curiosity about people. My dad was a natural at selling, and he was going to need the money. He was happy to work hard for me and dress me in little blue and white sailor dresses. He also took me to the popular program, Indian Princesses, which was for fathers with daughters ages five through twelve. It was meant to develop the foundation for a lifelong relationship between them. The club made their own drums by stretching tan sheets of rubber over metal coffee cans, and they wore feathers on their heads.

My dad's favorite event to enjoy with me, though, was to take me to see plays at UNC's theater. He became lifelong best friends with Howard Adcock, the theater director there. My dad took me backstage to meet the talented cast members that were Dr. Adcock's understudies. One of my earliest memories was of seeing the play *Grease* with my father. The production crew had driven a shiny, red T-Bird onto the stage for the musical number.

Over the years Wesley would take me to see many plays, such as *Hello Dolly, Victor Victoria,* and *Cabaret.* We saw the production of *The Sound of Music* nine times.

My mom and dad bought a townhouse when I was a toddler and moved into the same development where my grandmother and grandfather lived. They were just a few doors down in the sage-colored two-story complex. We stayed there for three years. Times were happy and prosperous. My father sold cars at the family dealership along with my uncles, Gordon and Tommy. Gordon and my dad had the same outgoing personality and came to be great friends.

The summer I turned five, my grandfather decided the family should all move to South Florida to open up another dealership. His partners would run the Greensboro operation, while he and his wife, Eleanor, moved to Pompano Beach.

His sons Gordon and Tommy would make the move, too, along with my small family. Thomas's plan was to one day retire in sunny Florida, while his sons took over the business, but first the families would each need a place to live.

The Apartments at Crystal Lake seemed as good a place as any to live while my mom and dad looked for a house near Pompano Beach. The ad for the beige stucco complex promised tenants could barbecue lakeside or go boating on Crystal Lake. They also offered extra storage units. It was an attractive feature for those moving from a two-story townhouse into a temporary one-story apartment. My father moved us into a ground floor unit with a large patio where he could grill steaks that he smothered with ground pepper. He quickly made friends with the blond, Cuban single mother next door, whose son was two years older than me. Soon he was grilling steaks for all of us.

My dad made friends often and easily, but there were times when he preferred long drives at night, alone. He would bring a bottle of liquor with him and be vague about exactly where he was going. One night he decided to take me with him. I was five. "Denise and I are going for a drive," he told my mother.

"But it's eight o'clock!" she protested. "I was just about to put her to bed." My father insisted and told me to put on shoes. I was in my pajamas when he put me in the car.

"Where are we going, Daddy?" I asked.

"Come on, let's go," he urged, pulling me out the door by my hand. He drove through the empty lot next to the Apartments at Crystal Lake, which was under construction. A billboard above urged people to pre-pay for condos that were being built there. Those getting in early would pay only half the cost of what it would cost to buy later, promised the ad. Our neighbor, who worked in real estate, was one of the first to take them up on the offer. The condos, however, were never finished, and all of her hard-earned money was lost.

I sat in the passenger seat of my daddy's black and white Chevy Nova and watched the headlights shine on the dirt in the dark. The erect sheets of woods that lined each side of the road were creepy at night. The place was like a ghost town. I was getting scared. Daddy was just driving and not saying anything. "I want to go home, Daddy," I whimpered, looking over at my daddy. He had a mean look on his face, and he was gripping the wheel so tightly with his hands. "Daddy, can't we go home?" I begged.

My daddy reached for his bottle of Scotch and took a swig. "Denise, be quiet! Stop whining!" he barked at me. I sulked and kept watching the lights on the road in front of me.

It was the first of many aimless drives with my father. His driving would come to frighten me more and more as his drinking worsened. My mother could not stop him from taking me out of the house. At least they would soon move away from the apartment with the scary construction site next door.

The house they decided to buy was located on a small island off Pompano Beach that fell inside the city limits of Lighthouse Point. Residents of the island had to cross a short, concrete bridge to get there. A ferry on the back side of the island took them to Cap's Place, a seafood restaurant that lured cats from all over the island due to the smell of the fish. My friends and I loved to play on the seawall there. We could also pet the dozens of cats that came to live underneath the restaurant between the pilings in the sand.

My dad loved the new house. My grandfather gave him and my mother the $80,000 for the down payment, which left them with a hefty mortgage. The place had three bedrooms and formed an "L" shape around a large, rectangular pool that was secluded by a tight wall of palm trees. They bought a thick, glass dining room table for entertaining that sat eight people and overlooked the pool through sliding glass doors.

The master bedroom also featured a set of sliding doors that offered a view of the pool. My dad loved to rise out of bed and dive into the water naked to the horror of Mrs. Wilson, the nosy neighbor behind our house. He accused her of spying on him through the wall of trees.

The palm fronds fell from our backyard jungle at a staggering rate. It became a Saturday morning ritual for me and my dad to gather them together for the trash men to haul away. Another ritual of ours was slated for Monday nights. My mother served us dinner on TV trays in the living room so my father and I could watch *The Sonny and Cher Show* together. We were both big Cher fans. My dad loved her diva persona, and I begged for a Cher doll for Christmas. I had all the doll's outrageous outfits. My favorite was Cher's mocha Jumperoo.

The excitement of the new house soon gave way to tragedy. My beloved Grandfather Williams, who used to read me stories underneath a blanket, was dying of pancreatic cancer. Bedridden in the hospital, he asked only that the family bring him the tomatoes he loved so much, having grown up on them in North Carolina.

Once he was gone, my two uncles fought over the money. Tommy, the oldest, was accused of embezzling by the family. Years would go by where no one but my mother would speak to him. Meanwhile, the mortgage on the new home quickly became a burden. My dad enrolled in school during the day to become a real estate investigator and took a job at the European Health Spa in Fort Lauderdale at night. The men's only health club was a landmark on Federal Highway. It had a large, golden statue of Hercules out front that proudly held up the globe.

It was there that my father met Rob and Mitch, two high

school football stars who had secured scholarships to Notre Dame and Vanderbilt. They were good-looking guys in top physical condition. Rob had dark hair, and Mitch's blond locks curled up around his ears. My dad met them in the sauna, where he liked to show people the towel trick. He handed them each a white towel as they sat on the wooden bench and told them to wipe off their arms. If they were a smoker, their sweat would turn the towel yellow.

Rob and Mitch did not smoke, but the ice was broken. My dad eventually convinced them to bring the entire high school football team over for a pool party. There were so many muscular youths in the pool at once that day that I got trapped underneath all of their kicking feet and almost ran out of air as I panicked.

Meanwhile, my father was panicking over mounting bills and bickering in-laws. He was drinking Pabst Blue Ribbon by the case and cheap Scotch by the liter. All the nights away from home at the European Health Spa were taking a toll on his marriage, as well. And his nights off were becoming regular episodes of drunken rages that were increasing in pitch. Often, I would hide on a high branch of the big southern magnolia tree out front to escape my parents' escalating arguments.

One night my mother had just finished reading me a bedtime story in my red, white, and blue room. She had painted each of the walls to form a giant flag. Strings of red and blue beads hung like curtains in the windows, and a large wooden piano took up most of the room. My mother switched off the light in my room and stepped out to see my drunken father in the hallway. They stood arguing there for several minutes until I finally got up to watch from the doorway in my nightgown. Suddenly, my father began pushing my mother toward me. With one final shove, he sent her flying into the piano as I darted out of the way. My mother's forehead split open on the sharp corner and blood spilled forth to form a pool on the white rug. The stain would never come out, and the rug would later have to be discarded. I screamed, and my father immediately bent down to help my mother. He apologized and led her to the vanity in the bedroom, where she could sit down. My mother saw the cut on her forehead and knew she needed stitches. "I've got to go the hospital," she cried. This sent me bursting into tears.

"I hate you, Daddy!" I screamed. "I hate you for doing this to Mommy!" His face fell with each word. He was crushed.

"Don't say that, sweetheart," my mother begged. "Don't ever say you hate your daddy." My mother needed fourteen stitches at the hospital. She had to drive herself because my father was too drunk to drive.

A couple of months later, my father punched my mother and knocked out her tooth. She ran to the next-door neighbor's with me behind her, pounding on the door and screaming, "Neil! Neil!" My mother spent the next two months sleeping in the hatchback of the Nova in the carport. I begged my mother to let me sleep with her, but she just told me to go inside, so I crawled into my daddy's bed instead. I knew he would never hit me, and he never did. Those were the last two months of my parents' marriage. I was seven years old.

That summer, my mother and I temporarily moved in with her mother, my Grandmother Williams. She had purchased a condo on the seventeenth floor of Galt Ocean Mile in Fort Lauderdale. The expensive, spacious unit had a balcony that was perfect for watching the annual Fort Lauderdale boat parade. It was right on the Intracoastal. I watched my mother and grandmother make sequined felt Christmas stockings that year. I had broken my left arm falling off a fence and had to wear a heavy, plaster cast until it healed.

There would be no more family Christmases with Daddy. He stayed behind in the house and got a male roommate until the place finally sold. Then he rented a two-story loft off Los Olas Boulevard in Fort Lauderdale that had a liquor store at the end of the alley. It had a floor to ceiling window that was thirty feet high and a lofted bedroom with a half-wall that looked down over the living room. My friend, Hollie Steinke, and I threw ping-pong balls down at my dad on the sofa when he was drunk.

My mother and I moved into the right side of a two-bedroom duplex in Pompano Beach. A single nurse lived in the left side and drove an orange Volkswagen beetle. She let me hide under her table when my dad got drunk and came banging on our door. Each time my mother would open it and endure choking by him. Never once did she call the police.

Finally one day, when I was twelve, my dad called and told me he was moving back to North Carolina. I would have to fly out to see him for the holidays now. There would be no more weekend and Wednesday night visits at his apartment. There would also be no more visits from him at ours.

CHAPTER 22
Leviticus 18:22

My husband, Rick Reilly, found himself in the back of a detective car in Delray Beach, Florida, on Monday afternoon, June 13, 1999. He did not like drama and had not wanted to come. Feelings like sadness were a waste of energy to him. Life was life. Shit happened, he thought, as he looked out the window. Meanwhile, he had a client that was in need of financing for the 180,000-square-foot facility in La Jolla that he wanted to build for the Genomics Institute. Rick felt he needed to be back in California instead of here in Florida dealing with his father-in-law's murder.

Boland spied him through the rearview mirror. "So, it must've been quite a shock to you to find out that your wife's father had been murdered," he remarked.

"Yeah. Hey, how long do you think this is going to take?" he asked the detectives, leaning over the seat. Boland and Venetucci glanced at each other. Rick was supposed to pack up Wes's belongings from his apartment in order to spare me the sight of the blood-soaked carpet that remained from my father's body. Any unwanted items were to be picked up afterwards by Goodwill Industries.

"Well, it's a one-bedroom, but his closets are pretty full," Venetucci answered. There was silence as the detectives pondered the contents.

"Oh," Rick remarked, leaning back in his seat once again. "Just getting hungry, that's all. Didn't have a lot to eat on the plane." They drove the rest of the way to Wes's apartment in silence.

Meanwhile, at Lake Worth Funeral Home and Crematory, the director was explaining the different cremation and burial options to me in his office.

"Basically there are three choices for your father," Victor Sharp explained. "His body can be interred by way of an earth burial, it can be entombed in a crypt within a mausoleum by way of an aboveground burial, or it can be buried at sea."

I forced myself to ponder the options. It was not something I wanted to think about.

"Now, should you not like the idea of the body being 'burned' and you prefer to have the body slowly return to the elements, you will want to erect a monument on the grave," he continued. "Perhaps you want to visit the grave in the days to come, and you find a graveyard more appealing than say, a columbarium."

I did not find either of them appealing. "My father has no family left in Florida. There would be no one to visit his grave if I bury him," I said.

"Then perhaps cremation is the best choice," the funeral director stated. "Now, in that case, I want to let you know that you still have the option of having the body present for viewing before the cremation, however, due to the manner of death, you might not want to exercise that option."

My father's body had long cuts on his face from the murder weapon. Though the stab wounds on his neck could be concealed by a collared shirt, the facial wounds could not.

"No, I suppose not," I answered.

"Fine," the director said. "You will then need to decide if you would like the cremated remains scattered or kept in an urn or other keepsake."

"I think I'd like to bury my father at sea," I decided.

"All right. That leaves the matter of the memorial service. There's a lovely chapel near the beach called Del

Lago Chapel. I'm sure you will be happy with the location," Mr. Sharp assured me. "All that's left is the scheduling of the cremation process."

"You may go ahead with it," I instructed.

The director looked puzzled. "I'm afraid your father's body has been reclaimed by the forensics department," he told me.

I knew nothing of the news. "Why?" I asked.

"In an attempt to obtain DNA evidence from the bite marks on your father's wrist," Mr. Sharp explained.

I was silent for a moment. It was like a cruel, comic tragedy. The murder was over but my father's body was still being tossed around. I had hoped to leave the funeral home with the arrangements behind me. Now I would have to go back to my mother's and wait.

On the way out of the director's office, he halted next to a narrow, gray marble slab of a table. There, in the stunted hallway off the tiny entryway, he grabbed a five-by-five scrap of paper off a stack and handed it to me. It was a crudely handwritten map to Del Lago Chapel. For the second time in four days, tragic instructions were being handed to me in the form of a note.

Once I was back in the car, the weight of the situation hit me. My father's body was being repeatedly probed in order to find out who had killed him, and the killer had marked up his face so that he was not fit to be seen at his funeral. It felt as if my father had been violated, both before and after death. I drove back to my mother's condo and placed a call to Detective Venetucci.

"How are you?" he asked gently.

"Not great," I admitted. "I'm trying to bury my father, and the funeral director said that you've reclaimed his body."

"That's right. I'm sorry," he apologized. "We want to rule out the possibility that your father bit his own arm," he explained.

"What?" I cried. "Why would he do that?" I asked.

"We're just being careful by erasing any reasonable doubt in the case of a trial," Venetucci told me. I digested this explanation.

"Well, when do you think you'll return his body?" I asked.

"This afternoon. The process shouldn't take very long," the detective answered.

"Okay. Thank you. I'll let the funeral director know. Have you found out anything about who killed my father?" I asked.

"Not yet," Venetucci told me. The DNA from Kevin Conner's swab samples had not matched the DNA from the crime scene, nor had those of Fred Bowery, Raymond Steel, or Wayne Clarke. The detectives had been disappointed at the news and had already begun interviewing other suspects.

***

Outside the condo, my cousin, Hoover Reeder, was getting out of his rented, blue Chevy Malibu, his orange hair shining in the sun. It was the reason for his nickname, Punkin. He had not seen me in over twenty-five years. I had been five and he had been eight when I had moved to Florida with my family. A lot had changed. Punkin was now six feet tall and 176 pounds. He leaned over the trunk in his black slacks and pressed white dress shirt to get his bag.

I saw my cousin from the window and came to the door wearing a black, strappy dress that flared above my knees.

"Hey, Denise," he exclaimed. "I'm your cousin, Punkin. Look at you! You look so purdy!" he said, giving me a big, family hug. "I'm so sorry about your daddy."

I invited him inside to await the arrival of three of my father's six sisters who had driven out for the funeral. Helen Wyrick, the oldest had died, Doris Long had not been feeling well, and Billie Mae Andrews didn't get along with Margaret Bartenfield, so she had refused to come. The sisters tended to fight. Bill and Margaret had not been speaking lately. Margaret had said she would not come if Bill was going to be there and vice versa. I had begged my favorite aunt, Margaret, to come, however. I needed her. I needed all of them and could not understand why they could not just put their petty differences aside, at least for the funeral. My husband was not there, either. Rick had promised to attend the funeral but had said the arrival of my aunts would be like a family reunion, and he was not technically family, except by marriage. Besides, he had said, he hated all that sad stuff. I felt abandoned by him and knew my aunts would wonder why my husband was not at my side in my time of need.

Punkin explained that he had flown in but that his mother, Hildred "Hon" Reeder, and her twin sister, Mildred "Pig" Moore had driven with Margaret in Hon's car. The twins refused to fly. They were "scared as cats" he said, and he had not wanted to drive through two states with three old women arguing, so he had flown in by himself.

The three sisters arrived within the hour, full of hugs and southern drawls. Hon's red hair had grayed like Pig's, which used to be chestnut brown, like Margaret's, so now the fraternal twins both had gray hair. Margaret had a mole on her left cheek that accented her sweet smile. She apologized for hemming and hawing about coming and explained that she and Bill just did not get along.

The five of them sat down in the casual living room, and Aunt Margaret began the barrage of questions that I had been dreading. "What happened to my baby brother?" she wanted to know, her voice full of pain.

What little I knew I did not want to divulge, but my father's sisters expected answers. They loved their brother, and he had been mysteriously murdered in his own home.

They wanted to know how and why. The reunion became more like a game of dodge ball.

"He was stabbed," I told her, hating the words. "The neighbors next door heard an argument, and the man found Daddy in the dining room the next day."

"Well, was he stabbed in the dining room?" Margaret pressed.

"No," I told her.

"Well, where was he stabbed?" my aunt wanted to know.

"In his bedroom," I said.

Margaret wanted details. "Well, if he was stabbed in the bedroom, how do they know it
wasn't a woman?"

"They don't," I admitted. That much, at least, was true.

"Why would anybody want to kill Wesley?" Margaret asked. "Did he have any enemies?"

"No," I answered. "They don't know."

"Was he robbed?" Pig asked.

"Yes. His stereo and two of his VCRs were stolen," I said.

"Well, was that why he was killed?" Pig asked.

"The police aren't sure. They said there was no forced entry," I answered.

"So it was somebody he knew?" Margaret asked.

"Yes," I said.

"Why didn't the neighbors call the police when they heard the argument?" Pig asked.

"I don't know. I wish they would have," I answered, sadly. The fact that the neighbors had not called the police had haunted me since the murder. I thought of it constantly.

"What time's the funeral tomorrow?" Hon asked.

"Nine thirty in the morning," I told her. "I'll get you the directions."

Punkin had not known his Uncle Wesley very well, and

he was used to staying out of the way when the sisters got together. He was there to comfort his mother, Hon, and he literally held her hand whenever he was there with us all. The tricky part for me came when Aunt Margaret finally asked for the detectives' number to speak to them herself.

I was evasive. Christians were strongly against homosexuality, and the Wallace family believed the verse in the Bible, Leviticus 18:22, that read: "You shall not lie with a male as with a woman; it is an abomination." My father had not wanted them to know about his sexual preferences, and I did not want to betray him, even in death. Margaret pressed further.

"What's the name of the police department that's investigating his murder?" she asked.

"It's the Lake Worth Police Department," I answered.

"Well, I want their number," Margaret said.

"I'll try and find out for you," I told her, stalling. I hoped my aunt would let it go.

The sisters reminisced about their brother Wesley for the rest of the afternoon, while I remained on guard about the circumstances surrounding his death.

"Your daddy sure did love you," Margaret commented. "He was always talkin' about how smart you are and all— that you got into that gifted program at school."

I listened to my aunt speak about my father and tried not to cry.

"I remember when Wesley married Lynda and they had the reception at the Starmount Country Club," Margaret began. "He was so proud of that, you remember that, Pig?"

"I sure do. Where is Lynda?" Pig asked.

"She's in China," I explained about my mother.

"It's a shame she couldn't be here," Hon remarked. "She sure has a nice place," she added, looking out at the pool and tennis court beyond the sliding glass doors of the condo.

"Lynda's daddy owned North State Chevrolet," Margaret recalled. "Did you know that?" she asked her sister, Hon.

"Is that right?" Hon asked.

"Yep. Wesley used to sell cars with Lynda's brothers," Margaret continued. "That was a long time ago. Things sure have changed."

"They sure have," Pig agreed. "Hey, don't you have a new baby boy?" she asked me.

"Yes. His name's Blaine," I answered. "I'll go get you a picture of him," I said, standing up.

"I want to know why Wesley was killed," Margaret whispered as I walked to the bedroom to get my purse.

"There's got to be more to the story," she rasped behind her hand. "Why was somebody at his house?"

I returned with the picture of my son and showed it to my aunts and cousin.

"Oh, look at that," Hon remarked. "He's got red hair like you, Punkin."

"Yep, he sure does," Punkin agreed. The talk turned to my life out in California for a while, but the murder was still very fresh on everyone's mind. There were so many unanswered questions and some of the ones that I had answers for, I kept to myself. It was an uncomfortable afternoon for me, and though I welcomed the company of my aunts, part of me looked forward to when they would leave and I could let my guard down.

I did not even want to talk about my father's hidden sexuality to my two girlfriends from grade school who were planning to attend the funeral. One was living in Boca Raton, and one had driven over from the west coast of Florida to be there for me. I divulged little more to them than I had to my aunts and cousin, though they asked just as many questions about the murder. And sadly, it would be my last chance to lean on anyone.

I no longer formed close friendships as an adult out in California. Instead, I chose to keep almost everything about my life to myself. Women I knew had tried to befriend me, but I have to admit that I made it hard for them to do so. One had attempted to indulge me in daily phone conversations while she walked on the treadmill in her home. After forty-five minutes of mindless chatter one day, she had insisted on calling me back after her shower. I could not stand the thought of it and refused to pick up the phone for a second time. Eventually she got the message and stopped calling.

On Tuesday, the following day, the memorial service was held at the historic, sunny Del Lago Chapel near the beach. A smartly dressed anchorwoman for Channel 4 News held out a microphone for me on my walk up to the door. "How do you feel about your father's killer?" she asked provocatively. My husband pushed the mike away with his hand, and for the first time since his arrival, I was grateful for his gesture.

Forty-five minutes later, the newswoman had the funeral director relay a message to me that she wanted an interview. The appalling question came at the same time I had taken my father's ashes in my hands. Without warning, the director had passed me the rectangular-shaped cardboard box. Most shocking was the weight. I had not been expecting ashes to weigh as much as a bowling ball, and I nearly dropped the box.

The panic of the moment seemed to linger with me during the entire drive to the Lake Worth Pier, which was not far from the Ritz Carlton, Palm Beach. It had been named after William Osborne Lockhart, a longtime Lake Worth resident and pier master, who was known for teaching kids to fish and his generosity to the poor and the homeless. My aunts followed behind in their car, taking in the magnificent view of the Intracoastal Waterway from the bridge. My father and I had sometimes gone to the pier to feed the seagulls, so

I decided I wanted to scatter his ashes there in the ocean. Rick and my aunts decided to stand outside their cars in the parking lot and wait while I did so.

I was alone as I stepped across the worn, wooden planks of the pier that were designed to break away during high waves and heavy storms. I knew my father's favorite fish, cobia, likely lurked underwater along with the African pompano and snappers near the pier pilings as I crossed. After passing a couple of anglers with their fishing rods, I made it to the end of the pier with the cardboard box. The sky was clear, and a warm breeze blew as I scattered my father's ashes off the north corner of the pier. Disturbingly, they blew in the opposite direction of the one I had meant for them to go. It was then that the reality of my father's death finally hit me. I could spend the rest of my days scouring the earth and still never find my father. He was gone.

The Wallace sisters were waiting when I got back to the parking lot on Ocean Boulevard. I heard Pig whisper to Hon and Margaret from behind her delicate, aging hand. "Do you think we should say something to her?" Pig asked. Her sisters both nodded. "We didn't know you were going to have Wesley cremated," Pig said to me as I stood with tears streaming down my face.

"It's just kind of a shock to us, that's all," Margaret gently explained.

"I guess we wouldn't be able to visit his grave anyway," Hon said sadly, "Seeing how it would be all the way down here in Florida and all."

"I'm sorry!" It was all I could manage to say. It had not occurred to me to consult my father's sisters about his burial. In hindsight, I realized that they had each known him long before I had even been born. I should have talked to them about it first. I hugged my aunts, said "good-bye" to them, and got back into the car. My husband and I then drove back to my mother's in silence. Not only did I feel guilty about not being there when my father had needed me, I now felt guilty about leaving my aunts without a place to grieve for him. Sadly, there was nothing I could do about it now.

CHAPTER 23
Hitchhikers and Addicts

My father left Fort Lauderdale and moved back to Greensboro, North Carolina in 1980. He now went by the name "Wes." I was twelve years old at the time and would have to fly on a plane all by myself to see my dad. He found a tiny apartment at the end of seven pueblo-looking structures in a row on Bessemer Court. It was apartment number thirteen. The units emptied into a shapeless parking area that consisted only of crude, white gravel. My dad still had his black and white Nova. He had driven it into a lake one night while drunk, but it still ran.

The little strip of apartments was only a block from the lovely bridges and creeks of Fisher Park, yet it oddly resembled something out of New Mexico. Large homes discreetly hid them from the lush green park's view on one side. A 7-Eleven blocked them from the main road on the other. The rent was fifty-three dollars a month—unheard of, even in 1980.

Many months would pass before my dad would hit bottom and step foot inside his first AA meeting. In the meantime, he drank enough beer and Scotch to fill two black, Hefty garbage bags each week with the empties. They sat outside by the concrete steps of his apartment until the trash men finally hauled them away on trash day.

As a chronic alcoholic, my father drank until he passed out each night. He awoke each morning only to vomit and crack open another beer. I made him bacon and eggs for breakfast during the summers and on school breaks. Even badly hungover, my father still managed to take me to tennis lessons and movies. We went ice skating, horseback riding, camping, and whitewater rafting. He always made plenty of quality time for me.

But we also still went on his terrifying night drives. My father had no business being behind the wheel of a car, and worse, he had begun to pick up hitchhikers. Young, scraggly men who looked like they had not bathed in weeks would often catch a ride from us in the backseat of the Nova. Many were alcoholics and drug addicts.

One night my father drove me out into a yellow field and parked. We sat quietly for a long time before he pulled out a manila file from his divorce case and began to rant. "Denise, your mama's a whore. Do you know that? Are you going to grow up and be a whore like your mama?" he demanded. "Are you?" Suddenly, red and white lights shone in the dark behind us. Two middle-aged police officers got out of a squad car and approached each of our windows.

"Sir, what are you doing out here with this little girl?" one of the officers asked.

"That's my daughter," my dad informed him. The officer looked as if he did not believe him.

"Is that your father?" the other one asked me. I nodded. The officers made us get out of the car so they could search it. A brown paper bag on the seat had caught their attention. One of the officers opened it and found it half full of bottle caps. "What are these?" he asked.

"That's my bottle cap collection," I told them. A further search of the car uncovered an empty syringe in the back seat.

"You collect them, too?" the other officer asked me.

"That belongs to the guy I gave a ride to today," my father explained. "I picked him up hitchhiking."

"Is that true?" he asked me. "Did your father pick up a hitchhiker today?"

I nodded again.

He believed me. The officers let my dad go with a warning. "I don't ever want to find you out here with your daughter again, you hear? Get her home. This ain't no place for a little girl to be at night."

The aimless drives stopped after that, but the terror did not. Soon my father was even rendering himself too drunk to drive. Instead, he began handing the wheel over to me.

On a snowy drive up the winding road to Little Switzerland in the Blue Ridge Mountains that winter, my dad found himself in such condition. We were on our way to go emerald mining. It had begun to snow, and my dad's double vision was even further impaired. Rather than pull over and risk getting stuck in the mounting snow, he merely slowed to a stop and switched seats with me. To my horror, he insisted I drive. He was too drunk. "I don't know how to drive, Daddy!" I panicked. "I can't even see over the wheel!"

My dad grabbed a bed pillow from the back seat. "Here. Sit on this," he slurred. "Driving's easy. You just watch the road and steer." He showed me the pedals. "Look, this one's the gas, and this one's the brake."

"But I can't reach the pedals if I sit on the pillow!" I cried.

My dad told me that he would work the pedals. Terrified, I slowly steered the car in the snow and tried to keep from sliding off the embankment. I had never been so scared in my life. The scenery of the snow and the pine trees was exceptionally beautiful, yet I knew it could instantly turn deadly.

I glanced over at my father as he cranked down the window halfway. He was letting the snow fall on his face in the hope that it would sober him up. My dad could see the road was coming to a three-way stop up ahead. In one swift move he slammed his foot down on the brake just before we went over the edge of the mountain. I had thought that the road continued down the other side.

Somewhat sobered by the near-death experience, my dad got out of the car to urinate. While turning the snow yellow, he gazed down at the snow-covered valley below. The distance seemed endless.

An officer driving by pulled over and issued my father a citation for public urination. Once again, the police missed the big picture. My dad was well beyond the blood alcohol limit for safe driving.

A little while later, we reached our chosen motel that was lodged into the side of the mountain. The view was breathtaking, and the room was cheap. To further save money, my father had brought a hibachi to cook hamburgers for dinner. Staggering to light the grill on the balcony, he found to his dismay that the snow was still falling. It kept putting out the flame. After several frustrating minutes, my dad got what he thought was a brilliant idea. He would bring the hibachi inside the room to cook the burgers.

Dinner turned out to be tasty, but it was getting a bit smoky in the room. My dad was too drunk to realize that some of the charcoal was still smoldering. Just before passing out, he told me to open a window. He was now hot, but he was too drunk to do it himself.

Upon the checkout inspection of the room the next morning, the hotel manager noticed a rather large hole burned into the beige carpet. After hearing that we had brought our grill into the enclosed room, he explained that he was not angry about the damage. Instead, he was grateful to see we were alive. Had I not opened the window, he informed us, we would have died from carbon monoxide poisoning.

Soon after the emerald mining trip, my father found

himself at the front of an AA meeting. Perhaps two near-death experiences in one day had been enough for him. He went cold turkey and suffered through agonizing convulsions on his bed. He would stay sober for two years before relapsing.

My father knew that narcotic addicts have an even worse relapse rate than alcoholics of 80 percent. That's why when a narcotics addict named Pete moved into apartment number fourteen next door, my dad gave me strict instructions. I was not to open the door for him for any reason, no matter what he said. No matter how long he knocked, I was not to open the door.

One day while my father and I were both home, Pete knocked on the door. He just wanted to borrow some butter, he said. I got up to go to the door when my dad stopped me. "Denise, I told you not to open the door for that weasel," he seethed.

"But you're home, Daddy. I thought you only meant when you're not home." The knocking continued. Pete just wanted some butter.

"Come on, bud," he begged. "I thought we were friends! Why you got to be so fickle?" The knocking became more urgent.

"Can't we just give him some butter, Daddy?" I asked naively. Instead of answering, my father slid the sliding chain into the lock. Pete heard it. He made a rush for the doorknob and the bottom lock was not locked. The door sprung open, stopping short at the chain. Pete pleaded through the opening for my father to let him in. He looked like a wild animal. My dad was not budging.

"You get out of here, Pete, and don't come knocking on my door anymore!" He slammed the door in Pete's face and locked it. We heard another slam as Pete went back to his apartment. Then we heard chaos. It sounded like he was tearing up his place for several tense minutes after that.

After all the years of hitchhikers and addicts, Pete was the one who had frightened me the most. He had seemed like a wolf in sheep's clothing at the door. I often wondered what would have happened if I had let him in. Thankfully, he only continued to live next door for a few more months and then disappeared one day.

Though I was somewhat safer with Pete gone, I was still plagued by asthma and allergies. Inhalers and vaporizers were always kept on hand, especially when the pollen count was high. Other environmental factors like trees, weeds, grass, and mold set off my allergies and irritated my lungs. They made me more susceptible to colds that lingered and morphed into bronchitis every six or eight weeks.

My father thought he had a solution. Mamie, a heavy black maid at the hotel where he bartended at the Red Baron Lounge, was nursing her third baby. She offered to give me some of the breast milk that she bottled for the infant before she left for work each morning. It contained taurine that was packed with immunities. I adamantly refused. I was not drinking breast milk that came from some strange woman's breasts. It was not going to happen. For the first time, my father did not push the issue. He told his well-meaning friend Mamie, "No, thank you," and that was the end of it—except for the humorous tale that he now had for friends.

My father had other well-meaning friends in AA that would help him in his fight to stay sober. The fellowship was a support network, a lifeline. That was the purpose of a sponsor. Everyone in AA had one. If a member felt the urge to have a drink, he was supposed to call his sponsor, who was to drop whatever he was doing and talk them through it.

My father's sponsor was his psychiatrist friend, Dr. Dave Clemmons. Though Wes was not diagnosed with anything such as bipolar disorder or schizophrenia, he had sought psychiatric treatment from his friend in the past. His issues were confidential between doctor and patient. By my father's account, the two seemed to only discuss my mother's chronic nymphomaniac behavior and split personality. The diagnosis had come from my father.

He was much more adept at diagnosing himself, at least as an alcoholic. Once an AA member lets go of denial and admits this fact about himself, it's customary for him to get up in front of an AA meeting and tell the story about how he came to stop drinking. In Dr. Clemmons's story, he had hidden a bottle of liquor under his side of the bed. While he was reaching for it one night, his wife entered the room. Upon questioning, he told her that she had caught him in the middle of praying. Touched by the discovery, she had quickly left the room and insisted that he finish.

I never heard my father's story of how he came to stop drinking. At the beginning of his sobriety, he attended meetings alone. In time he would bring me with him for support. As his awareness grew from other members' stories, he would have me attend Alateen, a group meeting for teenagers living with alcoholics, and Al-Anon, a meeting for families and friends of alcoholics. The meetings give members much needed support and advice regarding their relationships with the alcoholic. Members were taught things like never argue with a drunk. Besides the fact that it could be dangerous, the drunk was not likely to remember the argument anyway, so it was pointless to try to reason with him.

Upon my father's alcohol relapse, I had taken to pouring out most of his glass of Scotch while he was in the bathroom. My friends would often see me doing this and inquire as to what I was doing. In time they would become the "lookout" for me and report of his return.

Sadly, the tactic was often used in vain. If my dad failed to pass out before he ran out of liquor, he would often get behind the wheel and return to the liquor store. Many times I was made to come along for the reckless drive.

The prospect of being alone with my dad while he was drinking was immensely frightening. I often found myself begging some of his friends to come along on outings with us. In one instance, my dad had promised to take me camping. Thankfully, his friend Tim had agreed to come along for the trip. He was a guitar player in a band at the Red Baron Lounge. I had been greatly relieved and was even beginning to look forward to the outing when Tim suddenly canceled at the last minute. I had pleaded with him to come, but he had been offered a gig and did not want to pass up the opportunity.

The night of the camping trip, my dad did a poor job of putting up the pup tent in his drunken state and it fell in on us during the night. Then it began to rain. He was too drunk to fix it, and I did not know how. We had to sleep that way until morning, when we discovered that wild animals had eaten the rest of the burgers that had been left on the hibachi outside the tent. I feared we had come close to being eaten by bears. The ranger had warned us that there were bears in the area. The culprits were more likely to have been raccoons, but we would never know for sure.

My father sometimes left me at home alone, as well, while he stayed out late at night by himself. Though I was free from his hazardous actions, I was often wracked with worry over my father, instead, which was not much better. One night, I stood at the screen door for what seemed like hours when he was extremely late returning home. I feared he had gotten in a car wreck and was amazed that he had not had one yet. My dad finally returned home at four in the morning to find me waiting at the door for him. Upon learning that I had been worried sick, he proceeded to laugh all the way to the bedroom, where he shut the door and went to sleep. He never offered an explanation as to where he had been.

I found myself wanting to spend more and more time with my friend, Alyssa, and less and less time with my father. Alyssa was Becky's daughter, my father's best friend from high school, who had let him try on her dresses. Becky had a Colonial style home on Magnolia Avenue in Fisher Park. The house had a large front porch that wrapped around one side, where a rocking chair sat from Becky's childhood.

There were many kids on Magnolia Avenue who were close to our age. Sometimes they hung out at "the court," a short cul-de-sac off the center of the street, which had a cement bench amid the well-manicured grass. Most summer days the pack hung out at Sheryl Jensen's house. Hers was the big one on the corner with the two white pillars out front. It was next door to Becky's. A black- and white-striped canopy over the front door gave the place a regal look that boasted of old money.

Becky and Sheryl were best friends. Their daughters, Alyssa and Patty, were also close, even though they were four years apart in age. At sixteen, Patty was the oldest on the street. She excelled at softball and considered herself the mother of the pack, calling me and the rest of us her "kids."

It was quite possible that the short-haired, freckled girl who looked like her mother would never bear any children of her own. Patty was a lesbian. She had a girlfriend named Charity who lived down the street. Charity had long, shiny black hair and a full face and jaw. She was a talented ballerina, and Patty often bragged about her to everyone. One day Sheryl walked in on the two of them in bed. She was enraged at the sight of the naked young girls in each other's arms. It was my father who talked her out of disowning her daughter.

Patty's bedroom often changed from one room to another as if she were searching for her own identity. Out back she swam freely in the large pool on the enormous patio. The kids all flocked there in the summertime. It was the only home in the neighborhood that had a pool. Wes, Becky, and Sheryl also spent many summer nights drinking out on the cement patio. Their loud laughter carried out onto the street in the night air.

One night, my dad got drunk and wanted to impress Becky and Sheryl with my newly acquired diving skills. As I walked out onto the diving board, he suddenly yelled at me to turn around. He wanted me to dive into the pool backward. "But I haven't practiced enough yet, Daddy!" I begged.

"Denise, just do what I tol' you!" he bellowed. The women could see how nervous I was and told him they did not need to see that particular display of acrobatics, but my father insisted. Terrified, I finally managed to do a backbend into the pool. I barely missed banging my head on the diving board before I hit the water. Becky and Sheryl were mortified. They begged my dad not to make me perform any more dives for the rest of the summer.

My father also pushed me to advance at tennis well before I was ready. After simply showing me how to swing my racket, he took me down to the tennis courts on the corner where a group lesson was being taught. I had never actually practiced with a tennis ball. The fifteen-year-old girls had been playing tennis for at least a year when my dad interrupted the class and told the instructor that I was fifteen and had a great swing. I could fit right in with the rest of them, he said. It did not faze him in the least that at thirteen, I was noticeably shorter than all the other girls. Once my father left the court, the instructor watched as I missed every ball. She then asked me if I wanted to join the thirteen-year-old class, instead. Relieved, I told her that I did.

My father did not always drop me off to the care of those running the activity but joined in himself. One summer he signed me up at Christian camp and asked me if I wanted him to come along for the week. He did not have a lot of money but managed to scrape enough together for both of us to attend. My dad always told me that money could not make me happy, that I could be just as happy with a poor man as I could with a rich man. One day I would find that out for myself, but that summer my dad and I set out on the two-and-a-half-hour drive listening to the eight-track tapes of Carly Simon and Cat Stevens. Father and daughter were happy to be together once again after the long school year apart.

By the time I was fifteen, I was wanting to spend more time with my friends and less time with my dad even though he was now sober again. One day I made plans to sleep over at my friend Alyssa's house. My dad dropped me off out front after a tense ride where he expressed his hurt that I always wanted to spend time with Alyssa instead of him. He drove away sad and left me feeling guilty.

Ironically, Alyssa had no plans to carry out the sleepover with me. She had lied to her mother and told her that she was spending the night at Jessica's house across the street. Meanwhile, Jessica had told her mother she was spending the night at Alyssa's house. The girls were actually sneaking out to a concert, and I had nowhere to sleep. Conveniently, Alyssa's friend Mikayla Pinkett had said I could sleep at her house that night. At sixteen, Mikayla was a year older than me. She was an athletic girl with a boyish smile. Alyssa often joked that Mikayla would make a good-looking guy so she nicknamed her Charlie.

I found Mikayla's room sparsely decorated. She had a framed picture of her old best friend on her dresser and a radio on the floor by her bed. Mikayla always went to sleep listening to the radio, she told me as she flipped it on. Michael Jackson's "Human Nature" was playing. It was 1983, and everyone had his new album *Thriller*.

Mikayla lifted the covers for me to get into the double bed first. I was wearing a long T-shirt and would sleep next to the wall. Mikayla got in next, in a pair of red satin shorts and a white top. We lay listening to the song for a few minutes. Then I turned over. Mikayla's face was an inch away from mine. I knew Mikayla was going to kiss me. I kissed her back. It would be three days before Mikayla would drive me home. She had not wanted me to leave. I told her that my friend Annie really wanted me to meet her little brother. Annie had been taken in as a foster child at Sheryl's house and did not get to see him very often. Mikayla was jealous. I thought it was ridiculous and insisted on going.

Back at my father's apartment later, my dad listened to me answer the phone that rang a dozen times. It was always Mikayla. "How come you stayed over at her house for three days?" he asked me.

"You said it was okay, Daddy," I replied.

"Well, why's she calling you so much? Denise, are you gay?" he demanded. He looked as if he wanted nothing to do with me anymore.

I just looked at him. "Yeah, Daddy, I'm gay," I said sarcastically. The whole idea of my being lesbian was ridiculous, I thought. A week later I was dating Keith Somers. He was a freshman in college that my father had let sleep on his couch until he was able to move into his dorm at the university. The young man had wanted to get out from under the watchful eye of his born-again Christian parents at their home. Keith was a bodybuilder. We dated all of the following year until my father found birth control in my purse and put an end to the relationship. Keith had been my first. To my father's relief, I was not a lesbian.

CHAPTER 24
Rolling a Fag

It was October 16, 1999. After his parents had thrown him out, Alberto Miliana, a young Puerto Rican male, had spent the night at Park View Motor Lodge in Palm Springs, Florida. The nearby hotel had large, clay-potted palms and an asphalt parking lot.

Miliana got up out of bed. It took him a moment to remember where he was. The thin, gold-striped comforter threw him for a second. He fumbled for a Pall Mall cigarette on the wooden nightstand. *Dammit*. There was no lighter. Well, he needed to take a piss anyway. He would check the bathroom.

Miliana stumbled to the john. Where the hell was the light switch in this place? They should have put the thing by the bathroom door so people could find it, he thought. He had no intention of paying the bill anyway. He was broke. He was also hungry. If he was going to skip out, he might as well have something to eat at the restaurant, too, he reasoned.

The hotel manager called the police when he saw Miliana's car pulling away through the office window. He had had his eye on Miliana from the moment he had checked in.

When Miliana had gotten about two miles from the motel, he noticed in his rearview mirror that a cop car was following him. Red and blue lights began circling on the squad car, and a siren began to blare. Miliana sped up and tried to outrun the officer. He swerved recklessly around a gray SUV in front of him. The male driver shouted at him from his car window, calling him an asshole. Miliana glanced in his rearview mirror again and stepped on the gas. He was now approaching 70 miles per hour on a two-lane road.

Up ahead, a red light was coming at him much too fast. A blue Mustang was already crossing the intersection in front of him. He was sure to hit it. Miliana slammed on the brakes, gripping the steering wheel as the squad car veered around him on the right and came to a barreling halt. Two officers jumped out of the car and pulled out their firearms. They demanded that he exit his vehicle and place his hands behind his head. Miliana was arrested and charged with fleeing and eluding along with petty theft.

While sitting in his cell, Miliana pondered a way that he could get out of doing jail time. It was not something he cared to do, and why should he? There were bigger criminals out there. Hell, he knew a guy that had done something worse than he had. Much worse. He decided to tell all this to the cop who locked him up.

Detective Venetucci was the one who took the call from the officer at the jail. Though none of the other leads on the Wallace case had panned out over the past four months, he still found himself listening closely to tips, though with great skepticism. Those arrested often had dirt on people they knew. This guy sold weed out of his apartment. That guy stole electronics off a truck. He was not about to send guys to stake out every small-time criminal who had pissed somebody off in his life. He would check out Miliana's story, though. It was part of the routine.

The detective drove the three miles over to the Palm Springs Police Department expecting the trip to be a waste of time. He told the cop at the front that he was there to talk to one of their arrestees, Alberto Miliana. The cop led him down a hall and pulled out a large key ring full of keys.

Placing one in the lock of a door, he turned it and pushed it open for the detective. Miliana was sitting on a cot inside a cell that was second to the last one in the row. The cop led Venetucci over to him and walked back out.

"You Alberto Miliana?" the detective asked.

"Yep," the young man answered.

"You got some information about a murder for me, huh?" Venetucci asked skeptically. "So let's hear it. Whatcha got?" It was a common ploy for a criminal to try to get out of his own mess by confessing someone else's. The detective had heard it time and time again. That was why when Miliana started telling him about a guy he knew who had "rolled a fag," he had started to leave. Then he heard about the items in the bathtub. Miliana knew about the bleach. Venetucci halted and turned around. Those details had never been published in the newspaper; they were confidential. That left only one way for Miliana to have found out about them. □

Ventucci walked out of the jail no less stunned than he found himself each time he listened to inside knowledge of a crime. How could someone keep something like that to himself when often the killer was not even able to do so? He headed back to the station with a name screaming in his head: Travis Jones. The same first name that Montegut had given them. Maybe he had caught a break in the Wallace case after all.

CHAPTER 25
Sex for Drugs

It was three o'clock in the morning on Wednesday, October 27, 1999. Travis Jones had still not been to bed. He had been able to score some cocaine the night before, but it had been in the form of powder. He had to cook it on the stove in order to burn off the impurities and melt the powder into BB-sized, smokeable rocks. The problem was that he was at his father's house now in Des Moines, Iowa. He had to be sneaky in the kitchen so that he would not awaken his dad and stepmother.

Travis thought he heard someone coming into the kitchen. He ran back to his room and hid in his closet for a couple of minutes. When he tiptoed back out, his small pot was still bubbling delightfully away on the stove. Travis jerked it off the burner to save what precious crack had formed its majestic shape before it all melted away. He had just cooked up his last ten dollars, and he was not due to get paid again until Friday. He would have to somehow make it through the next two days. Or steal from his stepmother's wallet. His dad usually had his wallet on him, but she could be counted on to leave her purse on the old, rusty trunk in her bedroom. Travis smoked the last batch inside his closet out of sheer paranoia that was prone to seizing him these days. He sucked the euphoric, white vapor through his amber-colored glass, round-bottomed pipe. The addict embraced the high that was becoming less and less intense until it was all gone.

Travis slipped on his jeans and left his father's house at seven in the morning. He had never gone to sleep. Outside, billowy clouds filled the gray sky behind the gold and brown leaves of the many trees. Travis wore a black T-shirt, Levis, and a pair of Puma sneakers. The young man lit a cigarette and treaded lightly down the concrete steps of the walkway behind the wooden rail in the grass.

Travis had been working at a gas station. It was down the road and within walking distance, though Travis preferred hitchhiking. His frail, blond pretty-boy looks got him picked up quite often by lonely men who wanted to talk. Or more. The taste for crack cocaine that Travis had developed a ravenous appetite for back in South Florida drove him to trade sex for drugs. Crack was more expensive in Iowa, but he still managed to score. He would pick up some more right after work with the ten dollars he had stolen from his stepmother's wallet—or so he thought.

Then he spotted Detectives Venetucci and Boland coming up the driveway.

Before leaving Palm Beach County, the detectives had gotten a court order from Judge A. B. Crouch in Norwalk, Iowa, to allow them to get fingerprints and palm prints from Travis. The young man's face showed no surprise, nor did he try to resist as Boland slid handcuffs on his petite wrists.

Venetucci stood guard outside the door at the Norwalk Police Department while the fingerprints were being taken. Travis was then driven to an Iowa dentist to have some molds taken of his teeth. Detective Boland had four cotton swab samples taken of the inside of Travis's mouth, as well, for the purpose of DNA testing. Upon their return to Florida, the swabs would be hand-delivered to a serologist and the molds to a dentist.

Travis was brought back to Florida by a private prisoner transport company. Upon landing, he was brought to "The Box" or interrogation room at the Lake Worth Police Department in handcuffs. A single hanging light shone down on him. The walls were blank, and his chair legs were straight while Venetucci's chair legs were on rollers. It was all done with the purpose of giving the detective a psychological edge. He could start off being three to four feet away, but if Travis was about to confess, he could easily roll within inches of him. Though Travis had been in police custody for eleven hours, no one had dared to interview him until now. His eventual defense attorney would surely move to dismiss any words that Travis uttered before being properly told of his rights. Even though Venetucci had Mirandized him upon his arrest back in Iowa, this still did not make his utterances defense-proof. Whenever possible, interrogations and interviews were to be conducted in front of audio and video recording equipment. Venetucci flipped them on methodically and took a seat in his rolling chair in front of the cold, metal table.

"Hey, Travis," he started off. Venetucci liked to treat suspects with dignity. He felt that if they could see that he viewed them in this way, the chances of communicating would start to open up.

Travis mumbled a response under his breath.

"You want something to eat or drink?" Venetucci asked, partly to break the ice and partly to ensure the kid could not later claim he had been hungry or thirsty. Travis asked for a soda. "I got Cherry Coke or 7UP," the detective offered.

"Cherry Coke," the suspect answered.

"You got it," Venetucci replied, then left for a moment to retrieve the beverage. He then returned and settled back into his chair on wheels to begin his questioning.

"What's your full name?" the detective asked.

"Travis Gene Jones," Travis answered.

"And your address?"

Travis gave him Dan Jones's address in Des Moines, Iowa.

"How long have you lived at your father's house?" Venetucci asked next.

"About four months," Travis stated quietly.

"Where'd you live before that?"

Travis paused for a moment. "In my apartment in West Palm until I lost my job."

"Where'd you work?"

"Personal Touch Detailing."

"Where'd you live after you lost your job?"

"On the street." The young man put his head in his hands.

"That couldn't have been too easy. What did you eat?"

"Hamburgers from McDonald's that they'd thrown out and stuff."

"Were you using?" the detective prodded, staring into the suspect's eyes.

Travis shook his head, which made Venetucci frown.

"You weren't doing any drugs?" he asked again. "What happened to all your stuff? You said you had an apartment, right?"

Travis nodded. "I lost it."

"You lost it?" Venetucci repeated. "You mean you put it somewhere and then forgot where you put it?"

Travis shook his head.

The detective wheeled his chair over and got in the suspect's face. "Ever hock any of it?" he asked.

Travis eyed Venetucci suspiciously. "A few things, when I ran out of money."

"Like what?"

"Microwave, TV, VCR," Travis answered. His voice waivered on the last word.

"And what pawnshop did you go to?" the detective wanted to know.

"I don't know," Travis whispered uncomfortably.

"What was that?" Venetucci asked.

"I don't remember."

Venetucci nodded. He really wanted to ask about the night Travis got picked up by Wes, but before he could, he would have to read him his Miranda rights again and more formally this time. He placed a sheet of paper listing the rights in front of Travis, and they went through them together one by one.

"You have the right to remain silent," Venetucci read. "Anything you say can be used against you in court," he reminded his suspect.

Travis nodded. Venetucci continued reading until he came upon the part about an attorney. He explained that if Travis could not afford a lawyer, one would be appointed for him. He also told him that if he wanted to talk without a lawyer, he could stop at any point to ask for one before answering any more questions.

"I want a lawyer," Travis said—those ominous words brought the questioning to a dead halt. Venetucci knew that anything Travis said after that moment, even voluntarily, could undercut the entire case against him. He gritted his teeth and took the hit.

"Okay," Venetucci sighed as he rose. He left without saying another word. Two more officers entered the interrogation room.

"I need you to stand up," one ordered. Travis rose obediently. The officer placed handcuffs around the young man's small wrists. He would not be buying that ten-dollar bag of crack tonight after all.

***

Travis Gene Jones was born in Des Moines, Iowa, on July 7, 1978, in a section called Kingman Place. The district contained a collection of American Foursquare houses that featured plain, handcrafted "honest" woodwork. The house that Travis lived in at birth included a basic square design that was two-and-one-half stories high. It had four large, boxy rooms on each floor, a center <u>dormer</u>, and a large front <u>porch</u> with a set of wide stairs.

Travis had been three weeks premature, therefore he lacked the baby fat in his cheeks that most infants who were carried to full term usually had. His father thought he looked like a small bird because he seemed to have no chin. Travis slept through most of the first three days of his life. He refused to drink any milk from the bottle his mother, Pamela Sue Jones, tried to feed him. Concerned, she called the doctor and asked what to do to get him to eat. He told her to try breastfeeding, but that did not seem to work, either. Only the wet, cold touch of an ice cube on his lips would awaken the child enough to prompt him to drink from a bottle. Within a few days, his cheeks filled out and the birdlike look of his face disappeared.

Travis's parents divorced when he was only one year old, but his father visited with him regularly. He was smaller than other children his age. In elementary school, he began to worry outwardly about his size. No matter how much his parents tried to reassure him, it never seemed to squelch the fear that he would be a midget of a person. His mother would later recall that Travis's pediatrician made the upsetting remark that he was in the thirtieth percentile of height for his age. "What does that mean?" Travis asked, his eyes scanning the chart that the doctor showed him.

"It means that 70 percent of the children might grow taller than you," the doctor said.

Travis feared he would remain the shortest in his class and never catch up with everyone. "I don't want to go to school," he told his mother the next day. "We're supposed to do pull-ups in PE," he cried, referring to gym class. "What if I can't reach the bar?"

"Aren't there a few girls that can't reach the bar either?" his mother asked. "I'm sure the teacher will have a solution."

This sent Travis running to his room. His mother had come to the door and insisted that he go to school. She would take him to the store afterwards and they would pick out a new pair of sneakers with a thick sole, she promised. This would make him look taller.

She knew he was sensitive about his size and got picked on at school, so she was reluctant to be as firm with him as some felt she should have been. With Travis's father gone from the house, often the only form of punishment was a mere "knock it off." Travis began to tune out the words as soon as he was old enough to brush his own teeth, which was something he often skipped. He also did not care to clean up the floor of his room, which was always littered with his favorite toys: ThunderCats. Travis's mother would ask him to put his ThunderCats to bed in their blue bin each night, but ultimately it was she who was left to pick up the orange, blue, and green action figures. Her son also had the maddening habit of throwing his clothes on the floor right in front of the closet where his hamper was kept. "Don't be so lazy," she would constantly find herself saying to him.

As Travis grew, his negative self-image worsened. He had no interest in sports like football and soccer that the others were playing, nor did he have any interest in playing an instrument. It was not that he did not like music. Travis loved bands like the Smashing Pumpkins and Weezer. He did not much care for Alice in Chains and Poison that a lot of twelve-year-old boys liked. Often, he would lie on the floor of his room with his knees up, getting high and listening to CDs by himself. Des Moines, being the most populous city of Iowa, had its ample share of weed. It was easy to get, even for an unpopular twelve-year-old with good grades and bad hygiene. Then his mother and stepfather moved to Delray Beach, Florida, and every drug became easy to get. Especially cocaine.

Coca, derived from the coca plant of South American countries such as Colombia and Peru, is ferried in to the United States by small planes or boats. In the 1990s, 90 percent of the cocaine shipped to the United States entered at points along the Florida coast through one of the most commonly travelled routes: The Windward Passage between Cuba and Haiti. During much bloodshed, the Colombian Cali cartel and the Medellin cartel, run by the incredibly violent Pablo Escobar, began to self-destruct. That 90 percent point of entry rate would then shift to Mexico by the year 2007.

That would be too late for Travis. At age eighteen, Travis's mother moved to Texas and he was left on his own. He had gotten a job at Personal Touch Detailing and rented a studio apartment in West Palm Beach. Around the same time, he also got hooked on crack cocaine the first time he sucked the white smoke through an amber-colored glass pipe. From then on it was days on end of smoking up jumbos that he had bought for ten dollars a bag. He would lie back on the bed and hold the rapturous smoke in his lungs like it was the nectar of the gods. Nothing had ever made him feel that good. The trouble was, the intense high was short-lived and immediately followed by intense depression, edginess, and a craving for more. Those ten-dollar bags started adding up. Things like food were going to have to go, not that he had much of an appetite anyway. Travis began living off Cheetos and Mountain Dew. He was also showering less. It was sometimes hard to tell what day it was when Monday ran together with Tuesday and Tuesday ran together with Wednesday.

Then one day he went to work and found that Personal Touch Detailing had been closed by the Palm Beach Auto Mall. He did not much feel like working these days anyway. All Travis wanted to do was get high. But the high was never as good as it had been that first time. He had been trying to get the feeling back ever since, but the problem with a three-day binge was that by day two you did not get high anymore. It was more of a rush, then nothing, followed by a craving, and on day three you needed the crack just to not feel like shit. And now there was no Friday paycheck to take to The Check Cashing Store on Atlantic Avenue. Travis had to pawn his stereo and TV just to buy more crack. When the end of the month came and he did not have the rent, the landlady taped a three-days-to-pay-rent-or-quit sign on his door. March had gone by so fast. Or was it April?

Crack-addicted Travis had been living on the streets for about four months. Instead of cleaning up, he chose to live near the tracks of Dixie Highway, like many other addicts. His meals often came from Dumpsters and homosexual men who slowed to give him a ride until one ride went wrong. Very wrong.

CHAPTER 26
The Gay Beach

Waves rolled up and tumbled onto the tide pools of California's Little Corona Beach. The white sand was lined with cliffs and parted by a small, jagged path of ocean water that spilled over onto smooth, gray rocks. My husband, Rick, and I strolled the smooth, fine sand. Rick dwarfed my small, athletic frame. I wore a long, flowing cover-up and my sandy blond hair fluttered in the wind as we wandered the little-known strip of beach.

"Perfect temperature, huh?" Rick asked me, looking up at the cloudless sky.

"Yes," I responded, agreeing with my husband as I always did. I flashed my Miss Congeniality smile and continued my delicate steps in the sand. We soon passed a volleyball game in progress. Something was very different about this beach. There were no women on it. The volleyball game was being played solely by tanned, chiseled men in colorful Speedos. We were near Laguna Beach—the city that had been nicknamed the Home of the Festival of the Arts. It had a 20 percent gay and lesbian population. This small section of the beach in Corona Del Mar called "Little Corona" had been taken over by gays.

Suddenly, my cell phone rang. It had been four months since my father's murder and each time it rang I still thought it was him calling. I was disappointed each time. "Mrs. Reilly, this is Marc Shiner," the voice stated. "I'm the prosecutor for the State of Florida. I wanted to let you know that we've found the man who killed your father."

I came to a halt in the sand. I was stunned. There was now a face to my father's killer. I dreaded the thought of seeing him in person.

"We need you to be at the trial," Shiner explained. "The jury needs to see your father's side. The killer's the worst kind of defendant. He's pretty and meek. He looks vulnerable, as if he couldn't possibly have killed anyone."

"How old is he?" I asked.

"Twenty-one. Like I was saying, if the jury sees that there's no one there grieving for your father, they could let him go. I've seen it happen before, believe me. The state will pay for your round-trip flight and hotel room. I could subpoena you, but I don't want to have to do that."

I thought over what the prosecutor said. "Okay. I'll be there," I agreed before hanging up the phone and slipping it back into my purse.

The trial felt like a door I did not want to open. I had tried so hard to stay on the outside of that door, and I did not want to know what was behind it. I could not imagine what would be there waiting for me. It was like the prosecutor was asking me to be some other person who lived on the other side of the door. That was someone else's world, not mine, but he was going to make me open it. I was not going to have a choice.

My husband was not happy about my decision to attend the trial. He asked if he had to accompany me. I responded to him by asking, "You want me to sit through my father's trial with the killer in that room by myself?" Rick felt the pressure. He decided he would make the best of it and view the trip to South Florida as a vacation.

CHAPTER 27
"The Guy Just Jumped on Me!"

The arraignment of Travis Jones was held in the prestigious Palm Beach County Courthouse on Friday, October 29, 1999. His court-appointed attorney, Mitchell Beers, a short, serious man with a sloping posture, submitted a plea of not guilty for Travis. He requested that bail be set at a low amount, claiming that the defendant was not a threat to the general public.

Marc Shiner, the bold assistant prosecutor for the State of Florida, had thick dark hair, a mustache, and a warm smile for the jury. Those who were being cross-examined by him were not so lucky.

Shiner had earned his BA from Hofstra University in New York and his JD from Nova Southeastern Law School in Florida. He had a reputation for handling complex litigation at both the state and federal levels. Throughout his career, he would appear as a guest speaker on Fox TV, CNN, MSNBC, O'Reilly, and numerous other national and local news programs.

Shiner had always considered himself to be a liberal man with strong morals. Eventually he would switch sides and become a defense attorney after winning a murder case against Nathaniel Brazill. The thirteen-year-old boy shot his favorite teacher for sending him home after he was caught throwing water balloons. Shiner did not believe children should be tried as adults and have to face the death penalty. The trial would prove to be an extremely difficult one for him emotionally.

Shiner vigorously argued bail should not be allowed for Travis Jones. He had already proven he was a flight risk when he left the state and fled to Iowa. Palm Beach County Circuit Judge Richard Oftedal agreed and denied Travis Jones bail. He would be transferred to Florida State Prison to await trial for several months. His step-grandmother, Nancy Young, would visit him often.

Mitchell Beers had earned his MBA from Xavier University and his JD from Northern Kentucky. He represented a significant number of high-profile clients such as professional baseball player Jeff Reardon. The pitcher was charged with the almost comical robbery of a jewelry store at the Gardens Mall. The four-time All-Star was declared not guilty by reason of insanity by Palm Beach County Judge Stephen Rapp. The circuit judge was convinced Reardon's robbery of Hamilton Jewelers was triggered by a potent mix of prescription drugs that he had been taking.

Travis Jones would not be so lucky. Beers made many trips to the prison to see him during his incarceration. "You've got to tell me what happened that night at the victim's apartment," he told him. "Don't leave anything out."

"The guy just jumped on me!" Travis cried. "He got on top of me and straddled me. Then he put his arm over my face. That's when I bit him." Time and time again they went over Travis's story about the night of the murder. Reliving the episode sometimes reduced Travis to tears. He had feared for his life that night, and the murder had been a last resort, he said. The attorney felt he was looking at a case of self-defense for his client. He carefully prepared a strategy to use on Travis's behalf in court.

Beers and Shiner entered Judge Oftedal's chambers regarding *The State of Florida vs. Travis Gene Jones* early in a game of poker. The prospect of the death penalty was tossed at Beers as proposed punishment for his client, and the argument of self-defense was thrown back at Shiner. Travis's attorney proposed his client would accept fifteen years in prison in lieu of going to trial. The prosecutor for the state declined his offer. He did not intend to inform me of it until I stepped foot inside the courtroom. Once I got there he would convince me that we should go through with my father's trial. He would have his day in court.

***

The Delray Beach I returned to in 2001 was a new one. I noticed the gas station near my father's old guesthouse had been converted into a diner. They had kept the red fuel pumps as a slice of Delray Beach history. There were also new sidewalks, palm trees, and streetlights.

These changes were the first phase of a multimillion-dollar West Atlantic Avenue facelift. The Art and Jazz on the Avenue festivals were held on East Atlantic Avenue five times a year. They traditionally stretched from the Intracoastal Waterway to Swinton Avenue near the tracks. This was the perceived racial threshold that divided the city's white and black neighborhoods. That January, the festivals expanded about two blocks west onto West Atlantic Avenue. The hope was that they would help to erase the dividing line.

My mother, Lynda, flew out for my father's trial, as well. She had sold her Delray Beach condo back in 2000 and moved out to Torrance, California, near me and her grandchildren. Therefore, she had to get a hotel room near the Palm Beach courthouse. My hotel room, however, was paid for by the State of Florida. I was surprised to run into my father's longtime best friend at the front desk, Howard Adcock, the theater director from UNC. Since the professor was to be a witness at the trial, the state was also paying for his room.

The aging theater director with Coke-bottle glasses

greeted me awkwardly, then quickly excused himself, explaining that witnesses were not supposed to discuss the case. Having not seen the professor in twenty years, I was somewhat hurt. Some of my best memories with my father had also been with Dr. Adcock at his theater, but now he was acting so strangely. After his testimony, I would never see him again.

CHAPTER 28
Out Cruising for Sex

The Palm Beach County Courthouse is a beautiful, buff-colored neoclassical structure that was first built in 1916 in West Palm Beach, Florida. The building on North Dixie Highway had only three floors and a basement when a sister building was built twenty-five feet to its east in 1927. In 1969, a modern addition was wrapped around the two buildings until three decades later when the city council voted to demolish it and the old courthouse was restored.

The trial of *The State of Florida vs. Travis Gene Jones* opened in the Palm Beach courthouse on February 26, 2001. Like Detective Venetucci, the state prosecutor instantly recognized me from the hundreds of photographs in my father's albums. He had been waiting outside the closed doors of the courtroom for me and held out his hand to greet me. "Mrs. Reilly, I'm Marc Shiner, the state prosecutor. We spoke on the phone," he reminded me.

I had spent many hours with Detective Venetucci and his partner after the murder, though Venetucci had done most of the talking and his partner had done most of the note-taking. Oddly, I thought the prosecutor and Detective Venetucci greatly resembled each other.

"I want to thank you for coming. I know it's a hard thing for you to do," Shiner told me. I nodded. He then directed my husband and me through a set of wooden doors. "Can you please stay here just a moment?" he asked me.

"Okay," I agreed.

The prosecutor then ushered Rick through a second set of wooden doors that led to the courtroom and instructed him to have a seat in the second row.

Shiner then guided me inside a conference room on the left and closed the door behind him. There, we sat down at the round, wooden table together. "We've received a plea offer from the defendant's attorney," he announced. "Mr. Jones is willing to accept fifteen years in prison rather than risk the death penalty if convicted of first-degree murder. What would you like to do?" he asked me.

"What do you think we should do?" I asked.

"I think we should go to trial," he stated. "The evidence is there, and the defendant deserves to pay for taking your father's life."

I thought this over for a moment.

"I don't take cases to trial that I don't think I can win," he assured me.

I sensed the prosecutor's compassion for my father and me and had not realized how much I needed someone to care. "Okay. If you think so," I agreed.

"All right. Let's go to trial," the prosecutor said, rising up from the table.

I joined my husband on the left side of the second pew behind the prosecutor's table. The first pew was reserved for legal assistants, Mr. Shiner informed me. My mother arrived shortly afterward and gave me a hug. "I'm here, honey," she said, taking a seat on the other side of me. The defendant's family consisted of his mother, stepfather, father, and step-grandmother. They sat on the right side of the courtroom, two rows behind the table where Travis and his attorney were seated. Dressed in simple clothing and wearing solemn expressions, the bunch looked as if they were attending a funeral.

And there he was. The killer.

All I could see was the left side of his small face. It was almost cryptic, as if he was not fully formed. Even the short Mr. Beers dwarfed him at the table.

Judge Oftedal, on the other hand, was a large man of warmth and patience. He had earned a BS from the University of Virginia in Nuclear Engineering and a JD from the University of Florida College of Law. The judge had recently presided over another Lake Worth murder trial that involved a backyard massacre at the height of what authorities would call a gang war. The trial for the murder of Wesley Wallace, however, was to be a battle of one on one.

Judge Oftedal was forty-five minutes late to the first day of the trial. The juror's chairs sat empty until the judge had the bailiff bring them in from a back room. The bailiff was a stocky man in his early thirties with a gun in his holster that was attached to a belt around his large waist. He sat in a chair against the wall beside the jurors, where he occasionally fell asleep during breaks. The court reporter, a severely overweight and bald man with glasses, looked to be about the same age as the bailiff.

Shiner, the state prosecutor, stepped to the center of the courtroom and began his opening statement in a crisp New York accent. "Good morning ladies and gentlemen of the jury," he said, looking each one of them in the eye. "I'd like to begin by telling you about a man named Wes," he said loudly as he paced the floor. "Wes was a lonely man who lived by himself. His only child and grandchildren lived all the way across the country, therefore, he had no family left in the state of Florida."

I felt the guilt setting in already. I had not been there when my father had been dying. Instead, I had been almost 3,000 miles away in California. My dad had moved back to Florida in 1987 to be near me, but I had moved away to Orange County less than a decade later. I had actually tried to get him to move out to Orange County, as well, but he had found it to be too boring there upon his first visit. He had mentioned that perhaps Las Vegas would be more exciting.

"He was a gentle man whose sexual orientation was his own business," the prosecutor continued. "Wes had merely been out for a drive on Congress Avenue one night when he saw Travis Jones walking on the side of the road. He felt bad for the young man and slowed down to offer him a ride. Travis took him up on that offer. He got in Wes's car with every intention of robbing him, and he let Wes drive him to his house so he could see what Wes had that he could steal." Shiner paused at that point, perhaps for dramatic effect. "The sex had been oral and consensual for both, after which, Wes had told him to leave. But Travis was not leaving without money. He threatened Wes with the broken, wooden-handled steak knife that he kept in his pants. The two struggled on the bed. Travis had cut Wes many times on the face and stabbed him several times in the neck. One of the stabs nicked his jugular vein. Wes was bleeding profusely as they fell to the floor, knocking the lamp off the table. He pushed Travis into the closet door and crawled down the hallway toward the front door of his apartment. Wes fell unconscious and never made it."

I watched the faces of the jurors as the brutal and sexual elements of the trial sunk into their minds. Surely they had not been expecting such a tale. Neither had I. I had seen my father be violent with my mother, but never another male and certainly not one who was his bed partner. The idea of my dad having sex with another man was quite shocking to me, yet at the same time it filled in a lot of gaps in his life. Now I understood why he had people-watched so much and talked about young men at length. He had seemed to be fascinated with one in particular, whom my friend Alyssa had a crush on when we were younger. I could never understand it at the time, but now it made sense.

"While Wes lay dying on the floor of the dining room, Travis coldly entered the bathroom to wash the blood off his hands. He then walked past the body to the kitchen and searched the cabinets for cleaning products in a calculated effort to destroy evidence. The murder he had committed had not affected his instinct for self-preservation nor his conscience. Quite the contrary!" Shiner yelled. "Now Travis was free to look around the victim's apartment and rip off whatever he wanted. He even stole the victim's car. It was all about Travis." The prosecutor's voice had risen with this last statement and carried a touch of both anger and sarcasm.

"Well, the trial isn't going to be all about Travis. It's going to be about the victim, too. By the time it's over, you all are going to know Wes like I have come to know him."

I was already beginning to question how well that was. The prosecutor had just described my father as a gentle man, which was far from the truth. I vividly remembered the pool of my mother's blood forming on the white rug of my room under the piano. It had not been the last time he had hurt her, either. Far from it. I tried to make eye contact with some of the members of the jury, but they had each been given strict instructions against such behavior.

Mr. Beer's opening statement took a decidedly different slant on that summer night back in June of 1999. "Mr. Wallace," as the defense attorney chose to call my father, "had been out cruising for sex. Poor Travis had been down on his luck and hungry after having lost his job. He had reluctantly climbed into Mr. Wallace's Acura that night, merely hoping for a meal. The youth had no interest in the videos that Mr. Wallace had invited him to watch. He was not a homosexual."

I noticed the disbelieving looks on the faces of some of the jurors. I, however, suddenly recalled Robert Downey

Jr.'s role in the film *Less Than Zero* where he had resorted to male prostitution due to his abuse of cocaine. Having grown up in my father's world of AA and NA, I was not naïve as to the lengths to which some addicts would go to obtain money and drugs.

My father had often sought out these types of men, yet, at the same time, he had warned me of the danger of associating with them. There were our regular drives by what was historically known as "Saloon Row" in old downtown Greensborough, North Carolina. My dad would point out of the car window at the bums loitering outside of what had become known as the Jones Building on South Elm Street. The old building that featured whimsical, upturned brick grooves and white Mount Airy granite served as a backdrop for the down and out. "See how their eyes are all red with bags under them?" my dad would say to me. "Those are drug addicts. Stay away from those kind of people, Denise. They're bad news." The fact that he had not heeded his own advice was disturbing to me as I listened to Beers's opening statement.

"It was the rumble in Travis's stomach that caused him to go along with the sex that Mr. Wallace wanted in exchange for money—money that was never given to him," Beers stressed. "Mr. Wallace had gone back on the deal and, instead, proceeded to attack Travis on the bed. The youth was no match for a man who was one hundred pounds heavier than he. Travis had feared for his life when he pulled out the broken knife that he carried solely for the purpose of opening cans of food. He had not meant to kill Mr. Wallace, who had been straddling him on the bed. Travis merely wanted to leave the apartment with enough money to buy something to eat. Since Wallace never made good on the deal, Travis made the stupid mistake of taking some of his items to sell instead. Everyone needs to eat," the defense attorney argued.

With that, the trial broke for lunch.

It seemed to me that Shiner felt much more confident about winning the case than Beers. There was something about the defense attorney's tone that made him already sound defeated, yet he seemed to strongly believe in his client's innocence. Would his belief somehow win over the jurors? I wondered. I got up to break for lunch, but the thought of eating only made me want to step outside for air.

CHAPTER 29
The Taking of Jake

The mood in the courtroom was somber when the elderly Rose Mancini approached the witness stand. She had hardly known my father, but as his next-door neighbor, she provided an unbiased account of the argument that had ensued between him and his killer that night. "It sounded like Wes was yelling at another man," Mrs. Mancini told the jury. "I heard him say, 'Get out! Just get out of here!'"

Frank Mancini got on the stand next and described the sounds he had heard coming from his neighbor's apartment that night. He had been asleep and had not heard the words his wife had heard. Instead, he had heard what sounded like a headboard banging against the wall. Mr. Mancini told the courtroom he had not wanted to get involved in his neighbor's business and had dissuaded his wife from calling the police. He now regretted his decision, and it would haunt him until the end of his days.

Venetucci was the next witness to testify. He was a familiar sight to me when he sat on the stand. I thought he looked extremely at ease. For the first time, I would hear details about the crime scene as the detective walked the courtroom through Wes's apartment. I was caught by surprise when an eight-by-ten-inch glossy, color photo of my father's face after death was passed around by the jurors. Even from my seat in the second row, I could see the many cuts on his face and neck. This was one of the last images taken of my father. He looked vulnerable to me as I looked at what the killer had done to him.

The prosecutor had been expecting Boland, but the detective was flat on his back from an injury, therefore he was unable to testify. Venetucci told the court he had worked with the Lake Worth Police Department for twelve years and had been a detective for nine of those years. The general assignment detective division handled everything from bicycle thefts to homicides, robberies, and deaths within the city of Lake Worth.

Shiner then moved to the discussion of the case by asking, "Did it take a while before you-all got what you considered to be the first major break in trying to solve the—"

"Yes," the detective interrupted.

"Tell us about when that was," the prosecutor ordered.

"It would have been on October 17, 1999," Venetucci told him. The detective explained that Miliana had been arrested by the Palm Springs Police Department on October 16 for defrauding an innkeeper.

Shiner had to remind him of the fleeing and eluding charge. He then asked about the period of time when the detectives were trying to solve the homicide case. "Did you or Detective Boland have any press releases sent out to the public to try and help solve this case?"

"Yes, we did."

"In this particular case, when you made out the press release or the police department made them out, was there any mention whatsoever in any of the press releases to the public as to how this man was killed, how Mr. Wallace was killed?"

"Prior to the arrest, no, there was not."

The prosecutor wanted to know if there had been any mention in any of the press releases about any destruction of evidence, such as when the tub was filled with water. "How about running water left on in the apartment, was that released?"

"No, it was not."

Shiner's purpose was to show that there had been no way for Travis's friend Miliana to have heard about the crime other than directly from Travis himself. Miliana's testimony was crucial for the prosecution's case, and it was going to be difficult for them to get him to testify against his friend when it came time for him to do so.

Shiner turned the witness over to Beers, who wasted no time in pointing out there had been a Crime Stoppers reenactment as well as a media release by the Lake Worth Police Department.

"The reenactment concerned the way Mr. Wallace died, didn't it?" the defense attorney asked.

"Yes," Detective Venetucci confirmed. "Well, it explained certain things the way things happened."

"That's what happens," Beers went on, "you get Crime Stoppers on it, and it explains how Mr. Wallace—the wounds, how he was killed in his apartment?"

"No, I don't believe it ever said how he was killed in his apartment."

"But there was a Crime Stoppers reenactment that was released to Channel Five?"

"Yes, there was."

"And that press release also went into further details where it indicated that the suspect left Mr. Wallace's apartment taking a Sony VCR, tabletop Sony stereo system, and then it was pointed out that Mr. Wallace was a homosexual who frequented parks, things like that, correct?"

"Without seeing it, I really can't answer."

The defense attorney then obtained permission from the judge to hand the detective a copy of the press release. "Media release dated June 23, 1999, by the Lake Worth Police Department. Just read it to yourself," Beers instructed

Venetucci, who quickly read over the page.

"Okay. And so confirming the fact that there was—the media release on June 23 talked about what was supposedly taken from Mr. Wallace's apartment, correct?" the defense attorney asked.

"Looks like everything but the Toshiba VCR," the detective pointed out.

Beers then steered the discussion to the interviews of Ritz Carlton employees and people on the streets. "You found out in the latter part of his life that he [Wes] was a homosexual, did you not?"

"We did do that, yes."

"I note in your report that you use the word 'heavy domination.' What did you mean by that?"

"It was information that was given to me by an individual."

At that point, Shiner objected as to hearsay, which was sustained by the court.

The defense attorney then reworded his question. "So you found out then, basically, without getting into what individuals told you, that again Mr. Wallace had a preference for other males?"

"Yes."

"And other young males?"

"Yes."

"And, again, from your report, you learned that Mr. Wallace was the type of individual that would, and I apologize for the wording, but the type of guy that would fuck them and forget them?"

"That's what I was told, yes."

"And then in your quest to locate this individual or the persons that were allegedly involved in this case, you went to a place called John Prince Park, did you not?"

"Yes."

"And you showed pictures of Mr. Wallace to the individuals in this particular park?"

"Yes, we did."

Suddenly, Beers changed topics, which seemed to confuse the detective. "You did visit the apartment, did you not?"

"Whose apartment, sir?" he asked.

"Mr. Wallace's apartment."

"Yes, sir."

"And you did observe—afterwards, you observed a number of videos, did you not?"

"Yes, there were quite a few videos."

"Did you ever notice a video in the plain view called *The Taking of Jake*?"

This provocative statement brought an objection from Shiner that was overruled.

"There were so many, I can't answer yes or no," Venetucci answered.

"So many videos meaning that it was a large collection of videos?" the defense attorney asked. He seemed to relish the chance to create such a graphic image in the minds of the jurors.

"It was a good collection of videos, yes."

"And there was a magazine that you recall or a—that was sitting right there that said *The Taking of Jake*, do you remember that?" Beers prodded.

"The name Jake sounds familiar. I want to say it was a pamphlet, not a magazine."

"Okay," the defense attorney conceded. He then went on to ask the detective about a press release regarding the discovery of Wes's car, which was not nearly as captivating a subject for the jurors as the pornography had been to them. Beers had managed to paint a portrait of Wes in the minds of the jurors as an obsessive sexual deviant by honing in on a particular pornographic video that featured heavy domination. Though he had been unable to get Venetucci to define the term, any jurors who were curious could potentially look it up later for themselves.

I found myself thinking back to the time after my parents' divorce when my father had accused my mother of selecting her boyfriend from the personals section of our local newspaper. "Your mama picked out a guy who's into S&M. He's sick," he had told me at the age of nine. At the time I had no idea what S&M was, yet I still found myself wondering how my father had known such a thing. Had my mother told him? If S&M was such a terrible thing, would she have done that? Now I found myself wondering if the sexual acts had been initiated by my dad and he had merely assumed that my mother had continued with the practice with another man. My view of my parents' virtues and vices was starting to shift.

Tyler Montegut was the next witness to testify. At twenty-five years of age, the thin African American was a fast talker.

"Mr. Montegut, isn't it true that you often purchase stolen items from people on the streets?" Shiner blatantly asked.

"Yes," the witness confirmed.

"And that you gave Mr. Wallace's Sony VCR to your girlfriend, Miss Heidel, to pawn?"

"Yes, I did," Montegut admitted. His criminal record had not been disclosed to the courtroom due to Beers's objection. Therefore, only half of Montegut's transaction with the defendant was allowed to be used as testimony. The witness had received strict instructions about admissibility before the trial, as had the prosecutor. They were not to make any reference to drugs.

Montegut described how Travis had come to his house at seven in the morning on June 6, 1999. Shiner asked if he had noticed any cuts on Travis's face or arms, and the witness said he had not. He was not aware that Travis had just killed a man and that the items he had brought with him had belonged to the victim. They lay in a shopping cart along with some other items that had not been obtained during the crime and were, therefore, left unmentioned.

Montegut then came to the part where Travis began to argue with him about buying the stereo. "He said he wanted to buy some rocks," the witness admitted.

Upon the slip, Beers instantly objected. He flew to his feet and approached the judge's bench, where he was joined by Shiner for a few moments of harsh whispers.

The witness had been clearly instructed not to use any kind of drug reference such as "rocks" and he had clearly disobeyed the court. He had not wanted to testify at all. In a loud voice, Beers firmly demanded a mistrial. Judge Oftedal ordered that the jury be temporarily removed from the courtroom while he weighed the decision about how to handle the matter at hand. While everyone watched in confusion, the bailiff escorted the jury out the back door of the courtroom.

Judge Oftedal took a few moments to decide what to do. He then ordered the witness's last statement be struck from the record. The jury was then led back into the room by the bailiff. The trial would go on, but Montegut would not be allowed to finish his testimony.

***

Downtown West Palm Beach had been almost completely abandoned by the late 1980s. The city remained a poverty-stricken, high-crime area until the 1990s, when it underwent a revitalization that was completed in 2000. The city poured millions of dollars into the renovation while striving to preserve its architectural details and charm. Now the downtown area was full of shops, restaurants, and entertainment venues like Tommy Bahama and Mojito Latin

Cuisine and Bar.

The attorneys and prosecutors of the courthouse took advantage of the new ambiance of their city. They liked to lunch across the street at Cabana, a lively Cuban restaurant that served local favorites like coconut rice. At night they sometimes frequented E. R. Bradley's Saloon. Years before, it had been located on the island of Palm Beach, where patrons had been known to dance on the bar. The restaurant transformed into a rowdy nightspot on the Palm Beach party scene after dark.

My husband, Rick, wanted to experience CityPlace, the $600 million upscale lifestyle center near the courthouse and downtown's popular Clematis Street. It had been described as the epitome of new urbanist multi-use developments. The mold-breaking, hurricane-resistant design featured retail shops, restaurants, commercial office space, and private town homes and condominiums. There was even a restored 1920s church that had been converted into a multi-purpose cultural center. He had chosen for us to dine at the Blue Martini Lounge, and he was enjoying his first Ketel One martini when I began to talk about the trial.

I was upset that drugs were not allowed to be mentioned as a motive for the murder since they were not a part of the crime.

"It's the law," Rick reasoned, quickly changing the subject to the view of the blue umbrella tables and wicker chairs on the patio. "This place is like an island resort, isn't it?" he asked lightly, looking around. "It's like being at an outdoor mall and the Bahamas at the same time." The cocktail was beginning to make him feel chatty. After getting a cold look from me, he began socializing with the couple at the next table.

I had absolutely no desire to talk to anyone who was not family and immediately saw there was no way to make Rick understand that. He simply would not get it. He could not relate to the need to share one's feelings on a personal level. At that moment I realized that was probably one of the very reasons I had chosen Rick as a partner. I had never wanted anyone to ask me what was going on in my head. There were skeletons in there that I had no intention of showing to anyone. Ever. Therefore, Rick had been the perfect choice. He had never asked me how I felt about anything other than perhaps a particular choice of restaurant. And I had never wanted to tell him how I felt about anything—until now.

When I tried to explain to him that I was not in the mood to talk to people, he seemed distracted and uninterested. In exasperation, I got up, threw down my blue cloth napkin and walked to the restroom. There, in line, I found a sympathetic stranger and soon found myself crying in the woman's ear. Not wanting to go back to the table in that state, I then did something I had never done before: caught a cab back to the hotel.

The first cab that appeared was simultaneously sought out by a drunken male patron from another bar. Not wanting to stand outside with tears streaming down my face, I agreed to share it with the boisterous thirty-something man, who was headed in the same direction. After several failed attempts to get me to accompany him to his hotel, he managed to cop a feel of my breast as I exited the cab. It was the perfect ending to a perfect evening during my week from hell.

CHAPTER 30
'Just Don't Bite Me!'

The trial resumed the next day with the next witness, a handsome, graying gentleman named Laurence Grayhills, who was a general practice dentist and an associate medical examiner forensic odontologist for the Palm Beach County Medical Examiner's Office. "We do identifications," the doctor explained, "usually examining either postmortem remains and ascertaining the identity of the deceased, or it also involves bite mark identification, et cetera."

Dr. Grayhills had his doctor of medical dentistry degree from the University of Florida. His forensic training had been done at the Armed Forces Institute of Pathology and the University of Texas and Marquette University. He was also co-chairman of the State of Florida Disaster Preparedness Team that had handled the Valu-Jet crash of flight 592 from Miami to Atlanta. The plane had crashed into the Everglades shortly after taking off from Miami as a result of a fire in the cargo compartment that had been caused by improperly stored cargo. The doctor had been involved in performing dental identification procedures on the 110 bodies that had been unrecognizable either facially or via fingerprints.

"Can you please share with us how you first became involved in this case?" Shiner asked Dr. Grayhills about my father's murder.

The doctor told the court he had first been contacted by Investigator Doug Jenkins of the Palm Beach County Medical Examiner's Office to examine the fifty-six-year-old

Caucasian male identified as William Wallace. The victim had what the medical examiner believed to possibly be two bite wounds, one on the right wrist and one on the back of the left hand.

"Can you tell us what your observation was, please?" the prosecutor continued.

"It was my impression that the wound on the right wrist was, indeed, a human bite mark," Dr. Grayhills answered. "And I could not make that—I could not make any statement as to the wound on the left hand as to whether or not it was a bite mark or not. It could have been caused by other objects."

Shiner then got permission from Judge Oftedal for Dr. Grayhills to step down from the witness stand to help explain the photographs of the wound on my father's left hand to the jury.

"This is the victim's left hand, the back of the left hand," the forensic odontologist pointed out to the jury in a photograph. "You'll see a large area of bruising and two very small dark marks. The medical examiner called me in to ask me if he thought those might be bite marks, and there's a possibility they could have been caused by a blow to the front teeth or to any teeth or to almost any object. I could not ascertain whether or not that was a bite mark or not."

"Could that have come from like a brass lamp possibly hitting them?" asked the prosecutor.

"Could have come from anything. I can't speculate," Dr. Grayhills answered cautiously.

"Is there any indication that that came from human teeth?"

"Well, it does have individual characteristics as teeth would, but there is no arch form so there's no curvature. It could have been caused by hitting the teeth. It could have been caused by something else."

"Are you aware of how much force needs to be exerted

in order to cause those kinds of bite wounds on the part of the human being?"

"The mouth is generating generally 250 to 300 pounds per square inch. Try biting yourself, and I guarantee you, you can't come anywhere close to that without reaching your pain threshold," Dr. Grayhills warned.

Shiner then proceeded to ask what would happen if someone wanted to bite a person using all of that force. "Would they take out, actually take out chunks of your skin and tissue?"

"Just like biting any piece of meat, you know you can take out a big chunk, sure."

The image of such a display of depravity was having a profound effect on some of the members of the jury. One female juror in her forties looked thoroughly disgusted as she heard the doctor's words.

The prosecutor was still not finished. "Have you seen cases or literature where there have been chunks of tissue from arms or legs or bodies that were bitten?" he asked.

"I think Mike Tyson demonstrated that to the world," Dr. Grayhills responded. This brought a smirk from one male juror.

When asked if any other molds of suspect's teeth had been delivered to his office other than Travis's, the doctor replied that two had been.

"Do you recall who they were?" the prosecutor asked.

"I don't know the first name. It was Conner, and the other was a Miliana," the doctor responded.

"Were you able to attempt to see if their teeth made or could have been responsible for the bite marks on Mr. Wallace?"

"Yes," Dr. Grayhills replied. "I ruled them out. There were major discrepancies in arch width, how big the curvature was, the exact number of teeth in the indentations, and from positioning."

After much questioning about the process of analyzing the bite mark evidence, Shiner then asked the doctor if he had an opinion to a reasonable degree of certainty whether Travis Jones was the person responsible for causing the bite wound on Mr. Wallace's arm.

"Due to the congruence of bite mark evidence," Dr. Grayhills responded, "there's a high degree of medical certainty that the bite marks were those of Mr. Jones."

The prosecutor had proven successful in establishing that Travis was most likely the one who had bitten the victim. Now the jury was left wanting to know why. "Have you seen the occasion where you felt somebody was in a defensive posture when they were bitten?" he asked.

"Yes, I have," the doctor answered. "And, of course, defensive posture is always protecting yourself."

"Is that a possibility in this case?"

"Sure."

"Is there a possibility that the assailant may have been on top of the person who was killed?"

"I don't see why not."

"Okay. But you can't tell this jury beyond a reasonable degree of scientific certainty how it happened?"

"No," the doctor admitted. The witness was then turned over to Beers.

"You mentioned briefly that it would take some significant force," the defense attorney began, "you can't qualify it, of course, but it would take some significant force on behalf of Mr. Jones to leave an impression like that on Mr. Wallace's wrist, would it not?"

"Yes, sir," the doctor confirmed.

"Or basically for anybody. And you indicated that if you—to try to bite yourself like that, it would certainly, obviously leave those type of dentitions in the skin certainly would hurt, would it not?"

"Yes, it would."

"All right. So the characteristic wound that we are saying now that came from Travis Jones," Beers stated, "the very characteristic wound on Mr. Wallace's right wrist was made by the mandibular lower teeth. Would you say—would you say canine?"

"Canine to canine," the doctor confirmed. "With two of the maxillary teeth off to the side in the opposing arch."

"All right. So if I were to walk up to you—" Beers began.

"You're not going to bite me, are you?" Dr. Grayhills asked in jest.

"No."

"All right."

"But if I were to walk up to you and—" the defense attorney paused to obtain permission from the judge to approach the witness. He then proceeded to roll up his sleeve. "If I were—let's face this way, but just don't bite me."

"Okay, I promise I won't," the doctor assured him.

The defense attorney then launched into several different scenarios in order to determine how the bite marks on the victim's right wrist could have been made, as well as the bruising on his left hand. One scenario even depicted the victim biting himself on the right wrist, which prompted re-direct examination by the prosecutor. Dr. Grayhills explained to the court that he had swabbed the victim's wounds for the purpose of salivary DNA analysis. He had then swabbed the victim's own mouth to rule out that he had bitten himself.

When both sides had finished with the witness, it was still unclear as to which bodily positions had led to the wounds on the victim's hand and wrist. What *was* clear, however, was the fact that they had most likely been caused while the victim was still alive. The forensic odontologist had come to this conclusion due to the fact there appeared to be no lividity or blood-pooling present along with the wounds. The evidence seemed to strongly suggest to me that Travis had been fighting for his life, which I found greatly disturbing, as I now had a son of my own. How could my dad had tried to take advantage of such a young man with so few years' worth of life experiences? Surely Travis had not been able to read people the way my father had been able to at his advanced age. He could not have known that he was walking into a losing situation with a man who was used to getting his way.

CHAPTER 31
Getting in through the Back Door

The next witness was my father's lifelong best friend. "Please introduce yourself to the court and also the members of our jury, please," the prosecutor began.

"My name is Howard Adcock," the witness told them. "I'm from Greensboro, North Carolina."

When asked about his background, Adcock seemed happy to explain he had received his BA and MA from Columbia University in New York, an institution that was known for the excellence of its theater program. After that, he had gone on to complete the residency for his PhD at the University of Delaware.

"Are you currently retired?"

"Yes, I've been retired eleven years."

"Will you share with us the type of employment?" Shiner asked.

"I was a university professor for thirty-nine years, the last thirty-four at the University of North Carolina at Chapel Hill. My official designation at this point is emeritus distinguished professor," Adcock answered.

"Are you currently married?"

"Oh no. My wife died twenty-four years ago."

"You live by yourself?"

"I live by myself, uh-huh, and I have a son and a daughter."

"Do you know of a man by the name of William Wes Wallace?"

"Yes, I knew Wesley Wallace for a long, long time," Adcock remembered sadly. "I would say at least twenty-five years."

"How did you know him? Through work, friendship?" Shiner prodded. "Can you explain to us a little bit how you got to know him?"

"I got to know him when he was married and they had just had a daughter and were living in Greensboro, North Carolina."

Just hearing the sound of Dr. Adcock's voice made me feel like my father was still in the room. Theirs had been such a close, warm friendship that had lasted until the end of my dad's life. Dr. Adcock knew my father perhaps better than anyone. He had clearly adored him and his effervescent personality that was overwhelmingly contagious.

"He—he—Wesley married Lynda Wallace into a relatively prominent family," the professor explained, to which Beers objected on the grounds of relevancy.

"Well, I'll give some leeway, but maybe you can move it on," the judge gently coaxed.

"I'm trying to figure out how you actually met him," the prosecutor asked.

"I actually met him in a bar," Adcock admitted.

"Okay," the prosecutor acknowledged.

"If you can," Shiner said, "What was the nature of your friendship or relationship with Mr. Wallace, can you share that with us, please?"

"We were like brothers. He had—should I go on?" the professor asked tentatively.

"If you need to explain the nature of your relationship, that was the only question," the prosecutor added coyly.

"He had a brother to whom he was never close, and I had a brother to whom I was never close, and we sort of filled in for each other. It was something that developed over the years."

"Did you socialize with him and his wife?"

"Oh, yes. We went on a trip to London together in the early seventies."

Beers then objected once again as to responsiveness and relevancy.

"I think it's somewhat responsive, but I think we can move it on," the judge ruled once again.

"What I'm trying to get to is: Did you do a lot of things together with Wes and his wife?" Shiner patiently explained.

"We did," Adcock confirmed. "After they moved to Pompano Beach, my wife and I came down and visited them, yes."

"Did you stay in close contact with him over the years?" the prosecutor asked.

"Yes. It was easier to have contact when we were all living in Greensboro, of course."

"Sure," Shiner agreed. "Let me ask you this: Did there come a time—I want you to be frank with us—when you found Wes was splitting up from his wife, did there come a time when you found that out, sir?"

"Say that—"

"Did there come a time during your relationship with Mr. Wallace and Mrs. Wallace that you found out they were splitting up?" the prosecutor repeated.

"Yes," Adcock admitted. "I can't recall how I found out about that," he added, bewildered.

Was Shiner trying to imply that Dr. Adcock and my father had been lovers? I wondered to myself in shock. The idea seemed ridiculous to me.

"Did there come a time you found about it?" the prosecutor asked again.

"After—after—after they split up, he came back to Greensboro for a while," the professor answered.

"Were you still in contact with him?"

"I was when he first came back to Greensboro, yes."

"How about his wife, did you stay in contact with her over the years?"

"No, I have not stayed in contact with his wife mainly because I'm up there and she's down here."

Shiner then chose to change topics. "Prior to Mr. Wallace's death in June of 1999, did you maintain the relationship that you had considered to be a brotherly type relationship with him, was that maintained through the years?"

"Yes," Adcock answered.

"Prior to June of 1999, when is the last time you had contact or had seen him?"

"The last time I had contact with Wesley—"

"Yes, sir."

"—was the week prior to the week in which he was killed."

"And how did that come about that you had contact with him?" the prosecutor wanted to know.

The professor explained that he had come to Florida and stayed at my father's condominium.

"Anything unusual happen during that week or was it a pretty non—non-eventful week, just friends getting together?"

"Well, the time that I was there, most people think was uneventful, but it was eventful for me because he had just gotten back from California, and he had pictures—"

The warmth returned to Dr. Adcock's voice with a swell of love that reached my heart. It felt as if I were a child in my father's arms again. I loved him so much, and for a moment he seemed to still be alive.

Beers objected for a third time with regards to relevancy. This time, the objection was sustained.

"Basically, you had a good time, is what I'm getting at,

good time with your friend?" Shiner asked.

Adcock agreed that he had and told the court that Wes had been very happy. "He was just as happy as he could be because he liked this new condo. I thought it was an excellent place to live," the professor added.

"Objection, Judge, relevancy," Beers interjected again. This time the prosecutor merely changed topics, therefore the objection was ignored.

"I want to ask you some questions about his lifestyle, okay?" Shiner said of Wes.

"Sure," Adcock answered.

"Did you ever discuss with Wes about his sexual preference, did he ever talk to you about that?" the prosecutor asked.

"Yes, over the years it would occasionally—he'd occasionally say something, and I'd reply. Discussions of sex were not all-consuming things with Wesley and me."

To this answer, Beers objected on the grounds of it being non-responsive. Judge Oftedal overruled the objection.

"But the topic did come up once in a while is what you're telling us?" Shiner pressed.

"I don't know that it was stated as a sexual preference," the professor replied. "The fact that he occasionally enjoyed being with men is what we talked about. Now, he would have occasionally enjoyed being with women at the same time."

Beers objected to this as speculation. This objection was sustained by the judge.

"Let me talk—let me ask you this," the prosecutor began again. "Did you actually witness Wes with other men? Were you ever a witness to this with your own eyes and ears? Did you actually see or hear him do that?"

"I never saw Wes have sex with anybody, male or female," Adcock replied.

"Did you know if—from your relationship with him and

knowing him as a friend—did there come a time that you found out that he enjoyed being with young males in the twenties, twenty years of age or higher, twenty, twenty-five, twenty-six, that kind of area?"

"Well, he—as I explained to Detective Boland, Wesley told me that he enjoyed being with young men, and I just assumed young men meant eighteen to thirty or thirty-five, something like that."

"Okay," Shiner said, regrouping his thoughts.

"The same age that I've been teaching for all these years," the professor added.

"Did you know anything about Wes's habit of keeping more than one particular wallet?"

"Yes, I knew about that because I knew that, occasionally, he was, he was bringing people to his condo or wherever he was living. And I said, this condo has nice things in it and somebody may want to take things or somebody may want to rob you when they get in the car."

"And you told him this?" the prosecutor asked, sounding incredulous.

"Yeah, because I've spent my life working with that age group, and I understand what their problems are. I was an administrator, brought to the university to head a department, and I was there and then I retired. We had 1,000 majors in the department, and when all the people couldn't take care of the problems, they ended up at my front door."

Beers once again objected as to the relevancy of all of this.

"Again, let's move on," Judge Oftedal urged.

"But I know that age level," the professor could not resist adding.

"Let me ask you some direct questions," Shiner said in an attempt to steer the witness's focus. "We're talking about two wallets. You said you brought up to him that people may come to his apartment and take things. What does that have to do with two wallets?"

To this question Adcock answered, "Yes, they can take things when they get into his automobile."

"How do you know he had two wallets?"

"Because he told me."

"Did he tell you *why* he had two wallets?"

"Yes," the professor answered. "The purpose of him having the two wallets was so if somebody wanted money from him, he could show them a wallet that had a very little bit in it," Adcock explained.

The warmth in Dr. Adcock's voice seemed to disappear to me. This was clearly a bone of contention between him and my father, and the room suddenly felt cold as if my dad had left. Soon Dr. Adcock would leave too, I knew, and I felt as if the past would be gone, as well. I wanted so badly to have it back.

"Were you aware whether or not Mr. Wallace believed in consensual sex or consensual sex while with somebody? Are you aware of what his preference was in that area?" Shiner asked.

"Yes, because Wesley was an old man, and I'm an older man, and we talked about how one finds sex when one gets old, and both of our attitude was that or his attitude, since that's what you're asking me—"

"Yes, sir."

"—his attitude was that he didn't believe in paying for sex. There was too much free sex around."

The prosecutor's questioning then veered off of sex and went on to food. "Did you ever eat at his house?" he asked.

"Oh, my, yes," Adcock replied. "Wesley was a good cook."

Beers objected to this answer as to relevancy. The objection was sustained.

"Was Wesley overweight?" the prosecutor asked.

"Oh, my, yes," the professor answered again.

"Okay. How was Mr. Wallace's health, do you know, if you know?"

To this question, Beers objected as to relevancy. His objection was overruled.

"Wesley was not in good health. We went walking on the beach, and he had to stop and rest, shortness of breath," Adcock explained.

Once again, Beers objected and, once again, his objection was overruled.

"Just trying to find out how you knew about his health and what your opinion is of his general health the week you saw him prior to his death," Shiner explained.

"I saw that Wesley was overweight, but he was just happy as a lamb," the professor responded. "He would get shortness of breath and—and I was walking regularly, therefore, I could out-walk him and since I was older than he was, he was really chagrined about that."

It was then Beers's turn to cross-examine. "I believe it's Dr. Adcock, isn't it?"

"Yes," the professor confirmed.

"Okay. You're a college professor and PhD?"

"Yes."

"So it's not mister—so if I properly address you, it's doctor. Is that correct?"

"Mister is fine also. I have never been sensitive about that at all, sir," the professor answered graciously.

Beers then reminded him that Detective Boland had found his name and phone number in Mr. Wallace's apartment. Upon being questioned, the attorney said, the professor had told the detective that Wesley was gay. Now the professor was contradicting himself by telling Beers that he should not have categorized him in that way.

202

"You also advised him [Boland] in June of 1999 that Mr. Wallace liked to pick up young males in their twenties and have sex," the defense attorney stated.

"I would not have said that exactly. If it's not a quote, then it's not inclusive," Adcock answered.

"Do you recall the officer asking you if you knew of any friends of Mr. Wallace that he had, and you advised the detective that he had none, and you stated that Mr. Wallace liked to live on the edge and pick up males in the park," Beers asked.

"If I did, it was part of a larger statement, because I don't speak in phrases," the professor insisted. "I would not have limited it to parks."

"So then you would have said that he also picked up young males on the streets, correct?"

"I would not have itemized things like that. I've never seen him pick up a male on a street. I have never seen him pick up a male ... because when we were together, he didn't do anything like that," Adcock told him.

"But you don't know what he did when you were not together, do you?" the defense attorney asked.

"No."

Beers then reminded him that Detective Boland had asked him if he knew anything about my father's decorator friend that I had told the detectives I had seen sitting on my father's bed. He said that he did not.

"You advised him 'no' but then went on to say to Detective Boland that Mr. Wallace kept two wallets, one with him with all of his items in it," Beers recapped for the professor, "and another one with nothing in it. That he would bring males home and keep his full wallet in his car and keep the empty one in his pocket. And that Mr. Wallace liked to go to a pie shop on North Dixie to watch guys walk by. Did you ever tell that to Detective Boland?"

"If I did I misstated because Wesley," Adcock explained. "I never heard of that pie shop until I came into Wesley's, and he had a pie there for dinner, my favorite kind of pie which we rapidly ate up and then we went to the pie shop to get another pie, oh, a day later." The courtroom was left hanging as to which kind of pie was the professor's favorite. "And it was when we went to the pie shop a day later that he says the street was all in disrepair, and that's when I found out that this was where one could find young men or older men or whoever wanted to be picked up." The professor was referring to the section of Delray Beach near Atlantic Avenue called Pineapple Grove Arts District. The area featured an extensive mix of cafes, restaurants, boutiques, galleries, and entertainment venues.

Beers then asked Adcock if it was true that he told Detective Boland quite specifically that Mr. Wallace enjoyed performing oral sex on males in their twenties. The professor replied that he had the highest regard for Detective Boland but that he could not believe that he would have said it that way.

"I would not have been that precise in what I was saying," he explained. "I don't know if he liked to have oral sex or whatever with men."

"Did you not indicate to Detective Boland that Mr. Wallace preferred males that were not feminine acting?" the defense attorney asked. Adcock agreed that he had told the detective that Wesley preferred construction-worker-type men. "And you further advised him," Beers continued, "that Mr. Wallace would probably not be with someone over forty years old."

"There's a big problem there because that was a supposition on my part," Adcock conceded. The defense attorney continued on as if he had not heard the witness.

"You told Detective Boland that Mr. Wallace had

incidents in the past where he would not pay males for sex, and they would try to take items from his home, and he would stop them," the defense attorney stated. "Didn't you advise Detective Boland that he would not pay for sex?"

"You're asking about the sex, not about the taking of things from the house?"

"I'm asking you—let's break it down," Beers offered.

"I'm not aware of anyone trying to take something from the home," the professor stated. It was apparent to everyone present that the professor was a well-educated man who was very careful with his words. He was not about to be intimidated by Beers.

The next line of questioning brought an immediate objection from the prosecutor. Beers then asked Judge Oftedal if they could approach the bench. "I agreed that I would not mention that he was masturbating to the pornographic movies and leave the bedroom door open, and I've cut out every portion of where it dealt with white male versus black males. But the point was that certainly I had [the] right to ask him about— he told the officer he had a great appetite for sex and each night he watched pornographic movies. That's all. Nothing about blacks. I would never go against that stipulation." When the defense attorney asked if there was any objection to that, Shiner opened fire.

"Yes, and I'll tell you why. Because he's getting in through the back door," he seethed, "that somebody's masturbating. How else would he know?"

"But the witness said he never saw him have sex," Judge Oftedal interjected.

"But Mr. Beers, what he is going to tell them is he allegedly saw him masturbating with the door open to pornographic movies," the prosecutor argued.

"I'm not going to say he was watching pornographic movies," Beers replied. "I can separate it. I'll separate the two."

Shiner was not satisfied with this solution. "He can correct me if I'm wrong, but part of our agreement was not to bring in anything about his great appetite for sex; that wasn't in there," he explained.

"Well, if that's a specific part of the stipulation, I'll sustain the objection. I frankly—" the judge conceded.

"I wasn't going to bring in anything about masturbation or watching pornography, the fact that he perused it," Beers assured him.

"If worse comes to worse, I will send the jury out and look at the original stipulation," Judge Oftedal promised.

"I'll separate the questions," Beers repeated.

"I'll take him at his word," Shiner curtly replied. At that point, the bench conference concluded and the judge apologized to the members of the jury for the interruption. "You may continue," he said to Beers.

"Thank you very much," Beers replied before readdressing Dr. Adcock. "Isn't it true that you told Detective Boland that Mr. Wallace had a great appetite for sex on July 20th of 1999 at 9:30 p.m.?"

"I may have, yes," the witness admitted.

"And isn't it true that you were in his apartment and you did observe a number of—on his bookcases there—you saw his apartment, did you not?" the defense attorney asked.

"Oh, yes," Dr. Adcock confirmed. "He had a new condo, and as soon as I arrived, he showed it to me."

"I understand," Beers said. "But in that condo there were collections of pornographic or collection of tapes, were there not?"

"I suspect," the witness replied. "I never did see them. I didn't count them."

"But yet you advised Detective Boland during the period of time," Beers stated, "that Mr. Wallace, each night, watched pornographic videos, didn't you?"

"If I'm answering that phrase, that's been taken out of context," Dr. Adcock said. "I'll have to say no."

"So you never advised Detective Boland that each night Mr. Wallace watched pornographic videos?" Beers pressed.

"Sir, I don't know what Mr. Wallace did on the nights when I was not there. You see, that says every night, that means every night of the year, doesn't it?" the witness asked.

The defense attorney then rephrased the question. "The nights you were with him, did you, on occasion, see him?"

"On occasion," Dr. Adcock answered. "From where I was sleeping in the living room, I could look through the door and see that Wesley was in bed and that—I could see part of the screen, so he was watching a porno video."

Beers then thanked Dr. Adcock for his testimony, and Shiner once again chose to question the witness.

"You told the jury that you believe that Mr. Wallace had a great appetite for sex?" Shiner asked.

"That's probably an overstatement," Dr. Adcock conceded.

"Well, as far as you know, did he have any inclination whatsoever," the prosecutor asked, "of performing domination or S&M type of violent sexual acts on any other human being? Do you have any knowledge of that?"

"Goodness, no. And Wesley and I traveled a lot together," the witness answered.

"Objection, not responsive to the question," Beers interjected. The objection was sustained.

"The question is," Shiner repeated, "Of all the time you spent with him, did you ever hear of a single thing like that?"

"No," Dr. Adcock answered.

"Did you ever hear of him having any sex with anyone that was not consensual in any way, shape, or form?" the prosecutor asked.

Once again, the witness answered "No."

"And you discussed personal matters with him throughout the friendship you've had with him," Shiner asked, "Intimate details that may have happened to you in your life or him in his life?"

"Yes, as brothers would, yes," Adcock confirmed.

The questioning then reverted back to Wes's health once again, but I was no longer listening at that point. My mind was still back on the sordid details of my father's sex life. It had not surprised me that my father had neglected to close his bedroom door in front of his friend. He had often urinated off the front porch of his apartment back in Greensboro in complete disregard for the neighbors or his own dignity. What surprised me, though, were the intimate details that he had shared with Dr. Adcock, such as the one about the two wallets. Surely he must have known how this would have looked to his friend, that he cheated and deceived people in this way. The private matters of my father had obviously been uncomfortable for Dr. Adcock to reveal in front of everyone. After his testimony, he had immediately headed for the door and left the courtroom and the state. I was never to hear from the embarrassed Dr. Adcock again.

CHAPTER 32
A Sex Act

On Friday morning before the jury was brought in, Shiner approached the bench before Judge Oftedal. After cordial "good mornings," the judge addressed the situation at hand. "Looks like Mr. Shiner has a matter before the court. Is that right?" he announced.

"Yes, sir," the prosecutor replied. "I alluded to Alberto Miliana, an essential witness in this case [who] has failed to appear for this trial." Shiner went on to explain that Miliana had been served a subpoena on Wednesday morning, and that he had had personal contact with him, himself. Detective Venetucci had also met Miliana over the weekend and told him to call him twice a day. Though Miliana had given the prosecutor a new pager number, he had not returned any of his calls, nor had he shown up for court. The man's family claimed they had not seen him in two days, but he had been seen the day before by a security guard where he lived.

The prosecutor wanted Judge Oftedal to issue a rule to show cause. He quoted a Florida statute that said if a person was a witness in a homicide or capital case, the court could issue a detention order and no bond warrant until the person was brought before the court.

"Has anyone been able to reach him by phone?" the judge asked.

"I tried," Shiner replied. "We reached his sister. The sister claims she doesn't know where he is." The prosecutor told the judge he had reached Miliana on Sunday, right before the trial had started. Miliana had assured Shiner he would be there on Wednesday, but he had not shown up. When the judge asked Shiner if Miliana was working, the prosecutor told him he was working in some type of telemarketing operation and he had given Shiner a phone number. The prosecutor claimed he had called the number repeatedly and no matter what time of day it was, all he had gotten was an answering machine. He said music had played, but there had been no voices.

When the judge asked Shiner what date he would like him to set for a hearing about the matter, the prosecutor answered that was the problem. "I don't know how they are going to serve him. If he doesn't answer the door, they can't break the door down." Shiner was therefore proposing the court issue a warrant to have Miliana brought directly before the court. He had tried calling Miliana and telling him that if he did not show up, the police were going to come and get him. He had even gone by Miliana's house the night before and left a copy of the subpoena by his door with a note saying Miliana had to be in court the next day. "The lights were on and the car was there, but nobody answered the door," the prosecutor said.

The judge asked Shiner if he knew the statute number for that particular criminal procedure. "I'd like to make sure I'm on firm legal footing before I send somebody out to be picked up," he added.

The prosecutor told the judge that he did. "I can assure the court that you would be," he said. With that, the jury was brought in.

It was soon clear something was going on with the trial. The prosecutor pulled me into the area between the wooden doors and confided to me that Alberto Miliana, their star witness, had failed to appear. "What now?" I asked him. Mr. Shiner assured me the police would pick Miliana up. "What if they can't find him?" I asked.

"They'll find him," he promised.

The next witness was Debra Glidewell, a studious-looking senior forensic scientist at the Palm Beach County Sheriff's Office crime laboratory in the serology/DNA section. Glidewell told the court she analyzed blood and other body fluids such as semen, saliva, and vaginal secretions. She held a bachelor of science in forensic science from the University of Central Florida and was currently a Master of Science candidate at the University of Central Florida. She had also spent a month at the FBI Academy in Quantico, Virginia.

The prosecutor began by asking the forensic scientist if she could tell the court what had been submitted to her for examination. "There's quite a number of items," she announced. "I'll just read them. Sexual battery evidence collection kit from William Wallace."

"Let me stop you there," Shiner interrupted. "What's a sexual battery evidence kit from William Wallace? What is that?"

"Well, that's a kit that's routinely taken to collect evidence when you believe a sexual assault might be involved in a particular crime," she explained. "The kit actually includes a blood standard from the individual, which is a known sample of drawn blood, depending whether male or female, vaginal swabs, oral swabs, rectal swabs, fingernail scrapings, and pubic hair combing."

"How about oral swabs if the investigators believe there may have been some evidence linking through oral swabs?" the prosecutor asked.

"Yes, absolutely that's collected," Glidewell confirmed.

"Please continue," Shiner asked of her. "What else was submitted to you?"

The forensic scientist told the court hair standards had been submitted from my father, as well as numerous other swabs from the body, such as the right arm, the left foot and the left hand. There had also been oral swabs from a number of interrogated suspects in the case, such as Fred Bowery, Raymond Steel, and Wayne Clarke. Glidewell continued with the list of items before her.

"What evidence did you have that made the police go out and try to match something to this particular case?" Shiner interrupted once again.

The forensic scientist explained there had been a large volume of evidence that she had received into the lab, and most, if not all, had an indication of blood on them. "The other evidence that I had was semen stains," she said. "I had semen that was found on tissues inside the house, and I found semen on the oral swabs of Mr. Wallace." Glidewell then read the other items on the list aloud. There was the swab from the bathroom sink, the bathroom wall light switch, the metal lamp shade, the light bulb, the bed headboard, the bedroom phone, the bedroom door, the bedroom closet door, a piece of Ritz Carlton paper, a white long-sleeve shirt, five Kleenex tissues from the trash, two tissues from the bedroom, a swab from the kitchen sink, a swab from the kitchen counter, four knives, a sample from the rear seat of the vehicle, and a plastic shower curtain.

"And you said there were other items that were submitted to you?" the prosecutor asked.

"Yes," Glidewell confirmed. "There was a queen-size fitted bed sheet, a full-size bed sheet, another queen-size bed sheet, two pillow cases, and three paper towels."

Shiner then asked the forensic scientist if she had any energy left for any more questions.

"I'm ready," Glidewell told him. She then went into a lengthy explanation of the procedure for DNA analysis, after which Judge Oftedal opted for a twenty-minute break. The trial would resume at a quarter past three, he said.

Shiner once again approached the bench in an attempt to get Judge Oftedal to sign the warrant to pick up Miliana. "I gave the court a courtesy copy of the State's motion for detention of an essential witness," he began. "We also gave the court a potential warrant to sign. We're asking the court to—"

"Maybe we can take this up after we finish with the next witness," Judge Oftedal interrupted.

Shiner knew that he did not have any time to waste. The quicker the court was willing to sign the warrant, he said, the quicker they could have the police start looking for Miliana. Right now they could only knock on his door, he argued. They could not go anywhere because they had no authority to take him.

"Suppose he's picked up over the weekend?" Judge Oftedal asked, considering the option.

"It's the State's request, since he's willfully failed to comply with the subpoena, he ought to spend the weekend," the prosecutor proposed. "He deserves to spend the weekend so we can secure his appearance for Monday. If he's let out, there's no way that he will show up, based on his past."

Suddenly, a new dilemma occurred to the defense attorney. If Miliana were to be picked up over the weekend, it was possible he could be placed near Travis, who was being held in West 3-A of the main detention center. "In all likelihood," Beers pointed out, "he would be placed in the south, but—"

Judge Oftedal interrupted him by speaking directly to Shiner. "Apparently you believe you know where this person can be located anyway?"

"I know where he was as of Sunday of last week. I don't know where he is today, Judge. I know where he lives but—it's the State's hope that we can find him rather quickly," the prosecutor admitted. He wanted to bring Miliana in immediately. Judge Oftedal finally agreed to sign the arrest warrant, and the sheriff's office sent law enforcement officers to pick up Miliana. They located him within an hour.

"Your Honor, the deputies tell us Mr. Miliana is now in-house," Shiner announced to Judge Oftedal an hour later, once Miliana had been brought downstairs.

"How long will he be on?" the judge wanted to know.

"Depends on his attitude," the prosecutor told him.

"We don't know, but certainly I have some extensive cross-examination of Mr. Miliana because he's a significant witness," said Beers.

Judge Oftedal was worried that if they waited until the end of the forensic scientist's testimony, Miliana would not be put on the witness stand until half past four. That would mean the jury would be forced to stay for another two to three hours after that. He was not about to keep them that late on a Friday. This led to another problem. Should they then incarcerate Miliana for the weekend or let him go?

"I don't think he's going to have any respect for the court, Mr. Beers, or myself," Shiner said. "With all due respect here, I don't think this young man will come back unless he's put in a police car with handcuffs like he was today."

Beers suggested the court talk to Miliana and tell him he had a responsibility to be back on Monday or he could be held in contempt.

"If the court considers releasing him," the prosecutor said, "I ask that he post a significant bond, which the statute allows him to post bond so he has—we have sort of some reliability, some indicia he will appear as opposed to, unless he had some real good reasons that he wants to explain to the court." Shiner then suggested they bring over a public defender as Miliana had the right to counsel.

"Well, my preference would be to get him on and off if we can avoid these kinds of problems," the judge stated.

"One alternative is to take his testimony now and get it over with." He then asked Glidewell if they could bring her back on Monday.

"I'm available on Monday," she told the judge.

"Can we bring him up and the court inquire of him?" the prosecutor requested.

"You can bring him up right now. Go ahead and bring him up," Judge Oftedal told a deputy sheriff. "You may want to hang around a little bit to make sure that we, in fact, have a witness who will be testifying," he told Glidewell, who agreed to do so. "Is he still in street clothes?" the judge asked the deputy sheriff, who assured him that Miliana was.

"There's also an issue as to whether or not it should be brought out that he was brought in by force today," Shiner pointed out.

"Who is going to want to bring it up?" Judge Oftedal asked.

"I'm sure Mr. Beers would and if he's going to," the prosecutor added, "I certainly think the State would be allowed to inquire as it goes to his state of mind."

The judge thought about this a moment. "Unless there's some objection, you're both free to go into it."

Just then, Miliana entered the courtroom through the side door to the right. He wore a black T-shirt, unhemmed jeans, and a foul expression on his face.

"You can stay right there for a moment, sir," Judge Oftedal told the defiant Miliana, who stood huffily in front of the doorway to the left of the witness stand. "Just so you're aware, the reason you wound up coming in through the side door rather than through the front door," he said, "is the State had indicated that you were an essential witness in this case; that you've been lawfully served with a subpoena; that you've refused, despite efforts to contact you and obtain your voluntary compliance. So that's the reason that this rather unusual procedure has been implemented."

Miliana stood listening to the judge, fuming at having been brought in by deputies in handcuffs. They had been removed just before he had been allowed to enter the courtroom, and he flexed his wrists back and forth now that they were off.

"So we made arrangements to go ahead," the judge continued, "at some other inconvenience, to take your testimony here today out of turn so we can bring the jury out now and go ahead, and so, hopefully, we can complete that this afternoon so it won't be necessary any longer to incarcerate you to make sure we have your testimony in this case. Do you understand that, sir?" he asked Miliana.

"Yes, sir," Miliana answered, finally grasping the matter at hand.

"Why don't we bring out the jury and swear the witness in," the judge suggested to the bailiff, who escorted the jury back into the courtroom. They each took their respective seats and listened carefully to Judge Oftedal's next words. "You'll notice Miss Glidewell is not on the witness stand," he began. "The reason we're going to have to actually interrupt her testimony," he explained in annoyance, "is we have something of a scheduling problem, so I think the State is going to call another witness out of turn, so we'll take that witness's testimony this afternoon, and we'll probably bring Miss Glidewell back later after this witness testifies."

Upon being told to do so, Miliana trudged reluctantly over to the witness stand and plopped down. The prosecutor poked at the defiant Miliana with the question: "Can you please state your name?"

The young man began to answer Mr. Shiner's questions in an irritated yet candid manner.

"Alberto Miliana," the witness responded. He told the court he was twenty-one years old and employed. When

216

asked about what kind of work he did he replied "computer entry database." He said he knew Travis Jones from where he used to live.

"Where was that?" the prosecutor asked.

"Victoria Woods." Seven hours after the murder, someone had spotted Travis in the gated subdivision of Victoria Woods with a shopping cart. They called the police at around ten or eleven in the morning to report a vagrant on the property. The officers had told Travis to "move along and don't bother the people here." He was no longer their neighbor.

"Did you go to school with Travis Jones?" Shiner asked.

"Yes," Miliana answered.

"What was the nature of the relationship, was it a good friend or acquaintances, did you hang out together; how would you describe it?" the prosecutor pressed.

"Good friends," the witness admitted.

"Did you lose any contact or did you stay in constant contact with Mr. Jones throughout the years?"

"Lost contact."

The friends had apparently parted soon after high school had ended.

"How in the world did you become a witness in a first-degree murder case?" Shiner shouted dramatically, turning around to face the courtroom with his arms spread apart.

"I don't know. It just happens," Miliana answered curtly.

"Did you tell the police or did you contact the police officer and tell him that you knew something?"

"Objection, leading," Beers interjected.

"I didn't finish the question," the prosecutor snapped. "That you knew something about a homicide?"

Once again, the defense attorney objected.

"Overruled," ordered the judge.

"Yes," the witness finally answered.

"Was that back in 1999?" Shiner asked, "Does that sound

right, about a year and a half ago?"

"Sounds about right."

"Just so everybody understands," the prosecutor stated, swirling around again, "When you told the police about this, the information you thought may have been important to them, were you in custody—were you under arrest?"

"No."

"Didn't you get arrested by the Palm Springs Police Department?"

"Oh, yes, I was under arrest," Miliana remembered.

"What did you get arrested for?"

"Fleeing and eluding."

"Trying to outrun a police officer in your car?"

"Yes."

"What else? Anything else?"

"Retail theft, petit theft," the witness stated.

"I'm sorry?" Shiner asked.

"Petit theft, something—"

"Was it for not paying a bill at a restaurant?"

"Yes," Miliana admitted. That, he understood.

"When you were arrested by the Palm Springs Police Department, did they tell you

anything of the nature, this is a way you can get out of this charge if you give us information on another case; did anything like that come up?"

"No."

"Did anyone tell you you were going to get a reward, promise you any kind of special treatment or money or anything of that nature?"

"No," the witness said again.

"Why did you decide to come forward and tell some information about a friend of yours, why did you feel that was important?" the prosecutor asked.

"I don't know."

"Just something you did?"

"Yeah."

"Did Mr. Jones ever do anything to you, personally, to make you want to see him suffer in any way, shape, or form?"

"No."

Shiner then took a moment to pace the floor and let the words of the witness sink into the minds of the jurors. "You said you lost some contact with him, but did you ever see him again after high school?"

"Sometimes," Miliana admitted.

"How did you see him again or how did you hook up with him again?"

"Picked him up on the side of the road."

"What was he doing?" Shiner asked.

"Walking."

"Before we go any further, you obviously don't want to be here today?"

"Not really. I'm supposed to be working right now."

"Were you pretty much brought in by force by the police?"

"Yes," the witness admitted.

"You said you saw Mr. Jones and you picked him up. How did you pick him up? Were you in your car?" the prosecutor asked.

"Yeah. I was in my car. He was walking down the street."

"Did he appear the same way he always did?"

"No, homeless."

"How could you tell he looked homeless?"

"Wearing the same clothes."

"You mean like dirty and disheveled and that kind of stuff?" Shiner asked, elaborating
for the witness.

"Yes," Miliana confirmed.

"Why did you decide to pick him up that particular day?"

"Felt like he needed a ride."

"Did he wave to stop you?" the prosecutor asked.

"I don't recall if he waved or if I just pulled over and picked him up," the witness said.

"Was he—did he have anything with him when you stopped?"

"A shopping cart."

"Did you see what was in there?"

"Some bags."

"Do you know what was in the bags?" Shiner asked.

"Dirty clothes and—I don't really recall what else was in the bag," Miliana admitted. "This happened like almost two years ago."

"And what happened with the bags? Did he put them in the car?"

"Yeah, we put them in the car. And then we dropped them off behind Inspiration House."

"What's Inspiration House? What's that?"

"It's like a gospel store, church books," the witness told him.

"Did he leave it out in the area or did he hide it so no one would see it?" the prosecutor
asked.

"It was pretty well hidden."

"How long would you say you spent with him that day, would you estimate?"

"Four to six hours," Miliana said.

"Did you reinstate your friendship with him?"

"Yeah."

"All right. When you were with him, did he appear to be injured in any way, shape or form?" the prosecutor asked.

"Yeah," the witness answered.

"What kind of injury did he have on him?"

"Cuts on his hand."

"How many?"

"A lot."

"Did he ever stay at your house or sleep at your house?" Shiner asked.

"No," Miliana answered.

"Did you ever offer him the opportunity to do that?"

"No."

"How come?" asked Shiner.

"I didn't like what he told me."

"What did he tell you?"

"He killed somebody."

Several members of the jury widened their eyes after hearing the words.

"Did he describe that person as a 'porno fag' to you?" the prosecutor asked.

"Yeah," Miliana confirmed. "He said he'd rolled a fag."

Miliana's eyes met with Travis's. His old friend looked defeated.

Meanwhile, my wall of protection was starting to crack. Up until this point, the trial had only depicted my father's body. Now I was hearing about his last moments on earth. For the first time, I broke down and the tears kept coming. They would not stop until the end of the trial.

"Did he tell you how in the world he wound up with this man?" Shiner asked.

"He said the guy picked him up."

"Did he tell you—did he tell you why he got in the car with him?"

"Yeah," Miliana answered. "To rob him."

"Did he tell you what the guy wanted from him?"

"Some kind of sexual favor or something." Miliana was growing more and more irritated. The line of questioning was making him uncomfortable, and it showed.

"All right," Shiner gently said to him. "Did he ever tell

you what happened between him
and this man?"

"Kind of," Miliana admitted.

"When he was telling you these things, did you believe him at first?"

"No."

"How come?"

"I didn't think he'd do something like that."

"Did he tell you the man was gay?"

"Yes."

"Did he tell you that there was a scuffle and the man died?" the prosecutor asked.

"Yes," the witness admitted.

"Did he tell you any other details about what happened that you could remember?"

"He said he stabbed him."

"Do you remember telling the police anything about a bathtub in this case?"

"Yes."

"What's a bathtub have to do with this case?" Shiner asked.

"He told me that he stuffed the bathtub or sink or something," Miliana explained.

"Did he tell you what he stuffed it with?"

"I don't know if he said clothes or a towel, I'm not sure."

"Did he tell you why he did that?"

"Clean up the mess." The witness was clearly agitated. He was beginning to speak in
stunted phrases.

"Did he ever show you a knife at all?" the prosecutor asked.

"Yes."

"What did it look like?"

"Four or five inches. Steak knife."

"Did it have a handle on it?"

"Yeah. Looked all broken up."

The questioning then moved on to Travis's flight. "Did there come a time when you took Mr. Jones to the bus station so he can leave town?" Shiner asked.

"Yes," Miliana said.

"Where did he tell you he was going?"

"Iowa."

"Do you know why he was going to Iowa, did he tell you?"

"To get away from all that happened."

"Did you loan him money or did you give him money to buy the ticket, the bus ticket to Iowa?"

"Gave him money."

"Do you recall ever seeing him with a stereo or VCR during that time period?" the prosecutor asked.

"Yes," the witness answered.

"Did there come a time that you started believing your friend was being up front with you in telling you what happened?"

"Yes."

"When did you start believing it?"

"When I seen it in the newspaper."

The effect of this testimony on the jury was sobering. It seemed to have a similar effect on Miliana as well. He suddenly began volunteering complete sentences.

"Do you remember reading details of the case where the newspaper told you that the man was stabbed and he was in [sic] pornography, did the paper tell you things like that?" Shiner asked.

"Yes, there was an article like that," Miliana said. "I read an article saying something about pornography or something."

"When you came in contact with him, did—did Mr.

Jones act like he was scared to death?"

"I don't recall."

"During all the conversations you had with him, did he ever tell you the man tried to kill him?"

"No."

"Did he tell you he killed this man because he wanted a sexual act performed or that he felt uncomfortable with the sexual acts that were going on?" Shiner asked.

"Yes," Miliana confirmed.

Beers objected to the question on the grounds that Shiner was leading the witness. Judge Oftedal agreed, and the objection was sustained.

The prosecutor then dropped the line of questioning. "Was this an easy thing for you to come in here today?" he asked.

"Not really," the witness answered.

"How come?"

"He's my friend."

"How come you didn't show up this week?"

"I've been working," Miliana replied. "I just started a new job. I can't tell them I had to go to a homicide trial."

The prosecutor summed up his examination by having the witness confirm once again that he had received no favors for his testimony.

Beers was then free to cross-examine the witness. "Right off the bat," he began, "you were in the Palm Springs Police Department on October 17th of 1999 and were arrested for fleeing and eluding, a felony, from police officers," he announced.

Miliana could not dispute this fact, nor did he try. Instead, he admitted the felony charge had been dropped to a misdemeanor.

"Do you recall Detective Boland telling you on videotape that he would talk to your probation officer and see what he could do; do you remember that?" Beers asked.

"I don't recall," Miliana said.

"You were in jail on a felony charge," the defense attorney explained. "When you gave this statement, weren't you fleeing from a police officer; weren't you?"

"Yes."

"And you were facing some serious felony charges when you gave that statement to the police."

"It wasn't that serious of—"

"Fleeing and eluding a police officer is not serious?" Beers argued in a loud voice.

"No," Miliana agreed. "It is serious."

"You didn't want to stop for police, did you? Did you?" the defense attorney yelled.

"It doesn't score out to prison anyway."

"What?" the defense attorney exclaimed. "It certainly scored out to county time, didn't it, for a year, didn't it? Didn't it?"

"It might have," Miliana admitted.

"Plus you were on probation and you could have done six months to a year on probation and that scored to a year, couldn't it?"

"It could have."

"I have no further questions," Beers barked, ending his cross-examination of the witness.

When Miliana's testimony was over, it was clear to everyone in the courtroom that I was crying. I loved my dad so much, and it was suddenly hitting me that he was really gone. And to hear it from someone who did not even know him or care about him was more than I could bear, yet it was still not over. Meanwhile, the court reporter could no longer keep his curiosity to himself.

"Who are you?" he asked me privately when I rose for the break.

"Denise Reilly," I answered.

"No, I mean, who are you to the victim?" he pressed.

"I'm his daughter," I told him.

The man looked surprised and confused. I now figured the rest of the courtroom must be thinking the same thing. Little did they know that I was just as surprised as all of them to be the daughter of a man who so often engaged in homosexuality, and the broadcasting of it felt violating to me.

I found myself washing my hands at the sink in the restroom at the same time as the alleged killer's gray-haired mother. Our eyes met in the mirror. Though no words were spoken, it was an icy moment where I felt the threat of the opposing team. Afterward, we returned to our opposite sides of the courtroom.

CHAPTER 33
Mick Jagger

Judge Oftedal began the court proceedings by welcoming back the members of the jury. He explained that they had taken a longer break between witnesses than they had originally anticipated. "We had a matter or two outside of your presence, but we're ready to proceed now," he announced. "Mr. Shiner, your next witness."

The prosecutor chose to call a serious-looking gentleman named Jon Russell Thogmartin to the stand, who told the court he had completed a degree from the University of Texas Health Science Center and done a five-year residency in anatomic and clinical pathology. At the time of the murder he had been the Chief Medical Examiner in Palm Beach County. Thogmartin explained he was board certified in anatomical, clinical, and forensic pathology. Anatomy being the study of solid human tissues and organs; clinical pathology being the study of fluids from human tissue such as blood, cerebral and spinal fluid, and urine; and forensic pathology as it applies to the legal system—in other words, traumatic deaths, murders, and unnatural deaths.

Thogmartin told the court that after measuring and weighing William Wesley Wallace in at six feet, 252 pounds, he had organized and photographed the body, making charts as he went along. He had also taken hair and nail samples and used a rape kit, which had included samples of swabs that had been taken from all of the victim's body cavities. "Obviously, you can't apply every sample," the doctor explained, "like one of them is vaginal swabs. Since this was a male person who did not have a vagina, I substituted penal swabbings."

"The rape kit that you mentioned," asked Shiner, "is that a standard protocol that you use in any case where you believe there may be some sexual activity that would have taken place in order to find the link with the person or persons responsible?"

"I would consider it routine," Thogmartin answered.

"Can you give us a brief overview of Mr. Wallace, in your opinion, as to a reasonable degree of scientific certainty prior to his death?" the prosecutor asked.

"He was mild to moderately obese," the doctor answered. "His heart base weight was a little enlarged; 550 grams for that size of a person is a little enlarged for a six-footer. His lungs, his other organs were in reasonably good health. His liver was normal. He had arteriosclerosis that put him into the 70 to 90 percent range, but they weren't completely blocked."

"What about his muscular ability, was he consistent with height and weight? Was he extraordinarily strong looking or—"

"He looked pretty much normal."

"For his age?"

"He didn't look like he used anabolic steroids." Thogmartin said the victim had looked like a normal fifty-six-year-old guy who probably had not had a lot of physical activity. "He also did not look like he was on the other end," he added, "he didn't have atrophy. He didn't look weak."

The members of the jury sat weighing the contradictory aspects of my father's physical condition. He had been a large man who had clearly outweighed his killer by about one hundred pounds, but he had also been past his prime. Had Travis been stronger than my father at that late point in his life, or had he merely been able to overpower him with the use of a weapon?

Shiner then asked about the next part of the medical examiner's procedure, when my father's alleged sobriety had been tested. Thogmartin explained that in cases of traumatic death where the injury had occurred within the last twelve hours, toxicology samples were drawn in order to test for the presence of drugs and alcohol in the victim's system. My father's results had proven to be negative. "After that, I can reasonably arrive at a cause and manner of death, and I did in this case," the medical examiner announced.

"Where are the primary injuries focused on this gentleman?" Shiner wanted to know.

"The neck and face," the doctor announced.

At that point, the prosecutor moved to offer two photographs of the deceased into evidence: State's Exhibit 78 and 79. He asked Thogmartin if he would hold them up high and show them to the jury. "He has facial injuries that are detailed in another drawing," the doctor explained, "neck injuries here, incised and stab wounds here, and abrasions here on the chest," he pointed out. "He also had abrasions and contusions. Abrasions here on the elbow, on the upper arms and—a contusion is a bruise," he added for the jury. "He had a bruise here with a couple of little scrapes on his hand. He also had what appeared to me to be a human bite injury here on his right wrist."

A few members of the jury sat forward in their seats and strained to see the photographs detailing my father's injuries.

"On the right side of his face, he had some wounds," Thogmartin added. "On the left side of his face, he had numerous incised wounds. These are more appropriately abrasions," he clarified. The medical examiner explained that a sharp instrument had been used to partially incise or scrape the surface of the victim's lips, nose, top of the head, and brow. There had also been a laceration or blunt force injury. "Something hit his face and caused a cut in his skin."

Shiner then moved on to another photograph from the evidence. "Any of the injuries in State's Exhibit 68," he asked, "any of these life-threatening?"

"Yes, this actually," Thogmartin responded. He then pointed to the two stab wounds in my father's neck that had been lethal. "I know there are a lot of wounds, but two of them severed a vessel here in the right side of the neck that caused bleeding to result in death."

I lowered my head into my hands after hearing the words.

"The wounds that are of merit here are number eleven and number seven," the doctor added. "This wound, number eleven," he pointed out, "partially transected the left external jugular vein." The other wounds—many larger in size than wounds number seven and eleven—had penetrated the neck to a depth of one-half inch, a quarter of an inch, and an inch and a half, but none of them had pierced any vital structures.

"Doctor, the jugular vein, you use the word *puncture* or *sever*?" the prosecutor wanted to know.

"Well, sever would be a term because it's a knife and it cuts," the doctor told him.

"But severed in this nature, based on your training and experience, would Mr. Wallace have lost a lot of blood?" It was a question that had members of the jury riveted.

"Well, he would have lost not as much as an artery, but when you have an internal and external jugular vein," the medical examiner explained, "blood comes out and air goes in, so those two things result in death. But there's blood on the body," he added, "lots of blood, and certainly there would be enough to result in death."

"When the jugular vein is severed in this nature," Shiner asked, "does the blood, does it shoot out or drip out?"

What? Does the blood *shoot out*? I could not believe the

question. It sounded like one that a movie-going teen would ask about the latest horror film his friends were describing to him in 3D. What else was the prosecutor going to ask before this was all over? What more was I going to have to hear about my dad and his murdered body in front of everyone in the room? The trial was becoming more surreal by the moment, and I was going to have to sit through it until the twisted, sordid end.

"It would ooze out," Thogmartin answered. "To squirt out, it would stream out of an artery. An artery would be bright red pumping of blood," he continued, "And the carotid artery is very close, but it happens that it [the knife] got the veins and missed the artery." My father had lost 200 cubic centimeters of blood. A typical adult has a blood volume of approximately 5,000 cubic centimeters or five liters.

The prosecutor now wanted to know if the doctor had seen any evidence that showed anyone had tried to stop my father's bleeding.

"Well, he had blood on his hands," Thogmartin said of my dad. Whether that had been the result of my father holding his own neck or not, he did not know.

Shiner then asked how long it would have taken for someone in that situation to die.

The doctor answered by saying, "If you're standing and your jugular vein is cut, you're eventually going to have lowered blood pressure and you'll feel faint and you'll drop. But then after you drop," he added, "there may be minutes of lingering and, further, unconsciousness would come before death."

"You would be certainly alert prior to unconscious for a period of time?" the prosecutor asked.

"You could be alert," Thogmartin answered. "He could have talked. There is no reason to believe that he couldn't talk. His larynx was intact."

Shiner then wanted to know if my father could have stood up.

"He could've gotten up if he had enough pressure to sit upright," the doctor told him.

But would it have made him weak? the prosecutor asked.

"It will make them weak," the doctor admitted. "I've found that the nature of the injury cannot predict the behavior of the decedent right before death," he continued. "I've had a case, for example, where a seventy-eight-year-old woman got shot right through the lungs by a nine millimeter and she was able to run about fifty feet before taking another shot."

Several female members of the jury looked horrified at the mention of such an elderly woman running for her life after being shot in the chest.

Thogmartin went on to say he had seen other people fall—after being hit with a similar round from a gun— who had dropped where they had been shot. "A lot has to do with how much movement is occurring after an injury," he said. "As long as the brain or spinal cord isn't hit by a knife or bullet, a person can move, and a lot depends on their determination and what their physiology is like."

Shiner then steered the discussion back to my father and asked if a lot of pain had been associated with his injuries.

"It depends," the doctor answered. "Pain is a subjective thing depending on the individual. If someone has a lot of adrenaline," he explained, "they are not going to feel a lot of pain. If someone has low pain tolerance, they will feel it." It was hard for him to say, he said.

After much more discussion about the size and nature of my father's wounds, the defense attorney then rose to cross-examine the witness. He, too, seemed to go on endlessly about the same subject until the judge finally grew visibly weary of it. "Mr. Beers, can we go to lunch on wound five?" he finally asked, to which the defense attorney amiably agreed. They would resume court at a quarter past one.

Once again, I ran into Travis's mother in the restroom. This time the woman looked frail and sad. I looked away and hurried into one of the stalls. I stayed there for several minutes until I was sure she was gone.

Once the trial resumed, the defense attorney moved on through my father's injuries at a painfully slow rate. "Now that wound, wound number seven," he droned, "could be considered, as you've indicated, a mortal wound?" he asked the medical examiner.

"Yes," Thogmartin agreed.

"And, basically, what that does is the jugular vein," Beers continued, "I know you've seen Mick Jagger up close, saw those veins popping out. Would that be an example of when one strains their voice and you can see their—"

"The vein you see in the singer's neck or somebody that holds their breath or bears down, that vein that bulges, that is the external jugular vein," the medical examiner explained.

Next, the defense attorney moved on to the next lethal wound, number eleven. It was important for him to poke holes in the prosecution's theory that Travis had meant to kill my father that night. He, therefore, sought confirmation from the doctor that wound number eleven was like some of the other wounds, even the non-mortal wounds that were only one centimeter in length. It was also only one-half inch to an inch deep. "That didn't go into the *internal* jugular or the branch of the *internal* jugular vein," he asserted; it had only partially severed the right external jugular vein.

"That is correct," Thogmartin confirmed. As to the rest of the injuries, the medical examiner could say that it was probable that all the stab wounds had been delivered with the same amount of force if they could assume the same blade had been used.

Beers then moved to further discount Travis's intention

to kill by getting Thogmartin to minimize the amount of blood found in the apartment.

"You see, here he's got blood on the bed," he pointed out in a photograph for the jury, "no blood in the hall, and then there's blood in what looks like an eat-in kitchen." The doctor explained that my father would have at least one external jugular wound or both at that point, and he would have covered them in some way or covered the distance before he made another drop. "I would expect there to be blood there, but there's not," he said.

By the time the cross-examination was finished, the jury would come away with the following questions that the physical evidence had posed: Had Travis meant to kill my father or had the defendant just been defending himself? Should there have been blood in the hall if the wounds had been intentionally fatal? The answers would never be clear.

CHAPTER 34
The Gay Cruising Park

It was finally time for the defense to call its first witness, John Latham. Latham was now a private investigator for Identifax of Broward County, but he had not been hired to testify in that capacity. His occupation actually had nothing to do with the case at all.

"Mr. Latham, good afternoon," Beers began.

"Good afternoon," the witness said.

"Where do you live, Mr. Latham?"

The witness told the Court he'd been living in Florida for forty-three years and he now lived in Pompano Beach.

"Married?" Beers asked, coyly.

"Single," Latham replied. He said he was divorced and had three children.

"Before you were a private investigator sometime in the year of 1998, 1999, in those years, what did you do then?" the defense attorney asked.

"I was a printer. I ran a printing company in Broward County," the witness answered.

"Mr. Latham, did you come to know an individual by the name of Wes?"

"Correct."

"And how did you get to meet this individual that you knew as Wes?"

"It's kind of a long story. It can't be just summed up in a couple of words. When I lived—excuse me, I'm kind of nervous ..."

"Take your time and take one thing at a time, without getting into anything he told you. I just need to know, how did you get to know Wes?"

Latham explained that while he lived in Lake Worth, he had a tendency to visit a neighborhood park in the afternoons. "I had a nice secluded spot, and I went there for peace and quiet, basically," he told Beers.

"What park was that?" the defense attorney asked.

"I forget the name of the park," the witness claimed.

"Would it help, John Prince Park?"

"John Prince Park, correct. Okay."

"Just take a deep breath and relax," Beers advised.

"Mr. Wes would ride through the park. And like I said, I had a secluded spot. So in the beginning, he would ride past the road." Latham claimed the two had not paid any attention to each other at that time. "One evening on my way home, around seven o'clock, I was on—it's the—"

"Let me stop you," Beers interrupted.

"Okay."

"The first time you got to know this person named Wes, tell us about what happened."

"Yes, that's what I'm getting at."

"Okay."

"On my way home one evening—I had a very distinct vehicle, a '67 Dodge van. And I was on this windy road on my way. I looked in my rearview mirror and saw Wes was behind me, but I had seen the vehicle quite a few times in the park."

"Why did you go to John Prince Park?" Beers suddenly asked, suspiciously.

"I had my three teenage kids and my sister living in a two-bedroom duplex, so I usually got off work around two, three o'clock in the afternoon, so it was a place to get away. I could get away from the noise and confusion of the printing company and the house at the same time," Latham explained. "So I'd go there, work on my car, my van, whatever I brought with me, watch the airplanes. I have a pilot's license, and I enjoyed sitting in the van watching the planes land. I would listen to them on my scanner, and it was just a getaway. So basically—"

"Prior to you driving your automobile, did this Wes ever come up to you at that time?"

"Not at that point. Like I said, I had seen him driving by the road quite a few times, but, no, I don't remember if he ever approached me before that."

Beers urged Latham to continue, while the members of the jury listened with great interest.

"I looked in my rearview mirror, and I realized that he was behind me, and it made me kind of nervous. This road, on the right-hand side, it follows a lake, so it's all parking all the way along the road. So I pulled over to the right, and he went past me and pulled in front of me. And I must have pounded my hand on the wheel or gave him a funny gesture or whatever because he drove off, and it made me nervous."

The story almost seemed like some kind of subplot of horror to me. I did not know what gay cruising was at the time, so it seemed to me as if my father had been stalking or *trolling* the witness.

"I drove home and, you know, like I said, I didn't know the guy, so it made me nervous. I thought he was following me," the witness explained.

"What about after that incident, did you—did he look at you—do you know if he looked at you when he pulled over in front of you when you were driving home?" the defense attorney asked.

"Oh, definitely, definitely," Latham assured him.

"Were there any words, without saying—" Beers asked cautiously. The witness had clearly been instructed by the court not to repeat any dialogue that had been exchanged between him and my father.

"There were no words exchanged at that time."

"Just a look on your part?" asked Beers.

"Correct," Latham answered.

"Then the next time—was there another time when you came in contact with this individual that you knew as Wes?"

"That's when we actually met. I was sitting in my spot in the park—" the witness began to explain.

"I don't mean to interrupt you, but you said it was secluded. Tell us about why it was secluded and where it was located in John Prince Park?"

"Okay. It was—I guess they would call [it] the south entrance of John Prince Park. There is [sic] no names of the roads or anything, but the reason it was secluded, there was [sic] two parking lots, and I would park in between the two of them underneath a group of trees, so there was no road to drive past me except for the main road, which was half a block away," Latham went on. "If you wanted to come to my position where I was sitting, you had to literally drive through the grass. There was no reason to come by me unless you wanted to talk to me, basically, is how it came down."

"Now this individual that you came to know as Wes, did he ever come to visit where you were in a secluded part of John Prince Park?" Beers asked.

It seemed to me the defense attorney kept referring to my father in a depersonalized way, as if he wanted to dehumanize him.

"Yes, that's what happened next. I can't remember a time frame, but it was two or three days later, and I was sitting in my driver's seat, and I was sitting there, and he drove up. I was sitting in my driver's seat, and he apologized for following me."

"Now, no telling me what he said," the defense attorney

instructed.

"I'm sorry," Latham uttered.

"But what—did he make eye contact with you?" Beers coaxed.

"Well, he pulled up right next to me and started talking to me."

"Did you have a conversation with him?"

"Yes, I did," the witness admitted.

"And what was your understanding of what he wanted from you?" Beers asked.

"Well, at that point, it was just a conversation as far as I was concerned."

"And then what did you see—how long did that conversation take place?" Beers wanted to know.

"Probably just a five-minute conversation. I really wasn't very happy about what had happened prior to that," Latham explained.

"And then what happened next? When did you see this—did you ever let him know that you didn't want him to do this?"

"No, but a lot of times he would just drive up, and if I was outside of my vehicle, I'd get in and sit in the seat and he'd kind of see me, and he'd drive up and just [make] small talk. He did this quite frequently."

"How often would you say that he did this while you were in John Prince Park, that he came up to you?"

"A lot. I'm not quite sure. This was a long time ago."

"Would you say thirty to forty times?" Beers guessed.

"Oh, yes, yes, more than likely, yes," Latham confirmed.

"And from those thirty or forty times that he came up to you, did you have an idea of what he wanted from you?" the defense attorney asked.

"Oh, I knew exactly what he wanted," Latham answered. "He wanted sex."

"Did you ever go back to his apartment?"

"Absolutely not."

"Would you—how would [you] characterize Mr. Wallace—Wes towards you, his attitude towards you?" asked the prosecutor.

"He was a friendly person," Latham admitted.

"Was he persistent or pushy?" Beers wanted to know.

"Oh, extremely. I mean, in the beginning, the conversations, when we got onto the sex conversations, I would just stop. I would just—I don't want to hear about it, I don't want to talk about it, change the subject or whatever," the witness continued. "So after a while, it didn't come to that conversation. It was just, more or less, he would stop by to say, hey, and wave to me, and things like that. But in the beginning, there was a lot of sex talk."

"How did it make you feel in coming up to you?" Beers asked.

"I didn't care for it," he said. "You try not to be a nasty person or whatever. I was there to be alone and to do my own thing, so I didn't really—I didn't take kindly to anyone coming up to me, so I wasn't very friendly. It surprised me that he continued to come up to me because I was very unfriendly."

The defense attorney then asked Latham what else he witnessed of my father.

"He cruised the park. I'd say his car would go by my vehicle twenty, thirty times. I knew what he was doing, that's why I wasn't crazy about the fact that he was constantly stopping by my vehicle."

"Did he ever make any motions to you with his hands or arms?" Beers asked.

"Yes," the witness answered, "every time he went by, he would wave after that, yes."

Beers then asked about the location of Latham's vehicle

in the park. "Did you drive over the grass?"

"Correct," the witness admitted.

"You were allowed to do that?"

"There were two picnic tables at this spot," Latham explained. "There was one where I sat and one about twenty, thirty yards. There was another picnic table so it was—it was a secluded spot, but it wasn't illegal to be sitting there or anything or Gaines Park rules," referring to a city park in West Palm Beach. Apparently the witness had forgotten which gay cruising park he was speaking about.

I felt the witness had avoided the question. He had been asked about parking on the grass, but he had answered about sitting at the table.

Beers let it go. He finished questioning the witness and turned him over to Shiner, who got right to the point after a quick greeting.

"Mr. Wallace, the first time you said he met you was, basically, he was behind your car and following your home?" the prosecutor asked.

"That's correct," Latham answered.

"And no conversations took place that day?"

"I don't remember it now."

"And the next time you saw him was at the park and he actually apologized to you for what he did, isn't that true?"

This brought a quick objection from Beers, which was sustained.

"Well, the next time you saw him, were you still as nervous as you were the first time?" Shiner asked, instead.

"I was very upset the second time because of what had happened the prior incident," the witness claimed.

"Without giving us what he said verbally, did he still try to put the moves or make advances on you the second time you met him?"

"Yes, oh, yes."

"Did he eventually—you said the conversation changed and you talked about other things, is that what you told Mr. Beers?"

"As time progressed, correct."

"How many weeks or months did you know him for?" Shiner asked.

"I'm not—I don't—I keep thinking to myself that it was about six months, but I'm not sure, it could have been longer, could have been shorter," Latham guessed.

"Isn't it true that a lot of times he would just drive by and wave hello to you?"

"Yes."

"Never tried to force you into the car?"

"No."

"Never pointed a knife or gun at you, did he?" the prosecutor asked.

"No."

"Never tried to hurt you in any way, shape or form, did he?"

"No."

"As a matter of fact, you described him as a fat, jolly, happy kind of person. Do you remember saying that to the police?"

"I don't remember, but I probably did," the witness admitted.

"Is that how you would describe him?"

"Correct."

"And even though you didn't agree with his sexual orientation, you didn't want him to do anything to you, he didn't do anything that warranted you to call the police?"

"No."

"Did you ever wave back to him when he would wave to you?" Shiner asked.

"Sure," Latham answered.

"Did you ever, even though you weren't looking for conversation, did you ever participate in talking to this man about different things going on?"

"Yes."

"Certainly if he had done something to threaten you, you would not have engaged in conversation?"

"Well, as time went on, he was very persistent, so as time went on, we became friendly," the witness admitted.

"But you would have called the police if you felt your life was in danger?" the prosecutor pressed.

"Objection, asked and answered," Beers interrupted.

"Overruled," ordered the judge.

"Right," Latham answered.

"You never had occasion to call the police?" Shiner repeated.

"No."

"Any redirect?" Judge Oftedal asked of Beers, who declined the offer.

"Thank you, Mr. Latham. You may step down," the judge ordered.

I stared at the bewildered members of the jury as the witness got up. What must they think of my father now? I wondered. I was not sure what I thought of him now, myself. Apparently he did more than people-watch when I was not around. A *lot* more, and it *was* creepy. Not just to John Latham, but to me. At this moment my memory of my dad was becoming a distorted image akin to one in a fun house mirror. Who the hell *was* this man Latham was describing? A stalker? Someone who trolled people? I no longer knew.

CHAPTER 35
In the Closet

It was now time for the alleged murderer's side of the story. Travis rose from the defense table and took a seat on the witness stand. For the first time, I had a full view of his face. At twenty-two years of age, he barely looked to be a man.

"Travis, good afternoon," Beers said, smiling.

"Hi," Travis answered meekly in return. It seemed to me as if the two had become

friends. I wondered how much time they had spent together preparing for the trial.

The defendant stated his name was Travis Jones and his birthday was July 7, 1978. He had never been convicted of a felony. The defense attorney then spent a good amount of time establishing that Travis was the product of a broken home. He'd graduated from high school with a 3.5 or 3.6 grade point average. His father and stepmother lived in Iowa, and his mother and stepfather had moved to Arizona. Travis had gotten a job at Personal Touch Detailing in West Palm Beach when he turned eighteen and was left to fend for himself.

Travis explained that the company had been closed by the Palm Beach Auto Mall. He had put in applications for other jobs and unemployment benefits but had no luck. Consequently, the witness had lost his apartment and become homeless. The defense attorney established that this had happened about a month before the murder. Travis had pawned his TV, VCR, microwave, and phone. "So you were familiar with pawning those items?" he asked. The defendant confirmed that he was.

When asked if he had a girlfriend during that period of time, Travis replied he did not, but that while he had been working he had one. Her name was Stephanie Brewer, he told the jury. She was a bartender at the Peek-a-Boo nightclub. Then the defense attorney got to the point. "Everyone wants to know, Travis, are you a homosexual?" he asked.

"No, sir," the defendant proclaimed.

"So you had no apartment, and you were homeless," Beers continued, "Tell us, how did you live? Tell us what your day consisted of, how you lived."

"I pretty much slept on bus stop benches, park benches, picnic tables," the witness explained.

"What did you do for food?" Beers asked.

"I could go behind a McDonald's or Publix or Winn Dixie. They throw out food

sometimes," Travis informed him.

"So did you have any type—did you use any knife or anything like that?" the defense attorney asked. The witness said he did.

"What did you have the knife for?"

"Open cans, food, canned goods, eat with. I didn't have a fork or spoon or anything," Travis explained. He told the jury he went inside the Dumpster behind McDonald's at night when they threw out hamburgers and extra french fries. When asked why he did not call his father and ask for help, the defendant explained he felt like a failure.

"So you lived this way on park benches and eating leftover McDonald's for, would you say, how many weeks?" Beers asked.

"Three weeks, four weeks," Travis answered.

"What were you—can you tell us what you were intending to do? Did you have any plans other than being a nowhere man, did you have any plans?" the defense attorney wanted to know.

"I wanted to go home to Iowa," Travis stated, "because that's where my family is." The defense attorney then moved ahead to June 6, 1999. He asked the defendant to tell everyone where he was in the early morning hours.

"I was walking down Congress Avenue. I guess it was around two in the morning, between two and three," Travis recalled. He probably had not eaten since the day before, he said. "I saw a white car pass by me. It was late at night so there was no traffic, but I saw a white car pass by me." The witness explained he was walking back from the Peek-a-Boo nightclub where he had gone to see Stephanie, even though she was no longer his girlfriend. He was headed back to where he kept his clothes.

"I saw it oncoming first," he said of the car. "It passed by, kind of turned around, and the guy was kind of looking at me as he passed by. I didn't pay much attention to it. I kept walking." Travis said the car made a U-turn and came back toward him. He was on the sidewalk and was just about to cross the street.

"Why didn't you cross the street?" Beers asked.

"Because this car parked in front of me," the defendant explained. "The man driving asked me if I knew where to go to have a good time, and I told him no."

"What else happened?" Beers coaxed.

"He asked me if I'd like to go to his house to watch some fuck movies," Travis answered. He said he told the man no, but that he was encouraging Travis to come along. He said it would be fun. After the second no, the man had said Travis could make a little money.

"What did you feel was going to happen?" the defense attorney asked. Travis said he kind of knew there would be some kind of sexual activity. "Then why did you go with him?"

"Because I needed the money," the witness answered. Beers told the defendant he wanted to know the truth about what happened when he got to Mr. Wallace's apartment. "He led me straight to the bedroom, which is in the back of the apartment. He told me to lay down on the bed and take off my clothes."

"Travis, have you ever been involved in doing anything like this before?" Beers asked. The defendant said he had not. "Was there a VCR in the bedroom?" Travis confirmed there was. He said Mr. Wallace put in a "homosexual tape," and it began to play.

"So you were in the back bedroom and you were asked to take off your clothes?" he asked. "What did you do? Did you say anything to him?"

Travis said he didn't. "I was uncomfortable, but I got on the bed," Travis explained. "He took his clothes off, and he got on the bed with me, and he started to take my clothes off, and he said—he said, 'Don't be shy,' and he stripped all my clothes off me."

"Did you ever say, 'I don't want to do this'?" his attorney asked.

"No, I didn't," the witness answered.

"When you were nude on the bed, what did he do to you?" Travis told the jury Mr. Wallace performed oral sex on him.

"After that, he tried to—he tried to get me to perform oral sex on him," the defendant explained.

"What did you tell him?" Beers asked.

"I told him no," Travis answered.

"And just tell me, what happened then, how did he become?" the defense attorney wanted to know.

"He was angry, very angry," Travis said, "He got up off the bed, and he screamed at me to get out, and he called me a cock-teaser."

"How loud did he scream?" his attorney asked.

"It was pretty loud," the defendant told him.

"And did you get out?" Beers asked.

"No, sir," Travis answered.

"Why didn't you get out?" his attorney asked.

"Because I didn't—I asked him what I did wrong, and he just screamed at me, get out. I was still naked," the witness explained.

"Did you ask him for anything?" Beers wanted to know.

"I asked him for a ride," the defendant replied.

"What else did you ask him for?" his attorney prodded.

"I asked him for the money," Travis said. "He said no. He told me to get out again."

"And did you get out?" Beers wanted to know. "Did you start getting dressed?" Travis

confirmed he started to put on his clothes.

"Where were you when you were putting your clothes on?"

"I was on the edge of the bed," the witness said. At that point, the defense attorney asked Travis to hold up a picture and show the jury where he was. "I was sitting on this side right here." Travis pointed to the spot.

"Where the blood is?" Beers asked.

"Yes, sir. I put my jeans on and my socks on," the witness told him. The defense attorney wanted to know if he had put his underpants and shirt on. Travis confirmed he had put on his underpants.

"And then what happened? Did you get out?" Beers asked.

"No, I asked him—I was still—I just put my socks on, and that's when I asked him about the money. He just, he just lost it," the defendant explained. "He, he was already screaming at me [and] at when I asked him about the money, he jumped on me."

"And what did he say about the money? What did you say, you have to get the—" Beers began for him.

"He said, if you want to get paid, you have to do what Daddy wants," Travis finished. "He got on top of me, and he put each leg on top of me. He straddled me," the defendant explained. Travis weighed only 160 pounds at the time. He said Mr. Wallace put his right arm over his face. His left hand was in his shorts. "He had his forearm over my face, and I bit him. I bit him pretty hard, and he pulled it back, and he screamed, and he hit me with the back of his hand."

Beers showed the witness State's Exhibit 75, the picture of the bite marks on Mr. Wallace's wrist. "Show us how, on me, how he had—how he put his arm on you. Just show me," he instructed. The defendant demonstrated the move for his attorney. He explained that my father was trying to force Travis to perform oral sex on him.

"What did you tell him?" Beers wanted to know.

"I was screaming at him to get off," Travis said.

"And what did he do?"

"After I bit him, he pulled back, and he hit me, and he leaned forward on me, and he was trying to smother me with his arm, it was over my neck," the defendant claimed.

I sat listening in horror from the second row. Suddenly, I recalled a frequently occurring event from my childhood—one that I had tried to forget long ago. When my parents had separated, and my father had moved to Fort Lauderdale, he would drive down to our duplex in Pompano Beach three times a week and choke my mother, who always let him inside their duplex. I had seen it over and over again, and I could see my father's face even now. Then I remembered another event that had happened when I was nineteen.

"And during the course of that time, did he say anything about giving Daddy what he wants?" Beers continued. Travis answered that Mr. Wallace had said it twice.

"I was trying to punch him, to push him," the witness said.

"What else did you do?" Beers asked.

"I was trying to squirm from underneath him. I was trying to scream, trying to push him off. I couldn't get him off," the defendant explained. "He was on top of me. He had his arm across my throat. He had his left hand, and he was trying to grab my crotch while he was on top of me, so I reached into my pocket, and I pulled out the knife." Every juror sat mesmerized, listening to the words. "I hit him with the knife in the neck."

"Did you feel that if you didn't do that—what would he have done to you?" his attorney asked.

"Oh, he was choking me," Travis assured him.

"Was he trying to get your mouth open?" asked Beers. Travis said he was.

"I was poking him in the neck. He was still—he wasn't getting off of me. I don't—he still had his arms around my neck and he [was] trying to grab the knife with his other hand, and we were struggling on the bed back and forth, and we ended up rolling off the bed and knocked everything off the nightstand next to the bed. And he grabbed the phone, and he hit me in the temple with it, the left side of my head," the defendant explained. His attorney urged him to continue.

"He was on top of me on the floor. I was trying to get him off of me with the knife, and I grabbed the lamp there, it was a lamp that fell off the nightstand. And I grabbed the lamp, and I hit him with it, and I thought the bulb shattered, but I guess it broke off and the light went off, it went dark," Travis said. "After I hit him with the lamp, I think it stunned him. I hit him hard and he was, he kind of eased up off of me, and I was trying to get off."

"Was he still on top of you?" Beers asked.

"No, he had kind of, he lifted his weight up off of me, and I was able to get up," the witness replied. The defense attorney asked what happened next. "He kind of slung me into the closet."

Beers then showed the defendant State's Exhibits 53 and 57. One was a picture of some blood on a shirt and one was a picture of a broken closet door. The attorney asked the witness what happened when my father slung him into the closet. "He came in after me," Travis said, "I was able—I crawled out from underneath." Having to relive the struggle was taking a toll on the defendant. He looked as if he was about to cry.

"It's all right," his attorney comforted him.

"He was just trying to reach in. He didn't follow me in the closet, he was trying to reach in the closet after me," Travis explained.

"Was he striking you?" Beers asked.

"Oh yes, yes, sir," the defendant answered. "Like I said, I crawled out from underneath the closet door, and as soon as I was getting up, [he] kind of ran with me into the door jamb. The bedroom door. I'm not saying he threw me into it. He kind of charged me, and I don't know, like tackled me into the door."

"So you were trying to get out of the room?"

"Yes, sir," Travis answered. "I hit my shoulder. I didn't know the door was broken, but I guess that's what happened. When we hit the door, we both kind of stumbled out into the hallway right in front of the kitchen and the dining room. There's a hallway right in between there, and after I hit the door, we kind of stumbled out there. And he was right on top of my leg, and we landed, and I was rolled here, and he was right there on top of me again. He went with the choking again. I was scratching him, pinching him, trying to push him off of me. And he just stopped, and he froze. For lack of a better word, he just froze."

"When you say froze, what do you mean?" asked Beers.

"I guess, passed out, lost consciousness," the defendant answered.

"Did you think you had killed him?" his attorney asked cryptically.

"I didn't check his pulse. I don't know." Travis claimed that he was panicked. "I didn't know what to—nothing ever happened like this. I don't know. First thing I did was, I went to the bathroom, and I turned the sink on and ran water over my hands because they were—there were cuts all over my hands." Travis said the knife was on the floor of the bedroom.

"You're sore from him choking you?" Beers asked.

"Very sore, yes," the witness answered.

"What did you do?" the defense attorney wanted to know.

"After I went to the bedroom, I had washed my—I ran the water over my hands, and there was blood all over my face and my chest. I washed my face with the water. I went to the kitchen, got some paper towels in the kitchen, I wiped my face and hands off, and there was an empty milk carton on the floor by the refrigerator, and I filled that up with water and I drank it," Travis explained. He said he put the milk carton in the bathtub.

"Now, there were some items that were found in the bathtub?" Beers prodded.

"Yes, sir," the defendant admitted.

"Why did you put those items in the bathtub, do you have any idea?" the defense attorney asked.

"I—it's—it was a stupid thing. I don't know, don't know the reason," Travis stammered. "I threw the sheets in there, the lamp, the milk carton. I put it in the tub, and I turned the water on. I don't know—I can't—there is no logical explanation for it, no real reason that I can think of, no."

"Well, did you attempt—was that your way of thinking,

well, maybe I can get away from this—let me finish—put the sheets, you didn't put all the sheets in there, did you?" Beers quizzed him.

"No, sir," Travis admitted.

"So you threw some pillowcases and sheets in this bathtub and turned on the water?"

"Correct," the witness stated.

"You just turned it on a little bit?" the defense attorney asked.

"Yes, sir," Travis confirmed. Beers asked what he did next.

"After I put everything in the tub, I saw the black bag, canvas bag, it was in the living room, right by the couch. I grabbed two VCRs, the stereo, and I threw them in there," the defendant said.

"Were you scared?" Beers wanted to know.

"Oh yeah, definitely," Travis admitted.

"How many trips did you make up and down the steps to Mr. Wallace's apartment?"

"Just one."

"Did you even know that he had died?"

"No, I didn't know," Travis answered. "I thought that, yes, it was very possible, but I didn't know."

The answer to this question was one that I had been waiting for since I had first learned of my father's murder. The defendant had left my father on the floor not knowing if he was alive or dead when he had been the only one there who could have helped him. Hearing the words sent pain shooting through my heart.

Meanwhile, the defense attorney continued to question the witness about the sale of the stolen items, while the members of the jury listened to the censored version of the event. Once again, drugs were not allowed to be mentioned during the testimony. Upon completion of Beers's direct examination, Judge Oftedal ordered a twenty-minute afternoon break for the court. The witness got up from the stand and returned to his seat.

At that point, I stood up and whispered to Mr. Shiner that I needed to talk to him. Once again we found ourselves huddled inside the space between the doors, but for the first time in the trial, it had been my idea.

"What's going on?" he wanted to know. The conference room was being used, so we stepped out into the hall. I went over to the window and saw a lone barge way out on the ocean. I felt like that barge, ponderous and lonely. Shiner walked up behind me.

"What is it?" he asked.

"You didn't know my father," I said, looking up at him. "He used to choke my mother."

Shiner listened patiently as I confided in him.

"There's more," I continued. I told the prosecutor about something that had happened when I was nineteen. My father had called me at seven in the morning one day. He had still been drunk; he was slurring his words. I had answered the phone, and he had said to me, "Denise, I think I killed somebody. Come pick me up."

Though I had been asleep, I had immediately jumped out of bed and run to get my keys. Then I had flown out the door barefoot in my nightshirt and driven to my father's home.

It had only taken me three minutes to pull onto the white gravel in front of his worn, white trailer. My father was already outside. He jumped onto the passenger seat next to me.

"Is he okay, Daddy?" I had asked him, assuming that it was a man. My father had only associated with men since his recent return to Florida in 1987.

"Come on, let's go!" he had ordered. I had backed out on the gravel and turned onto Lindell Boulevard. Again, I had asked if the guy was okay. Instead of answering, my father had told me to take him to the repair shop on Fifth Avenue, where his car was being worked on.

I had feared the worst. I dropped my father off at the shop and drove back to the trailer to see if the man needed help, figuring I would at least have a few minutes while my father paid for the repairs.

Pulling up out front again, I sat in my blue Saturn for a couple of minutes staring at the trailer. What if the man was dead? Would that make me an accessory to murder? Would I tell the police and risk my father? No, I decided.

I started up the car and decided I would drive home and watch the news for the next couple of weeks to see if there were any reports of a body or a missing man. I never saw any, and my father and I never spoken about the incident again.

Shiner was shocked that I had never asked my father what had happened, even years later.

"What do you want me to do?" he asked.

"I want you to tell the jury," I told him.

The prosecutor explained that since I had never seen a body, I was not technically a witness. It was hearsay and, therefore, was not admissible in court. The only thing he could do was ask my mother if my father had ever hurt her. She was the only one who could testify. Shiner told me he would talk to my mother.

I then returned to my seat in the courtroom next to Rick. "What was that about?" he asked. I relayed the discussion that the prosecutor and I had had out in the hall. "Why don't you just leave it alone?" he suggested. "It's their job, not yours," he said, turning back toward the judge.

Why did he not understand? I wondered incredulously. The kid was facing the death penalty. He did not deserve to die. I listened as the prosecutor then called the defendant to the stand once again.

"Mr. Jones," he began, "Was Mr. Wallace's life worth thirty dollars, in your opinion?"

"No," Travis answered.

"I want to ask you, specifically, about—first of all, who gave you permission to steal these VCRs?"

"Nobody."

"What right did you have to take these things?"

"I didn't. I had no right, as I remember."

"You took both of them, not just one."

"That's correct."

"Without anyone's permission?" the prosecutor repeated. "While this man lay there bleeding did you ever attempt to put a towel around him, or a tourniquet?"

"No," the defendant replied.

"Or pressure in an attempt to prevent him from bleeding?"

"No."

"Did you ever knock on the neighbor's door in the senior community and say, 'The man next door needs help'?"

"No. I didn't," Travis admitted.

"The medical examiner told us it could take up to ten minutes for him to die; do you remember that testimony?" Shiner asked.

"Yes."

"You were listening, weren't you?"

"Yes, I was."

"Did you go over and feel his heart to see if it was still beating?"

"No, I didn't."

"Why not? What can an unconscious man do to you; what could he do while he's laying there bleeding," the prosecutor added.

The line of questioning was searing to me.

"What could he have done to you? Nothing, right?"

"No, nothing," the defendant admitted.

"But you didn't think to do that, did you," Shiner added, turning around to face the courtroom. "All you could think about was taking his property, right?"

"No, sir."

"You didn't think about taking his property?" the prosecutor asked again.

"I wasn't thinking about taking his property."

"But you did."

"I did," Travis admitted.

"You certainly did. Now, you told this jury, you couldn't think of an answer why you would turn on the water in the tub, right?"

"Right."

"Were you trying to clean up the crime scene, you didn't want to get caught?"

"That's not true," the defendant argued.

"Did you want to get caught?" the prosecutor asked.

"Caught? I don't—"

"Did you want to get caught when you were in that house? Did you want the police to find out that you did this?"

"I didn't want anybody to know that I did it."

"Exactly. And what you did was try to cover up what just happened, right?"

"No."

"So you took the sheets in there and the lamp that had blood on it and put them in the water to dissolve the blood or what other legitimate purpose?" Shiner asked.

"I was panicking," Travis admitted. Obviously, I thought. The prosecutor was clearly trying to establish robbery as the motive for the murder, despite what I had told him. There was nothing I could do about it but wait to see if my mother would take the stand the next day.

By this point in the trial, the memories I had of my

father had melted and warped as if someone had thrown my collection of his photos into a bed of flames. I would later find myself picking through those that had remained untouched and posting them onto a collage in my mind.

CHAPTER 36
A Struggle on the Bed

The sun was in its hiding place behind the clouds at nine in the morning on March 6, 2001, when the trial resumed. After a crisp "good morning" from Judge Oftedal, the prosecutor began the proceedings by giving the defense attorney a new copy of the jury instructions. "And there's a whole new set for Your Honor," he told the judge. "There's one thing that I changed that is different than we talked about to let you know, on 3.04 (d) justifiable use of deadly force."

"Way down on the first page: 'However, the use of force likely to cause death or great bodily harm,' do you see that paragraph, Judge?" the prosecutor asked.

Could this change be due to what I had told Shiner about the incident with my father? I wondered.

"Yes," the Judge answered.

"I inserted 'or' in between because the standard instruction had that and the instructions from yesterday from Mr. Beers did not have 'or' and that's also a correct statement of the law, you need to have an 'or' there."

That was it? I wondered incredulously. He added the word 'or'?

Just then, Beers made an announcement. "I'm renewing my motion for judgment of acquittal after the defense case for the same grounds as I requested after the State rested," he said. "And even further, the evidence shows that this was a self-defense issue and it was not a robbery case. Based on those grounds, I'm renewing the motion to judgment of acquittal."

Without hesitation, the judge answered his request. "For the same reasons I've indicated before," he stated, "I do believe the State has met its burden and it's sufficient to survive a motion for judgment of acquittal, even at this stage, so I'll deny that motion." He then ordered the jury be brought in. "Mr. Shiner, are you ready to begin?" he asked.

"Yes, sir," the prosecutor replied. It was now time for the closing arguments.

Marc Shiner had lain awake most of the previous night going over the words in his head, words that he had spent many emotional days preparing. As the prosecutor, he would go first."Good morning, members of the jury," Shiner began. "I told you from the very beginning in my opening statement this is going to be a very sad case. And you heard all the facts in this case and you heard, basically, that this case involves two very sad stories, two lonely people."

Once again, I felt the guilt of having been almost 3,000 miles away from my father when he had needed me.

"And you-all said when you came as jurors, you understand homosexuality may be an issue in this case and we are not going to be biased or prejudiced because of that," the prosecutor stated, looking straight into the eyes of the jurors and pausing. He then began to pace the floor in the center of the courtroom.

"The testimony started last week after a long jury selection with Mr. and Mrs. Mancini," he began. Shiner reminded the jury that the elderly couple had nothing to gain in the case. They were not friends with anyone, really, nor were they biased or prejudiced in any way.

What Mrs. Mancini had to say, however, differed greatly from what the defendant had to say, Shiner explained. "She said when she was awakened at around three in the morning, she heard loud banging and commotion, and she heard her neighbor, who she knew for at least a month, Mr. Wallace say, 'Get out! Just get out of here!' Why is that important in this case if that really happened?" Shiner asked the jury. He recounted how Mr. Beers, a good attorney, had thoroughly cross-examined all the witnesses and that, "She never wavered from that," he yelled. "'I knew for a *fact* it was his voice, I could recognize it.'"

As for Travis, Shiner poked holes in his claim that he was acting in self-defense and that my father was "trying to choke him with his neighbors right next door in a senior community." If that was so, he argued, then "how did it quiet down like she told you, like her husband told you, for another five minutes or a few minutes, enough for her to believe that it was some sort of lover's quarrel?"

"So he brings him back to his house so he can kill this man," Shiner proposed. "Is there any evidence of that in this case? Mr. Wallace, no matter what you want to think about his sexual lifestyle," he continued, "is there any evidence, whatsoever, other than this defendant telling you that?"

Shiner claimed the physical evidence was also inconsistent with what Travis told them. "Not just with the Mancinis," he claimed, "but with every single person in the case. In order for you to believe this defendant when he gets on the stand," Shiner went on, "why does he sit in this chair and tell you all, why does he stare at you, each one of you, in the eye as he recounted, I wasn't there to rob him?" The prosecutor explained that Travis knew now that there was something called "felony murder," that if the victim had died during the course of events considered to be a robbery, it was called felony murder. "The bottom line is, he took those items while the man lay there dying, blood coming out of his neck."

This fact seemed clear to everyone in the courtroom. Where the facts became murky, however, was when one went about examining the victim's wounds. This was an area of mystery that would spawn two completely different interpretations by the prosecution and the defense.

"Mr. Beers went through every single one of the medical examiner's wounds," Mr. Shiner surmised. "They're all a quarter to a half-inch deep. Why doesn't he stick it in four or five inches?" he asks about Travis and his knife. "What was he doing, torturing him—give me the money—while he's sticking him fifteen, twenty, thirty times? Why did he mess his face up like that? Why is he carving his face? How did he have time to cut the cord on the bed?"

Mr. Beers, however, clearly saw the lack of depth of the wounds as a sign of self-defense. Upon his turn to speak, he would describe the neck wounds of the victim as having been inflicted from the bottom up instead of from the top down. Travis claimed to have been straddled and choked by my father, who was larger than he. It was a scene I could vividly imagine, a scene I had witnessed many time before with my mother.

"Do you believe this man was choking and killing this young man?" he asked the jury. "What physical evidence is there to show that?" Shiner said he saw the defendant as a star witness for the state. "He comes in here and says my neck was sore. I couldn't—I had to drink a half-gallon water, and I threw the jug in the tub."

Shiner then fast-forwarded to roughly seven hours after the murder, when an officer had apparently been called to Victoria Woods. Someone had spotted a vagrant on the property and called the police. Travis had mistakenly thought the officers were there to arrest him. "He didn't try to run," Shiner marveled. "He didn't even like freak out or go crazy like most people. He didn't say: 'Someone just tried to kill me.'"

Upon the officer's examination by the prosecution, Shiner

had asked him about Travis, "If you saw he was injured, he was a homeless guy, would you call the ambulance?" 'I sure would,' the detective answered. 'I do it all the time.' When asked if he saw any injuries on the defendant, the detective answered only, 'I saw a couple of cuts on [his] hand, a couple of little bruises.'" He had not seen any life-threatening injuries.

Shiner went on to say the detective was probably embarrassed, that he had run into someone who had committed a murder and even had the murder weapon on him. Travis told the officer he had a partially broken knife in his back pocket. He explained he used the knife to open cans of food. The detectives threw it in the garbage, Shiner said. They did not want to be bothered with it. They could have arrested Travis. It was a gray area, but it was not a big deal to be carrying a steak knife. They told Travis to go on his way and not to bother the people there. He got up, pushed his shopping cart, and left Victoria Woods.

Regarding the victim's stolen property, Shiner asked the jury about Travis, "Do you believe that he sold Mr. Montegut the property? Of course you do," he answered for them. "There can be [no] doubt about this because this defendant told you Mr. Montegut was telling you the truth." They differed on the facts, however, Shiner remarked. The defendant could not even be straight with the jury on that. And how did Travis carry the stuff down the stairs? How did he have time to clean up and find a bag to put the stolen property in? "His hands weren't shaking enough," Shiner told them. "He certainly knew he lived in an adult community where people could possibly be looking out windows."

Mr. Shiner backtracked, then, to the murder. "Could he have stabbed him on the bed like he told you repeatedly and they roll onto the floor?" Shiner asked. "And then he said, 'I got the knife. The light was out, but I found the knife, and I kept stabbing. He threw me into the closet.' How come there is no blood trail from the bed or closet area to where the man is found?" The prosecutor told the jury to take the pictures back there and look at them.

Mr. Shiner professed that Travis's story was not consistent with the evidence at the scene. It was more consistent, he claimed, with a fight with a man where the man was trying to protect his property. "Where is the man's watch, Travis?" he asked the defendant. "How come the police never found a watch?" Travis had claimed he did not know. "He can't even be straightforward about that," the prosecutor spat, "because how would it look to you if he took a watch off a dying man's wrist?"

As to the covering up of the crime, Shiner began by asking the jury about Travis, "How come his fingerprints aren't anywhere in the house? Why aren't the police telling you they found eighteen or nineteen fingerprints? How come his fingerprints are not in the man's car? Is this a man running for his life?" he argued.

The prosecutor told the courtroom he was sorry to see the defendant was homeless and that he found himself in bad circumstances. He was also sorry my father was lonely enough that he had to cruise the streets to look for men. "It's a sad story," he said. "That doesn't give this defendant the right to kill him just because he was homosexual, just because he didn't want to pay him, just because he couldn't get what he wanted."

Because the mention of drugs was not permitted at the trial, the prosecutor tried to leave a blank hole in the minds of the jurors for them to fill in for themselves. "Why didn't he take his food if he was so hungry? Why didn't he raid the cabinets? Why didn't he stock up on groceries?" Shiner asked them. It was clear food was not what the defendant wanted. What did he want then? "Why does he have to take physical property that the man worked for? He had [an] honest job. Why did he have to take his property?"

Once again, Shiner returned to the murder. "How come his blood is not on the bed if the man is trying to kill him, swinging at him, punching him, choking him? Why is all the blood in this case belonging to Mr. Wallace? How come? How come every shred of evidence in this case comes back to Mr. Wallace except in the bathroom where he went to clean up?" he went on.

The covering up of the crime scene was gone over again, as well, but this time the tone was a mocking one. "Is this a man who was scared to death?" Shiner asked the jury. "I'm not leaving yet. I'm scared to death. He almost killed me and the man is gurgling or the blood is coming out of his neck. He can't get up, but I'm going to stay here and go to the bathroom and clean my hand and clean my chest where I have blood on [sic] because I don't have a shirt on. Let me go get some sheets, fill the bathtub. Let me turn the water on. Let me dilute that blood. Maybe I can clean this all up," the prosecutor mocked. "When he realized that the product of what he did was a lot more than he could handle, after all the noise, and he knows the neighbors were probably going to call the police—this all took time. He said, 'I have to get away. I've got to get out of that.'"

At the end of his turn, Shiner shared some insight with the jury. "You have an unusual chance in this case where someone actually got on the stand," he told them. It was a rare thing when the accused actually got on the stand and told the jury he did those things. That only happened, he said, because the detectives did a phenomenal investigation where they tied up the loose ends. "They worked for months talking to hundreds and hundreds of people, everyone who he worked with, and they started finding out about his lifestyle," Shiner explained. "Without Mr. Miliana, [Travis would] still be in Iowa, in his fantasy world, thinking no one is going to catch me." The prosecutor then paused for effect. "And it doesn't matter if you believe he intended to kill the man or not. What other intent could he have had when he's sticking him, carving him up? What other intent could he possibly have had to want to kill?" Shiner yelled.

"Anyone who has a knife, who's sticking it in someone and cutting him will know, you've got a good chance of killing them. It doesn't matter if six of you think it was first-degree premeditated and six of you think it was felony murder," the prosecutor explained, "As long as all twelve of you agree either way it was proven beyond a reasonable doubt, then he's guilty of first-degree murder."

I sat staring at Shiner as he thanked the jurors for their time, patience, and attention at the trial. He was a handsome and charismatic speaker. With his charm and intelligence, he had basically erased the motive of self-defense from their minds and told them how to think. It had been a brilliant speech that I doubted Beers could top. The court then took a ten-minute break.

Out in the hall, I leaned against the wall and watched as the prosecutor spoke with his legal assistant by the window. He was just doing his job as the law required of him, I knew. Unfortunately, life sometimes fell just outside of the lines.

When court was back in session, Beers rose to speak before the jurors, wearing his meek and familiar smile. Like Shiner, he agreed that my father's case was a very a sad one. He expressed to the court that he had seen both the pained faces of my father's family and Travis's family. "This was a moment in a young man's life," he continued, "where his life was threatened, and we cannot choreograph exactly what happened two years later and nothing was made up." He then told the jury, "I don't like the fact that the implication is made that we took evidence and we said, now, 'Travis, this is what happened, so you've got to say this before a jury.' Because he had a right not to testify," he informed them all, "but he wanted to, and he wanted to explain to you and look you in the eye and tell you what happened."

The defense attorney portrayed the defendant as "a young man who [was] homeless, who didn't even go to Winn Dixie to steal food, to steal anything out of the cases, to put it in his shopping cart; a young man that had never been convicted of a felony or any crime of dishonesty, nothing." Beers called Travis "a nowhere man" and said he was a proud young man whose life was at stake. "And I'm telling you, with all due respect, that from the evidence itself," Beers went on, "from a conflict of evidence, that there's a reasonable doubt whether or not Travis killed him because we know he was in the apartment and that was told to you by opening statement, but whether or not he used or he was justified in using force likely to cause death or great bodily harm to save himself from a man who was six feet tall, 260 pounds, from a young, skinny kid that's homeless, that's skin and bones.

"So we go back to that fateful morning on June 6th of 1999. We go back to a young man who, having lost his job and lost his apartment, is walking along the street, is walking along minding his own business. He's not looking for 7-Elevens to rob and goes in there, yes, I have the intention to rob and shoots somebody.

"Mr. Wallace pulls up in front of him and stops as Travis is walking across the street. Mr. Wallace is a man with a voracious appetite for sex. He was not unhappy. He was a happy man because he enjoyed—he found his niche. And that's okay as there's nothing wrong with being homosexual, gay, so long as you don't try to force your body and force yourself on some innocent young person. That's okay. I have no problem with that. But I'll tell you this," he went on, "and I'll look each of you in the eye and tell you that homosexuality and his aggressiveness had every part to play in this case. And I disagree vehemently with the government's contention that that's not—does not play a part in this case. It plays a big part because you heard Dr. Adcock come in here, a friend of Mr. Wallace and testify." The defense attorney placed his hands on his notes.

"He testified that he continued to bring young men to the apartment. And I asked him if he remembered talking to Detective Boland on July 20th and he said this man, Mr. Wallace, would probably not be with someone over forty years old, that [there were] incidents in the past where he wouldn't pay. Does that fit with what happened here?" Beers asked. "That he had great appetite for sex, and that each night he watched pornographic movies, leaving his bedroom door open for a man like Dr. Adcock who stayed with Mr. Wallace. That he kept two wallets, one with money in the event that someone wanted to get paid because he didn't pay for sex. A man that was described by Detective Venetucci as someone that would, excuse me for the expression, but fuck 'em and forget 'em.

"From the testimony of John Latham you learn how persistent a man Mr. Wallace was." Latham claimed that Mr. Wallace approached him twenty to thirty times. "Here's a man that Mr. Wallace followed. Here's a man that wanted sex from John Latham, and Mr. Latham didn't want anything to do with him. And that first time when Mr. Wallace followed Mr. Latham and Mr. Latham stopped and gave him a dirty look, you think that Mr. Wallace would go away.

"But no, that was not the type of person he was. Mr. Wallace, he wanted to get what he needed and he wanted," Beers insisted. "The persistence fits what happened in that apartment, that condominium on Lake Osborne Drive on June 6th, the persistence of Mr. Wallace to get what Daddy wanted. That was his persistence. That was what he wanted."

As to Travis's flight to Iowa, the defense attorney had this to say, "Well, why did he run to Iowa? He ran to Iowa? Well, he didn't. He bought a bus ticket June 9th. He saved himself half price. He waited a week. Is that somebody that had committed a robbery? If a young man is going to rob a man, does he let a man take advantage of him sexually? It doesn't make sense. It will never make sense. The evidence doesn't show it, and the evidence in any case shows the contrary, that he was listening to Mr. Wallace, that this young man was gullible to believe that that man with that sexual appetite was going to pay him and take him back to where he kept his clothes."

"But no, Mr. Wallace didn't do that. Mr. Wallace puts in a homosexual tape. Does that fit? Because that same VCR that Travis took from the apartment, takes the same VCR that Montegut saw. And what was in it, a VCR homosexual tape? Does that fit with [what] he says? Of course it does.

"Then what happens is that Mr. Wallace undressed Travis," Beers continues. "Travis does something that he has never done in his life before: he prostitutes himself, and Mr. Wallace gives him oral sex.

"But Mr. Wallace is not satisfied. Mr. Wallace is persistent. We know that. We know how he watches people in the parks. This was a young man that he had just taken advantage of. Now he wants more, and Travis says to him, 'I just want some money.' Is that so hard to believe? 'I just want—take me back to [the] car' and starts getting dressed. And Wallace, who has been sexually unsatisfied," Beers went on, "he says, 'Get out, get out.' Well, Travis would have gotten out, just give him a little money or just take him to his clothes. Fuck 'em and forget 'em, that was Mr. Wallace." This time Beers did not ask the court to excuse his expression.

"Then is it so difficult to understand that this man with this appetite says to him, 'You're now going to give Daddy what he wants,' and gets on top of him." Beers then admitted that Travis should have left the victim's apartment when he told him to leave. "And what did Travis say?" Beers asked the court. "'Get off of me, get off of me.'" The defense attorney then claimed he did not know what the Mancinis heard, that the voices were muffled.

As for Travis, Beers announced, "You heard what he said. He called him a cock-teaser. If Mr. Wallace goes to that length to find people, he's not going to give up. He's going to be relentless. He becomes the raging bull." Beers then corrected my father's weight to 252 pounds, as Dr. Thogmartin had pronounced it to be at his death. "And he is facing this young man, and he is trying to get this young man's mouth open. And Travis doesn't want it."

A photograph of a bite mark on my father's right wrist, State's Exhibit 75, was then held up. Several members of the jury leaned forward to get a closer look. They were all captivated by the fight scene being dramatically described before them. "Here's a bite mark that was characterized by Dr. Thogmartin as a very, very significant bite mark. Here's a bite mark characterized by the dentist, forensic dentist Dr. Grayhills.

"Who bites somebody like this? Somebody that's going to rob somebody and intends to kill them, or somebody that is defending himself from a man who is attacking him?" The defense attorney told the jury that the evidence showed that Mr. Wallace was pushing Travis's head down, and Travis bit him. There were mandibular marks, the lower partial of Travis's teeth in Mr. Wallace's wrist.

"You heard Travis say that he took his hand, and he smacked Travis across the mouth. Well, look at State's Exhibit number 73 and my exhibit, Defense Exhibit number 8. This is a close-up of Mr. Wallace's left wrist with two, what appear to be teeth marks."

Beers then moved on to State's Exhibit 58. "There is blood on the bed. Where is it taking place? On the headboard, top of the bed where Travis was, where he was straddling Travis. Travis's head was on the bed. He pushed him back. Travis had his clothes. He couldn't get on his shirt or those pants. He kept a little knife. Was that knife used to go out and rob people?" Beers asked the jury. He told them Travis used that knife when everything else failed, and he was placed in a life-threatening position, a horrible position.

"I don't know if we could ever describe the horror that someone could go through like Travis went through," Beers mused for everyone. "So he pulls out his knife and Travis is trying to extricate himself from this horrible situation, and there's a violent struggle."

The defense attorney then held up State's Exhibit 1. "Look at the door jamb," he demanded of the jury. "Look how it's broken off." Beers said my father threw Travis against the door of the closet, "Someone that was a hundred pounds heavier." He claimed my father could be a linebacker on a football team. "He takes the knife, and he doesn't stab him in the heart. He doesn't jab him in the jugular vein." Beers then asked that the jury "Think about a person on top of you. Think about a person that will not get off you." A person so heavy that you cannot get him off of you, he said. "So what the young [man] does is, he does little stabs underneath or just on the sides of the neck." The evidence showed the wounds were incised wounds, not stab wounds. The defense attorney explained that "Mr. Wallace was losing blood, but he was still strong enough, he was still strong enough to push him, to throw him into the closet, to throw him against—to push him against the door to break it with enough force to break that metal hinge on that thick door. He was still strong enough to do that. And then he was losing some blood, and he collapsed."

The defense attorney had just dramatically described the last moments of my father's life. I cringed at the thought of the violence that had occurred. My father had seemed to have been some kind of bogeyman who kept getting back up in the midst of his fury. It was as if *Grimm's Fairy Tales* had somehow come to life with my dad as the main character. Such an ending to his life was ugly and meaningless. It was hardly the father I wanted to remember.

"I'm here to show you why the evidence indicates why Travis is not guilty. Justifiable use of deadly force. An issue in this case is whether the defendant acted in self-defense," Beers announced. "And the use of force not likely to cause death or great bodily [harm] is not justifiable if Travis Jones, initially, provoked the use of force against himself unless, unless the force asserted towards the defendant was so great that he reasonably believed that he was in imminent danger of great bodily harm and had exhausted every reasonable means to escape the danger other than using force likely to cause death or great bodily harm to William Wallace." The defense attorney searched the eyes of the jurors as he ended his argument. "You must judge him by the circumstance that he was surrounded by at the time the force was used."

With that, the trial ended. My mother had never gotten on the stand to speak, and now it was too late. Judge Oftedal gave the jury explicit instructions regarding the charges. If Travis was convicted of first-degree murder, he could face the death penalty or life without parole. If he were convicted of second-degree murder, he could face ten years to life. If convicted of third-degree murder or manslaughter, he could face a maximum of fifteen years. A sheriff's deputy announced shortly afterward that lunch had arrived for the jurors. They then retired to their chambers to dine on Italian food and decide the fate of Travis Jones.

My husband and I left the courtroom with my mother.

Once we were outside in the hall, Rick cheerfully announced, "Well, the trial's over. All that's left now is the verdict, and who knows how long that's going to take?" He then glanced at his watch. He was thinking of catching a plane and getting back to the office. After all, he had been gone a week. I could handle the rest without him, right? "If you want me to stay, I'll stay," he offered casually.

I looked at him without surprise. "Just go," I said. We would separate a year later.

That night my mother and I dined at Dirty Moe's Oyster Boat on Atlantic Avenue. We sat silently eating rock shrimp at a picnic table beneath the torn, ragged netting overhead. Worn-out fishing gear sat on a wooden rail to our left, and a collage of business cards littered the wall to the right. When we were almost finished with our meal, I finally asked my mother about the incident at the trial. "Why didn't you say anything about Daddy choking you?" I asked.

My mother set her piece of shrimp back down in the basket. "Because I want that man to get punished for what he did to your father," she said.

I wondered how my mother could eat at a time like this. I had barely touched my food, myself. Afterwards, I went back to the hotel room and lay awake most of the night alone. The thought of my father's actions and the killer's fate stayed on my mind for hours that night, as I now bore guilt about both of them. The wake-up call from the hotel clerk jolted me awake at seven. It was time to get ready to go back to the Palm Beach courthouse and await the verdict.

CHAPTER 37
Verus Dictum

Court resumed once again at nine in the morning on Wednesday, March 7, 2001. It was now time for the verdict. Twelve jurors had finished convening behind locked doors the previous evening after five hours and thirty-two minutes. They were now ready to pass judgment on the defendant whose level of guilt still seemed murky to most. The trial had lasted a harrowing seven days.

Sheriff's deputies escorted my mother and me down the aisle to the second row on the left. Travis's family was then escorted down to the second row on the right. They held hands and leaned on each other, while my mother and I sat inches apart and kept our hands to ourselves. Only a handful of spectators graced a few of the remaining pews.

The Honorable Judge Richard L. Oftedal spoke from his high stand. "I'm told the jury has reached a verdict," he announced. "Bring the jury out."

The bailiff promptly opened a door on the back wall and escorted the jury into the courtroom. Each marched in with his or her head held high, looking straight ahead. They waited for the judge to tell them to be seated. "Would the clerk please publish the verdict," he asked.

"In the Circuit Court of the Fifteenth Judicial Circuit, Criminal Division for Palm Beach County, Florida," the clerk began, "We, the jury, find as follows: as to Count 1, we find the defendant guilty of manslaughter, a lesser included offense as contained in the indictment. As to Count 2, we find the defendant guilty of grand theft, a lesser included offense as contained in the indictment."

Travis's family cried in each other's arms while I cried out loud to myself.

Filings by the prosecution and the defense had already been submitted to Judge Oftedal. They contained summaries of how each side would try to define Travis and how each wished for him to be sentenced.

The prosecution described Travis as a callous thief without a conscience—someone who preyed on lonely men for money and items he could sell. He used pretty boy looks to get picked up by unsuspecting victims, they said, then stole whatever he could get his hands on.

The defense portrayed Travis as a hungry, innocent young man who had lost his job. He was not a homosexual, just someone who unfortunately found himself in a desperate situation that early morning of June 6, 1999.

Before the hearing, the prosecution and defense had struck a deal. Beers, the defense attorney, would be allowed three speakers to tell about why Travis should receive the minimum sentence. Shiner, the prosecutor, would be allowed only one speaker, but he would get the coveted position of going last.

Travis's father rose and stepped up to the podium to face the judge. His son sat fifteen feet away to his right in a gray suit and starched white shirt with a thin, navy-blue tie. His knees knocked together nervously beneath the sturdy oak table.

Like Travis's mother would do when it was her turn to speak, Travis's father defended himself in a speech that was mostly about himself. His son had been dealt a set of divorced parents who had been busy trying to run their own lives. If they had once competed for custody of Travis they now competed for the chance to shift the blame for whatever had gone wrong with him.

I listened with pity to the guilt that each one harbored. I knew my father had played a much heavier hand in the struggle that night than either of Travis's parents knew and, sadly, would never know.

Then it was Travis's turn. With his head down, he shuffled over to the podium and forced himself to look up at the judge. What he said took me by surprise.

"I know the victim's daughter thinks I'm a monster," he began. His head turned slightly to the right as he sought me out for a moment before losing his nerve. "But I'm not," he went on. "I didn't mean for any of that to happen that night. I don't know what happened." Travis started to cry.

Beers spoke softly to him from their shared table. "It's all right, Travis."

I believed him, though it still didn't ease the pain of losing my father. The two issues had split apart for me during the course of the trial and now they no longer overlapped. What happened next, however, surprised me. Marc Shiner came up behind me and whispered that it was my turn to speak next. I had no idea that I was supposed to stand up and tell everyone in the courtroom what I thought about my father's murder.

Shiner proceeded to shock me even further by telling me that my address was to become a matter of public record. Travis would have access to it upon his release from prison. Once again, I had been given more information than I could emotionally process at one time. I stared back at Shiner with questions in my eyes.

"You can either take the witness stand or stand at the podium, whichever you'd prefer," he instructed gently.

"I'll just stand here," I managed to say as I made my way over to the podium. Now Travis sat in my full view. Once again it felt surreal to me.

"Mrs. Reilly," Shiner coaxed, "why don't you start by telling us about your relationship with your father."

The thought of baring information of such a personal nature to the room was unbearable to me. "I *really* don't want to talk about that!" I reeled. My pain was stunningly palpable to everyone present. It could not have reached them more if I had answered his question. The prosecutor then tried another approach. "Why don't you tell us how you feel about what happened that night?"

I looked as if he had asked me to kill my father myself. "How do I *feel* about it?" I spat. There was no reason to add any more. Everyone in the room could sense the mixture of shock, disgust, and pain that I felt.

"I feel bad for *this person's* parents, that's how I feel," I began. Travis glanced over at me with sadness and shame. I could not bring myself to speak his name. "My father was in AA. He'd been sober for the last ten years, and I was proud of him for that," I announced through bitter, mixed tears. Travis's mother, father, and step-grandmother kept their eyes fixed on me, tensely awaiting what I was about to say. "I went to meetings with him when I was young. Sometimes we went to NA, as well. I think that drugs make you do things that you never thought you'd do, and I think that *this person* is going to regret them for the rest of his life." Travis looked down at the table. "And I want you to decide, Your Honor, with all your years of experience. Even though drugs weren't allowed to be mentioned in this trial, I think they had a lot to do with this case, and I want you to decide."

I stared at the judge with a combination of pain and strength. The facts of the case and testimonies of the witnesses who had known my father had been powerful, as well.

Judge Oftedal spoke directly to Travis. "Stand up, please," he ordered. Travis rose to his feet to accept his fate for the travesty that had happened, which still felt like a nightmare to him. "Mr. Jones, I could sentence you to the maximum of fifteen years today," he announced. "But I don't think you deserve it and, frankly, no one's asking for it. I don't know if you have a drug problem or not, but Mrs. Reilly seems to think you do." Judge Oftedal then did something odd. He accidentally sentenced my father instead of Travis Jones. "Taking into account all the things said here today, feelings on both sides, I'm going to sentence Mr. Wallace [sic] within the guidelines to ten years in the Department of Corrections, receive full credit for all the time that he served, sentence to be followed by five years' probation during which time I would require that he undergo a substance abuse evaluation, period testing."

In all the years of court proceedings, Judge Oftedal had never made such a Freudian slip as he did that day. An apology was neither expected nor necessary. Everyone in the courtroom had felt the twists and turns of the victim and killer during the trial. It was not surprising that he would make such a mistake as to sentence the victim.

I had done what I could to come forward with the truth about what had happened back in 1987, when my father had told me that he had killed someone. I had wanted to make up for having concealed that truth all those years. All I could do now was hope that my words in the courtroom had at least helped spare the defendant an additional five years in prison, though the judge seemed to have doubted Travis's guilt, as well. The *Sun Sentinel* ran the following story about the trial:

"A 22-year-old man was sentenced to 10 years in prison in the stabbing death of a Lake Worth man. Travis Jones could have faced the death penalty if the jury had opted to convict him of first-degree murder. Instead, it found him guilty of manslaughter. Jones testified that he stabbed William Wesley Wallace, 56, in self-defense during a violent June 6, 1999, struggle in Wallace's apartment. Jones said an enraged Wallace attacked him when he wanted to leave the apartment after performing a sex act. Circuit Judge Richard

Oftedal also sentenced Jones to five years of probation after he is released."

Shiner was waiting outside in the hall for me when I came out of the courtroom with my mother. "The defendant's mother and grandmother would like to say something to you," he told me.

When I turned around, Travis's mother stepped over and gave me a hug. "I'm so sorry!" she said.

"I am, too," I told her, hugging her back.

Then it was the step-grandmother's turn to give me a hug. "God bless you," she said.

"You, too," I said to her with tears streaming down my face. The prosecutor watched from the side in disbelief.

I met him in his office after the trial was over. "You know, in all my years of practice, I've never seen the two families of a case even speak to each other," he said to me.

"They didn't do anything wrong," I told him, laying the receipts for my airline ticket and hotel room down on the desk in front of him. There was still the matter of the release of my father's possessions that had been held until the end of the trial. Other loose ends were left hanging in the air as well. Shiner was the first to address them.

"You know I asked your mother if your father had ever been violent toward her," he began. "I told her what you said about seeing him choke her on more than one occasion."

I listened quietly and relived the memories in my head to myself.

"She said he never hurt her, that the most he ever did was knock her glasses off one time. Why do you think she doesn't remember?" he asked, curiously.

I looked up at him. The trial had worn on me to the point that nothing surprised me anymore. Only one thought drifted into my mind: Things are not always what they seem.

The End

AUTHOR'S COMMENTARY

From the moment I arrived in Florida alone to meet with detectives Venetucci and Boland, they immediately sensed that I lacked a network of support. Over the course of the investigation, they would try and fill the void left by a mother who was out of the country and a husband who probably wished he was. Not that the full weight of the situation had hit me. The father that the detectives were describing to me was far from the one that I was sure would be calling me as soon as I got back to California. But the call never came. Denial is a powerful tool that I had been sharpening since 1987 when I had made the decision not to go look inside my father's trailer or go to the police.

It was probably Marc Shiner who pushed me up to the window of my illusion and got me to break the glass. He made my attendance at the trial mandatory, and I will always be grateful to him for that. It was also Shiner who continued to call and check on me long after I flew back to California. It was as if he knew he might be the only one who did. Which is one of the reasons I enrolled in film school at the University of California, Los Angeles once I got back home. My means of expression had always been writing as opposed to talking even when there had been someone there to listen.

But I did not jump right in. For a while I studied comedy, and over the course of writing six screenplays I eventually switched to thrillers. However, I always knew the story I would tell about my father would be written as a book, like the *Detective Brown* series I wrote in the third grade. I had been blown away after reading *Encyclopedia Brown* and wasted no time in ripping off his name. So much for the days of innocence. And my new story would drag up all the dirt and grime of my past and leave me in shreds.

Once I finished the first draft of my book, I decided to take a novel rewriting class at UCLA. In the course catalog, I came across the instructor, Dan Fante, who was also an author. Dan's father was the late John Fante (also an author) who was hailed as "my God" by author Charles Bukowski because of the braveness of emotion in his writing. His son Dan's motto was "if you like your prose vodka-soaked, soulful, and bleeding on the page, then Fante is your man." I knew that Dan would be the perfect instructor for my book and was beyond excited when I got accepted into his class. I then proceeded to bore my family with my chatter about it for weeks: I was going to study under the tutelage of the great Dan Fante, author of thirteen provocative books. They probably grew tired of hearing it. After all I had been studying writing for years. Should I not have given up on what was probably a pipe dream by now?

The drive over to my first novel rewriting class was hell. It dawned on me that not one person had read my book yet, but within the next three hours, a famous author (and son of a famous author) was going to tell me what he thought of my writing. I was exhilarated, yet terrified. I felt as if I might jump out of my skin. This was it, I thought: the moment of truth. Dan had a reputation as being hardcore, offensive, and not for the faint of heart, therefore I knew he would not hold back when critiquing his students. Some of us would be slaughtered.

The first one to share a chapter of their book with the class was a male student who made the unfortunate mistake of including a colon in the title of his book. "It's a working title," he explained.

"Yes, it is," Dan growled. The rumble of his presence could be felt by us all. Some of us slinked further into our chairs.

Eventually it became my turn to readChapter one of this book to the class, while they all followed along with a copy of the pages I had printed out for each of them. When I finished, Dan was quiet for several moments. He was reading back over the part to himself where my father's elderly neighbor had discovered my dad's body. Finally, he spoke out loud to no one in particular. There was a note of surprise in his voice: pleasant but obvious surprise. "This is *really* good writing," Dan uttered. I thought I might die. It was even better than the moment when he had held up a hardcover copy of his latest book, *Point Doom,* which was in the process of being made into a television series. The story featured sex, violence, murder, and depravity. It was clear that Dan and I were of the same vein. He loved the seediness of my story and was fascinated with my father's character. The fact that my father was an alcoholic only made him more endearing to Dan. The rewrite was going well.

I still had three questions, however. First, when should I bring in my character? Second, how much should I bring in my character? And third, what should I put in the middle of the book? The rest of it I pretty much had down—or so I thought at the time. The answers to the first two questions were answered by Dan during one of the many discussions that we had before class. I always made a point to arrive before everyone else for the purpose of picking Dan's brain. After all, how many chances would I have to ask a published author anything I wanted? Especially when I did not even know any. I only knew filmmakers and screenwriters. The third question was answered the night I brought in aChapter about my father's friends. I knew that what I really wanted to show in the book was my father's personality, because I had never met anyone like him.

"I'm salivating over this character," Dan said about my dad. Then came the answer I had been seeking. "These areChapters," Dan announced. "Each one. Every friend is aChapter." And there were the fifty pages I was looking to fill.

But my writing did not all go that smoothly. As with all writing, there was pain and therapy to be had. Mine began the night a fellow writer in the class corrected me about the term homosexuals would have used for my father. "He wasn't that type of *queen,*" my classmate said.

"But my father wasn't like that," I assured him. "He was six feet, 250 pounds," I told him.

"He was still a queen," my classmate insisted. Then he saw my face. "They would've called him a queen," he shrugged.

I was shocked at the notion and vehemently denied the prospect that my father had been a queen. "But," I stammered, seeking out Dan for support, "he wasn't like that—he was ... he was strong. He used to lift weights."

Dan saw me struggling and reliving my memories. "He was a security guard, right?" he asked.

I nodded.

"And a trainer? He was a big guy?"

"Yes," I eagerly agreed.

"Denise, honey, we need to *see* that," Dan firmly urged. "Was he in the closet? Did everyone know he was gay? We need to be able to picture your father, honey."

And there it was. The root of the problem. If I did not want to see my father, then how was I going to write about him?

Soon I found myself having to immerse myself in the world of the gay man, which was definitely new to me. I was by no means naïve to the world of alcohol and drugs, but gay men were new territory.

That weekend I went to a homosexual nightclub called "Rage" in West Hollywood. There I took in the colorful scene and listened in on the conversations of sweaty, shirtless men. Another night I went dancing at an old converted monastery called "The Abbey" across the way. The classy, statue-studded establishment is known as "The Best Gay Bar in The World." Aside from the action, they also serve excellent food.

It was at these places that I found the father I did not know, and despite what some might think, it was not the homosexual aspect of his nature that bothered me. After all, I lived in LA, where it was trendy to be gay. What really upset me was the fact that my reality was not real. Everything I thought I knew had changed. I felt like the robot of a movie I had seen who spent most of her life believing she was real only to find out that her memories had been implanted. None of them were hers.

Like my memory of John Prince Memorial Park. There were fundamental problems with theChapter I brought in to class about it mainly because I had no idea that the park my father frequented was a pick-up place for gays. This was soon explained to me by my classmate, who quickly saw through the censored testimony of one of the witnesses at the trial. The witness had also frequented the park but claimed he went there to "listen to the planes land on his scanner." My classmate was not buying the man's story. I was going to have to do some digging. I was also going to have to go through the court transcripts again.

As I began reading through the transcripts from the trial for the second time, one thing became overwhelmingly clear to me: A trial is a performance put on by actors on a stage otherwise known as attorneys and prosecutors. Some of those actors are better at their craft than others, but the transcripts strip their performances away, leaving only the facts behind. Without the tones and inflections of their voices, the truth becomes the reigning presence. Denial loses its inherent power of deflection, as well.

It was very difficult for me to read the forensic testimony, which described in great detail the violence acted out by both my father and his killer. Reading Travis Jones's recantation of the crime was especially hard. But the hardest part might come as a surprise to most. There was a point during my writing where I had gone onto Google Earth in an attempt to view the yellow guesthouse where my father had lived back in the 1980s. I must have searched for it for a good thirty minutes, but to no avail. I kept trying to move the toggle around a hedge and was sure that the house was just beyond it. If I could just get the tool to work right, I thought, I would be able to enter the house and see my father one last time. Tears sprang to my eyes as I tried as hard as I could to work the toggle and get past that hedge.

The guesthouse is probably gone. As I mentioned earlier in the book, South Florida is an ever-changing mecca, where places come and go, as well as the people of its story.

Hollie Lynn Steinke, one of my best childhood friends from the book, is one of those. She passed away much too soon in 2003 at the age of thirty-six. We have all known girls of extraordinary beauty, but Hollie was also a sweet, loving soul. We were in the gifted program together at Deerfield Beach Middle School back in the 1980s. There, we expressed our talents in the adjoining art class and entered the poetry contests of *Cricket Magazine*. Sometimes, on the weekends, we visited my father at his loft in Fort Lauderdale and dropped ping-pong balls down on him when he was drunk. We had not yet turned the corner of puberty but were already getting a glimpse of some of the vices that would claim so many of the lives in the mecca of South Florida.

PICTURES

Wesley Wallace holding his baby daughter, Denise. He was ecstatic when he found out he was going to be a father.

Wesley playing with his daughter, Denise, when she is one-year-old at their first home on Westmoreland Drive in Greensboro, NC.

Wesley and his bride, Lynda Williams, after their wedding at Starmount Presbyterian Church. They were both twenty years old. Wesley's fellow seaman friend, Dutch, is in the backseat. He would accompany them on their honeymoon.

Wesley and Lynda at a party in Greensboro, NC. Wesley was very social, so they threw many parties after they were married and attended many parties. According to Lynda, it was a whirlwind.

DENISE WALLACE

Wesley and his brother-in-law, Gordon Williams, standing in front of an ice sculpture at a National Automobile Dealership Association conference in Las Vegas, Nevada. Wesley's father-in-law, Thomas Williams, was appointed president of the association that year.

Wesley and his daughter, Denise, on a trip to Grassy Key, FL to take Denise's oldest daughter, Marissa, swimming with the dolphins.

The Prosecutor for the State of Florida, Marc Shiner, who sent Travis Jones to prison for the murder of William Wesley Wallace.

Detectives Steve Venetucci, and Dan Boland who investigated the murder of William Wesley Wallace.

Detective Dan Boland and his daughter, Kiley, who followed in her dad's footsteps and became a detective for the Delray Beach Police Department.

Detective Boland of the Lake Worth Police Department.

Wesley's killer, Travis Jones, at twenty-one years of age. Travis was convicted of manslaughter and received ten years in state prison.

Lieutenant Paul Patti, who told detectives Venetucci and Boland to "just work the scene."

Denise's childhood friend, Hollie Steinke. Denise and Hollie threw ping pong balls down on Wesley when he was drunk in his Fort Lauderdale loft apartment.

Denise being walked down the aisle by her father, Wesley at thirty years of age.

Wes's homosexual pornography video collection.

The dining room of Wes's apartment, where the killer attempted to clean the blood from the murder.

Wes's apartment on Lake Osborne Drive.

The bathroom at Wes's apartment, where the killer had tried to bleach the evidence from the murder.

Wes's bedroom, where a violent struggle took place between Wes and his killer.

The closet door of Wes's bedroom, which was broken during the violent struggle between Wes and his killer.

The dining room of Wes's apartment, where Wes's body was discovered by his elderly neighbor.

Wes's 1986 Acura, which underwent cyanoacrylate fuming.

Wes's second wallet, which was discovered underneath the floor mat of his car.

The kitchen of Wes's apartment, where the killer sought out the bleach to soak the evidence from the murder in Wes's bathtub.

COMING SOON FROM
WILDBLUE PRESS:
ROUGH TRADE by STEVE JACKSON

RIGGAN, ROBERT L

Name: RIGGAN, ROBERT L   DOC Number: 100589
Age: 55   Est. Parole
Ethnicity: WHITE   Eligibility Date:
Gender: MALE   Next Parole
Hair Color: BLONDE   Hearing Date:
Eye Color: BLUE   This offender is scheduled on the
Height: 6'00"   Parole Board agenda for the month
Weight: 190   and year above. Please contact the
                         facility case manager for the exact
                         date.
                         Est. Mandatory
                         Release Date:
                         Est. Sentence   12/11/9998
                         Discharge Date:
                         Current Facility   FREMONT
                         Assignment: CORRECTIONAL
                                       FACILITY

CURRENT CONVICTIONS

Sentence Date	Sentence	County	Case No.
04/18/1999	Life Without Parole	JEFFERSON	97CR1006

Read More: **http://wbp.bz/rt**

ROUGH TRADE

Joanne Cordova was a former Denver cop-turned-crack addict and hooker who, in the past, had submitted to violent sex with murder suspect Robert Riggan in exchange for drugs. Here is the riveting story of Riggan -- a monster who preyed on women, his final victim, and the woman who pulled herself out of a seething criminal underworld -- and her own private hell -- to testify against him and see justice done.

Updated from the true crime library of New York Times Bestselling Author Steve Jackson has updated his classic true story about life's tragic turns, murder and redemption. Played out in the Colorado mountains, the underbelly of Denver's seedy Colfax Avenue, and during an intense death penalty courtroom battle, at its heart it is the story of three people and the role both fate and choices played in their tragic tale.

Check out the book at: **http://wbp.bz/rt**

More True Crime You'll Love
From WildBlue Press.

Learn more at: http://wbp.bz/tc

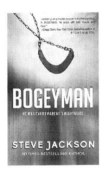

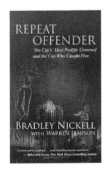

www.WildBluePress.com

Let Someone Else Do The Reading.
Enjoy One Of Our Audiobooks

Learn more at: http://wbp.bz/audio

Please feel free to check out more True CRIME books
by our friends at

www.RJPARKERPUBLISHING.com

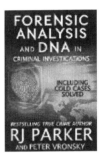

33991171R00172

Made in the USA
Middletown, DE
03 August 2016